MW00513044

A SCHOOL OF THE CHURCH

A School of the Church

ANDOVER NEWTON
ACROSS TWO CENTURIES

—◦◦◦—

Margaret Lamberts Bendroth

WILLIAM B. EERDMANS PUBLISHING COMPANY
GRAND RAPIDS, MICHIGAN / CAMBRIDGE, U.K.

© 2008 Andover Newton Theological Seminary
All rights reserved

Published 2008 by
Wm. B. Eerdmans Publishing Co.
2140 Oak Industrial Drive N.E., Grand Rapids, Michigan 49505 /
P.O. Box 163, Cambridge CB3 9PU U.K.

Printed in the United States of America

14 13 12 11 10 09 08   7 6 5 4 3 2 1

Library of Congress Cataloging-in-Publication Data

Bendroth, Margaret Lamberts, 1954-
A school of the church: Andover Newton across two centuries /
Margaret Lamberts Bendroth.
p.   cm.
Includes bibliographical references.
ISBN 978-0-8028-7123-7 (alk. paper)
1. Andover Newton Theological School — History.
I. Title.

BV4070.A56B46   2008
230.07'3427444 — dc22

2008012448

www.eerdmans.com

To Nick Carter

Contents

—ᴐᴠᴐ—

Acknowledgments

⎯⎯⟋⟋⟋⎯⎯

Many able people contributed to this book. Sharon Taylor, who helped conceptualize the initial project, freely offered research help in two key areas of Andover's history, its role in the foreign missionary movement and the ins and outs of the nineteenth-century Andover controversy. Diana Yount, the Trask Library archivist, not only read every page of the manuscript and saved me from some embarrassing errors, but provided wonderful access to archival and printed sources. She also shared information about dates and donors, and proved herself a true ally on many different occasions. My dear colleague Barbara Brown Zikmund offered invaluable advice and perspective on the final version; I simply cannot thank her enough.

I am grateful to Andover Newton faculty — including Bill Holladay, Gabriel Fackre, Earl Thompson, Mary Luti, Max Stackhouse, Jerry Handspicker — who offered key perspectives on important events and people. My friend and colleague Patty Appelbaum read and critiqued the manuscript in its early stages, with gracious suggestions for improvement.

Thanks are especially due to my wonderful staff at the Congregational Library — Claudette Newhall, Jessica Steytler, Robin Duckworth, John Simon, and Beth Spaulding — who somehow knew exactly when to offer encouragement and when to allow me necessary space and time to finish this project. The Library's board members were extremely patient and supportive throughout.

Extreme honesty would require me to individually thank the makers of Starbucks coffee and Diet Coke for providing regular shots of caffeinated energy, and to the Boston Red Sox for keeping me focused on the long haul, and just as often, terribly, terribly nervous. But in truth, my wonderful husband and children finally made this project possible, stepping over boxes of files and stacks of books, and putting up with a lot of late-night and early-morning grousing. Thanks, as always, for keeping me laughing.

Introduction

—⟨⟩—

The history of Protestant theological education in the United States is surprisingly unexplored territory. Stories of individual schools abound, of course, many of them written, like this one, to commemorate an important chronological milestone. But that close-range perspective tends to obscure what has been truly remarkable about the training of American clergy for the past two centuries. Beneath that upper crust of university-affiliated divinity schools — Harvard, Yale, Union, and Chicago — are a hundred tales of institutional resilience.[1]

Independent seminaries have faced enormous difficulties. For one thing, they do not enjoy an economy of scale: just like any professional school within a well-endowed university, they must have a scholarly library, a first-rate faculty, a full range of administrators and staff, a dormitory and a cafeteria, and a building and grounds crew. But unlike a medical or law school, they produce relatively few wealthy alumni; indeed, tuition costs for Protestant clergy have a natural ceiling. In fact until relatively recently, most divinity students paid only a small boarding

---

1. The best sources are two volumes by Glenn Miller, *Piety and Intellect: The Aims and Purposes of Ante-Bellum Theological Education* (Atlanta: Scholars Press, 1990) and *Piety and Profession: American Protestant Theological Education, 1870-1970* (Grand Rapids, MI: Eerdmans, 2007). The other "classic" studies include Robert L. Kelley, *Theological Education in America: A Study of One Hundred Sixty-One Schools* (New York, 1924); William Adams Brown and Mark A. May, *The Education of American Ministers,* 4 vols. (New York, 1934); H. Richard Niebuhr, Daniel Day Williams, and James M. Gustafson, *The Advancement of Theological Education* (New York, 1956).

cost; seminaries relied on the largesse of local churches and a few key benefactors to keep the furnaces stoked and the lecture rooms humming. That meant, of course, that these schools were quickly vulnerable to the adverse currents of Protestant denominational life — when the new pastor proved a disappointment or when certain new theological ideas became a problem, it was natural to blame the seminary.

Though institutional histories are not particularly fashionable in scholarly circles these days — to many people they bring to mind a litany of capital campaigns, curriculum reforms, and building projects — they do important work. Beyond the normal scholarly purposes of a book like this, its larger intention is to offer Andover Newton's friends and supporters a sense of their school's uniqueness and its contributions to American religious life.

Without doubt, Andover Newton has an important history. When Andover Seminary opened in 1808, it was the first theological school in the United States, and indeed the first American graduate school of any kind. During a time in which most clergy either learned on the job or sat for a few months with an older colleague, Andover's three-year curriculum provided the basic template that all other seminaries would follow, even today.[2] Newton Theological Institution adopted the Andover model when it was organized in 1825 as the first graduate seminary for Baptist clergy. In the nineteenth century, Andover achieved near mythic status as the birthplace of the American foreign and home missionary movements; its students and faculty were central to the formation of the American Board of Commissioners for Foreign Missions in 1810. In the mid-nineteenth century intrepid "Andover Bands" of young graduates planted Congregational churches in the wilds of Iowa and Minnesota, Kansas and Maine.

The faculty of both schools made important intellectual contributions: Andover's Moses Stuart introduced critical study of the Bible into the United States and Newton's versatile Alvah Hovey produced an astonishing range of historical, biblical, and theological works that became classics of nineteenth-century Baptist orthodoxy. After the Civil War, Andover's embattled faculty were the leading voices of the New

---

2. A good overview is provided in Natalie Naylor, "The Theological Seminary in the Configuration of American Higher Education: The Ante-Bellum Years," *History of Education Quarterly* 17 (Spring 1977): 17-30.

Theology, an early and influential form of Protestant liberalism. And many years later, Andover Newton faculty still continue that scholarly tradition, from theologians and ethicists like Nels Ferré, Gabriel Fackre, Max Stackhouse, and Mark Heim, to historians and biblical scholars like Gerald Cragg, Phyllis Trible, and William Holladay.

Andover Newton has also been a pioneer in the professional education of clergy. After the two schools affiliated in 1931, they introduced clinical pastoral education into the seminary curriculum; within a few decades, psychological training for prospective clergy would become a standard element in twentieth-century theological education. During the 1960s, Andover Newton's innovative Church and Ministry department introduced a "teaching parish" model of field education engaging seminarians, clergy, laypeople, and even seminary faculty into a single shared enterprise. The list could, and does, continue in the chapters to follow.

I have often envisioned this project as a kind of family album for all of the people who have been associated with Andover and Newton over the years. As such, it includes a broad array of posed portraits and candid snapshots, records of important events and casual get-togethers. There are a few universally beloved figures — and many more whose pictures no doubt stir up a host of ambivalent and widely disparate memories. Imposing a narrative on that family album has not been a simple task. Many times over the past year I have envisioned a host of Andover Newton people busily leafing past the text and going straight to the index, all of them expecting to find that one name or event indispensable to a decent history of their school. That impulse is understandable, and I have done my best to accommodate it where I could, realizing that it is in the end impossible to fulfill.

But there are larger stories to tell. To begin with, this book is not a history of just one school, but of three different institutions. Andover was the intense and often troubled offspring of New England Congregationalism, at the center of frequent theological and social debate. The literature on the school's intellectual contribution is vast, beginning with Leonard Bacon's anniversary account written only fifty years after its founding, and including many of the best historians in the American religious history guild. Newton carried the burden of Baptist ambivalence toward higher education for clergy, its own prospects rising as the denomination moved toward middle-class respectability in the late nineteenth century. Not surprisingly perhaps, the written history of Newton is only scattered and occasional; this treatment is the first to consider its entire development in one piece. The third school, Andover Newton, came of age in 1931 during a time of national and international crises, and in the last waning decades of mainline Protestant hegemony. It rode the crest of religious prosperity after World War II, endured the travail of the 1960s, and experienced head-on the erosion of the mainline denominations in the late twentieth century. Its story has never been written — all the more reason for this book to finally make its way into print.

The scale of difficulty for a narrative like this one is considerable, for Andover Newton's story intersects with many others. It overlaps with the history of both theological education and American education more generally, including two hundred years of curriculum development, pedagogical techniques, and changing student cultures. It tracks the development of Protestant thought, from Jonathan Edwards to the liberation theologians of the late twentieth century. It reflects the shifting institutional concerns of Congregationalists and Baptists, and it is situated within the local history of the city of Boston and the region of New England. It is deeply entwined with the complex histories of race and gender in American society. In some way or another, all of these tributaries, large and small, contribute to the single narrative laid out in the following chapters.

In many ways, however, the real story of this book is about mainline Protestantism. Not surprisingly, given the disastrous membership losses of the past few decades, scholars have devoted enormous time and energy to explaining the ultimate failure of moderate to liberal Protestant denominations. Especially alongside their entrepreneurial evangelical cousins, mainliners have often appeared inarticulate and tired, a wispy shadow of the Protestant "establishment" that for much of the nineteenth and twentieth centuries produced a steady stream of university presidents and statesmen.[3]

Andover Newton's story brings the discrete truths of local history to this larger theoretical perspective. There is no denying the hard reality

---

3. The "establishment" concept comes from William R. Hutchison, *Between the Times: The Travail of the Protestant Establishment in America, 1900-1960* (Cambridge, MA: Harvard University Press, 1989).

of decline, even marginalization, which has befallen white northern mainline denominations. But that sociological fact should not obscure the determination, resilience, and creativity that have kept many a local congregation or an educational institution going on year after year, sometimes for centuries. As the following pages show, Andover Newton proved remarkably adept at reinventing itself and moving on, sometimes in the face of overwhelming human error and even tragedy. That persistence reflects the particular genius of mainline Protestants: if evangelicals excel in spreading the word and moving on, their mainline cousins have their own talent for understanding and maintaining institutions, sometimes under deeply adverse conditions. Multiply Andover Newton's story many times over, and what emerges is a story of "grassroots liberalism" in the twentieth century, largely untold but crucial to understanding the persistence of religion in the modern era.

In American religious culture, theological seminaries rarely operated as ivory towers or monastic retreats; the more apt metaphor is that of the crossroads or town square. Over the course of the past two centuries, all of the great personalities and most colorful controversies in American church life found their way onto a seminary campus. Many of the most surprising or troubling ideas originated there, perhaps around a faculty lunch table or in a late afternoon seminar. It is not too much of an exaggeration to say that a few hundred small, mostly independent and often poverty-stricken institutions stoked the engines of intellectual change in American religious culture. All of the many nuances of what it meant to be an evangelical or a liberal, a Lutheran or a Methodist or a Baptist, were regularly rehearsed in seminary dorms and lunchrooms, faculty offices, and classrooms. These stories all deserve retelling. Understanding what makes a particular institution "tick" is an important key to that vast great puzzle of religious belief and behavior at the heart of American culture. Andover Newton's history is central to that larger tale, important not just to its friends and supporters but to anyone curious about the complex fortunes of Christian churches in the modern age.

CHAPTER ONE

Andover Seminary and the Origins of Theological Education in America

———✺———

Andover Seminary was the gifted child of New England Congregationalism. Bright with promise, its founding began a new era in the
education of Protestant clergy: Andover's three-year curriculum, introducing a wide array of knowledge and skills necessary for the would-be
pastor, forever altered the shape of ministerial training in the United
States.

But the school's family lineage was complex, and its origins shaped
by controversy. Andover Seminary came into the world charged with an
ambitious — some would say impossible — task. Not only was it to res-
cue the family fortunes from troubles down at Harvard; Andover also
bore the mark of its founders' soaring intellectual aspirations. As the
school came of age in the early nineteenth century, faculty and students
dedicated themselves to theological inquiry, harvesting the best scholarship from Europe and working to instill the life of the mind in American churches. During those early years, few worried about the possibility of colliding purposes.

The events in this chapter, roughly covering the school's first half
century, document the ambitious hopes and the deepening contradic-
tions that would define Andover for the rest of its independent existence. Of necessity, the opening narrative includes a good deal of background, especially on theological matters which may seem a bit arcane
to present-day readers — though others will no doubt find the story lines
vastly oversimplified. The important thread is the interlocking concerns, both practical and theological, that brought Andover into being.

Trouble at Harvard

As the nineteenth century opened, American Congregationalists were a vigorous group, justly proud of a theological tradition stretching back more than two hundred years.[1] The self-conscious heirs of New England's original band of Puritans and their complex cultural legacy, Congregationalists and their plain white meetinghouses still enjoyed pride of place in small towns from Cape Cod to the upper reaches of New Hampshire and Vermont. Indeed, across the New England states, from the colonial period up through the early nineteenth century, Congregationalism had been the legally established faith; in many parts of New England, Baptist dissenters paid a tax to support the old Puritan parish, or risked going to jail. Massachusetts, the last state to bow to the First Amendment's disestablishment of religion, would not do so until 1833.[2]

If this famously independent collection of Yankee individualists thrilled to any common achievement, it was Harvard. The original Puritan settlers had established it within a few years of their arrival from England, determined to ensure the future of their new settlement with an intellectually rigorous school for clergy. Since its founding in 1636, Harvard had required of all its students a reading knowledge of Hebrew, Aramaic, Greek, and Latin, as well as training in logic and rhetoric. Even as its curriculum gradually broadened to include history, literature, and science, students still sat through weekly lectures by their college president, who warned them against the dangers of drifting doctrine and admonished them toward deeper piety.[3]

But now, nearly two hundred years later, a crisis was brewing at the Cambridge school. In 1805, Henry Ware became the Hollis Professor of Divinity, ascending to a powerful role as New England's leading theologian, the primary bellwether of Protestant orthodoxy. The Hollis chair had been originally endowed in 1720 by a pious Baptist layman, and came with a stringent pledge of adherence to Calvinist doctrine. That

1. For a standard history, see John Von Rohr, *The Shaping of American Congregationalism, 1620-1957* (Cleveland: Pilgrim Press, 1992).

2. Edwin S. Gaustad, *Dissent in American Religion*, rev. ed. (Chicago: University of Chicago Press, 2006).

3. See George Marsden, *The Soul of the American University: From Protestant Establishment to Established Nonbelief* (New York: Oxford, 1994), pp. 33-44.

promise was intended as a safeguard for the future clergymen Harvard would train and for the countless ranks of laypeople those men would one day serve.

Intellectually, Henry Ware was more than up to his teaching role, but theologically he was a problem. When he ascended to the post at Harvard, Ware was a liberal, sympathetic to the Unitarian doctrines emerging within the relatively loose confines of the Congregational family in New England.

Calvinists in the Age of Reason

Orthodoxy had always been a tricky business in New England, where theological debate had been firing printing presses ever since the first group of settlers arrived in the 1620s. The core of Congregational polity — and, of course, of Protestantism itself — was the integrity of individual belief. The original settlers came to Massachusetts to free themselves from the arbitrary rule of kings and bishops and to create church communities peopled by "visible saints," those truly converted by the inner work of the Holy Spirit. But as the original communities grew and became more geographically dispersed, New England's religious leaders found it increasingly difficult to hold the doctrinal line. Always reluctant to rein in the faithful with rituals or creeds (this was, in their view, the fundamental error of their Anglican opponents), New England's clergy chose to maintain correct doctrine through a carefully articulated consensus, monitored by an educated core of scholar-pastors and watchful laypeople in the pews. Harvard College, it goes without saying, was central to this ambitious project.[4]

The Unitarian controversy began as a Calvinist family quarrel. During the eighteenth century, New England intellectuals wrestled deeply with the challenge laid down by the Enlightenment critics of Christianity. Indeed, Calvinist theologians on both sides of the Atlantic Ocean struggled to respond to the deist argument that belief in miracles, prov-

---

4. On church governance see, for example, Edmund Morgan, *Visible Saints: The History of a Puritan Idea* (Ithaca, NY: Cornell University Press, 1965) and James F. Cooper, *Tenacious of Their Liberties: The Congregationalists in Colonial Massachusetts* (New York: Oxford University Press, 1999).

idence, or, in fact, a Christ who was both human and divine defied all the principles of logic and common sense.[5]

Liberal Congregationalists, many of them centered in the Boston area, rejected the bottom-line rationalism of the Enlightenment skeptics, but they were sympathetic to the idea of a reasonable faith. In their view, true belief did not require miracles or supernatural revelation; it could just as easily come from observation of the natural world, whose regularity and order testified daily to the wisdom of a divine creator. The seeming arbitrariness of orthodox doctrine was a deeper problem, however. Calvinism, a taut system of ideas centering on God's sovereignty over creation, often clashed with the democratizing spirit of the age. In the wake of the Revolutionary War and all of its leveling passions, the old assumption that God's decrees were beyond analysis or question came under increasingly hostile scrutiny.[6] "We have not only a right to think for ourselves in matters of religion," Old West's pastor Jonathan Mayhew declared, "but to act for ourselves also." Even God adhered to the "eternal *laws* of truth, wisdom, and equity, and the everlasting *tables* of right reason — tables that cannot be *repealed,* or *thrown down* and *broken* like those of *Moses.*"[7]

The liberals' opponents, led by Northampton's Jonathan Edwards, were also sympathetic to the Enlightenment call for reasonable religion, but they held the line on supernaturalism. They insisted that, properly understood, Christianity was indeed a religion of rationality and intellectual rigor. Adopting what came to be known as the "commonsense philosophy," Edwards and his followers argued that that the plain meaning of religious truth was not beyond ordinary human understanding. The line of argument came from the Scottish Enlightenment, and the response of thinkers like Thomas Reid and Dugald Stewart to the radical skepticism of David Hume. As Reid argued, normal people (all those except philosophers and the insane, at least) could not help believing in basic foundational assumptions — the truths of mathematics and logic, the fact of one's personal identity, the reality of a low doorway that

5. The best overview of the Enlightenment's impact on American religion is Mark Noll, *America's God: From Jonathan Edwards to Abraham Lincoln* (New York: Oxford University Press, 2000).

6. The story is ably told in Gary Dorrien, *The Making of American Liberal Theology: Imagining Progressive Religion, 1805-1900* (Louisville: Westminster/John Knox, 2001).

7. Mayhew quoted in Dorrien, *The Making of American Liberal Theology*, pp. 3-4.

even a skeptic would stoop to enter. In the same way, God had created human beings with all intellectual faculties necessary for receiving God's word — in other words, a universal "common sense."[8]

In effect, they placed Christianity firmly in the camp of enlightened reason, but continued to insist on the validity of religious experience. Even the difficult Calvinist doctrines of predestination and divine sovereignty, Edwards argued, did not require blind faith — they were accessible both to the heart and the mind of the honest believer. Writing vigorously from his small parish in western Massachusetts, he argued for "balance of divine sovereignty and human responsibility, grace and law, piety and moralism." Rejecting the extremes of Enlightenment rationalism and a strictly emotional basis for the truth of Christianity, Edwards insisted on a reasonable and thoroughly supernatural basis for orthodox Calvinism.[9]

But circumstances hampered his case. In the 1730s and 1740s, the Atlantic world was aflame with religious revival, a widespread yearning for vividly experiential, personal piety during the Age of Reason. In North America, the so-called "Great Awakening" swept up and down the colonial coastline, propelled by the outstanding pulpit presence of English revivalist George Whitefield, the fiery Tennant brothers, and by Edwards himself. To the gratification of some, and the deep dismay of others, this heady public preaching produced vigorous experiential results. While converts wept and cavorted with joy, critics like Cambridge pastor Charles Chauncy denounced the "Shriekings and Screamings; Convulsion-like Tremblings and Agitations, Strugglings and Tumblings" they witnessed under revival preaching.[10]

Under the weight of these contending forces, Congregational orthodoxy began to splinter. In the late eighteenth century, few religious leaders proved as adept as Edwards in maintaining both the validity of

---

8. Marsden, *The Soul of the University,* 86-93; Mark Noll, "Common Sense Traditions and American Evangelical Thought," *American Quarterly* 37 (Summer 1985): 216-238.

9. Douglas Sweeney, *Nathaniel Taylor: New Haven Theology and the Legacy of Jonathan Edwards* (New York: Oxford University Press, 2003), p. 27. The best single account of Edwards' career is George Marsden, *Jonathan Edwards: A Life* (New Haven: Yale University Press, 2003).

10. See, for example, Harry S. Stout, *The Divine Dramatist: George Whitefield and the Rise of Modern Evangelicalism* (Grand Rapids: Eerdmans, 1991); Chauncy quoted in Dorrien, *The Making of American Liberal Theology,* p. 2.

religious "affections" and the rational basis for Christian belief. Old fault lines of disagreement between liberal and orthodox Calvinists began to widen into a multitude of sectarian divisions. Many of the pro-revival Congregationalists, known as New Lights, drifted toward the Baptist fold, drawn by the symbolic power of immersion in the waters of baptism. On the other side of the fence, Old Light Congregationalists opposed the emotional excesses of the revivals as an affront to reason. In the increasingly complex topography of late-eighteenth century New England Congregationalism, this anti-revival group took on various labels, including "liberal" and "Arminian," reflecting their commitment to reason and their aversion to Calvinism. In 1825, when they formed a separate body, they would be called Unitarians, because of their emphasis on the humanity of Christ and wariness toward the orthodox doctrine of the Trinity.[11]

The formal split in 1825 was only one dimension of religious change. As is always the case with religious divisions, the "schism," as it was called on the Congregationalist side, was extensive and deep, rending individual congregations as well as personal relationships. In fact the rift between Congregationalists and Unitarians permanently altered the New England landscape. In many local disputes, the original parish fell into Unitarian hands, and the orthodox resettled in nearly identical new white buildings, staring resentfully at their old opponents from the far end of the town square.[12]

Training the Orthodox

Not surprisingly then, when Harvard announced Henry Ware's candidacy for the Hollis chair, battle lines formed quickly. Even Harvard's president Samuel Willard announced from his deathbed that he "would sooner cut off his hand than lift it up for an Arminian Professor." Jedidiah Morse, the leader of the orthodox forces, warned that the Ware appointment could have a "ruinous" effect on the churches of

11. C. C. Goen, *Revivalism and Separatism in New England, 1740-1800: Strict Congregationalists and Separate Baptists in the Great Awakening* (New Haven: Yale University Press, 1962).

12. Robert B. Hanson, *Dedham, Massachusetts, 1635-1890* (Dedham, MA: Dedham Historical Society, 1987), pp. 201-215.

New England. With a liberal at the helm at Harvard, the faith of the churches would inevitably become "less pure, their discipline less strict, [and] the standard of christian [*sic*] morality lowered, . . . til at length the spirit and power of our religion shall have evaporated, and its very forms be abolished."[13]

But theology was only one part of the problem. The furor over Harvard's Hollis professor also unearthed a systemic flaw in the instruction of fledgling clergy. Since colonial days, young men (and they were, of course, all young men) who felt a calling to the ministry had taken all of their training "reading divinity" under one person, a gentleman of demonstrated erudition and proven piety. It was his responsibility to introduce his charge to all of the subtleties and the grand themes of orthodoxy, preparing him for the day when wary colleagues and vigilant laypeople would listen intently for any departure from Calvinist rigor.

As Cotton Mather explained the general practice of the early eighteenth century, the requirements for ministerial office were rigorous, but not always well defined. New England congregations expected their ministerial candidates to have led a "blameless life," to be motivated by "evangelical principles of Love to CHRIST and Souls." The young pastor was to be acquainted with three learned languages, and the "Sciences commonly taught in the Academical Education." The main requirement was a probationary sermon, after which he would be examined by other clergy, who would ask about the depth of his theological study — had he read Ames' *Medulla Theologia*? — and raise "errors" for the young candidate to refute. But even this practice proved difficult to enforce. "Several *Associations* of *Pastors* in the Country have begun to execute these PROPOSALS," Mather noted. "But they are not until this Day *fully* Executed."[14]

By the late eighteenth century, most pastoral preparation followed the method described by Joseph Bellamy, who had been trained in turn by Jonathan Edwards. The teacher of some one hundred students between 1742 and 1790, Bellamy typically presented his charges with a

13. Willard quoted in Samuel Eliot Morrison, *Three Centuries of Harvard, 1636-1936* (Cambridge, MA: Harvard University Press, 1936), p. 188; Jedidiah Morse, *True Reasons on Which the Election of a Hollis Professor of Divinity in Harvard College, Was Opposed at the Board of Overseers, February 14, 1805* (Charlestown, MA: By the author, 1805), p. 28.

14. Cotton Mather, *A Faithful Account of the Discipline Professed and Practiced in the Churches of New England* (Boston, 1726), pp. 118-121.

long list of theological questions, and then sent them to the "ablest treatises" to extract the answers on their own. Over the ensuing months, or in some cases years, Bellamy often took time to converse with and critique his students, and even listened to the occasional fledgling sermon. But for the most part the young men worked independently. In this manner, men like Bellamy and his colleague Nathaniel Emmons, who trained some ninety ministerial students before the end of his career in 1840, effectively guaranteed the doctrinal rigor of New England pulpits. But again, in practice it should be noted, only a minority of Protestant clergy received even this much systematic training.[15]

During a time in which a Congregational minister's primary responsibility was the doctrinal content of his Sunday sermons, close-grained intellectual instruction served an obvious purpose. Local churches selected their pastors on the basis of their obvious piety and leadership abilities, but the bottom line was pulpit presence. Typically New England Congregational clergy spent their entire career in a single church, where they visited the sick, rebuked the sinful, ministered the sacraments, but above all delivered a clear message from the Word of God week after week.[16]

Eighteenth-century clergy training created a pattern of informal mentoring that would become the general rule in law and medicine. When all but a tiny few had anything near a college education, and many decades before the establishment of the American Medical Association or the American Bar Association, professional education was basically an extended internship. Future clients pinned their hopes not just on the diligence of the student, but the trustworthiness of the teacher.

By modern standards, therefore, ministerial training was terribly narrow. It focused almost entirely on the reading of books with relatively little attention to the methods of biblical exegesis or knowledge of

15. Leonard Woods, *History of the Andover Theological Seminary* (Boston: James R. Osgood and Co., 1885), pp. 20-26; James W. Fraser, *Schooling the Preachers: The Development of Protestant Theological Education in the United States, 1740-1875* (Lanham, NY: UPA, 1988); William Warren Sweet, "The Rise of Theological Schools in America," *Church History* 6 (1937): 261; Edward A. Park, *A Memoir of Nathanael Emmons: With Sketches of His Friends and Pupils* (Boston, 1861), pp. 215-265.

16. Donald M. Scott, *From Office to Profession: New England Ministry, 1750-1850* (Philadelphia: University of Pennsylvania Press, 1978), pp. 1-17.

historical context that might have expanded their meaning. No one either taught or learned much about homiletical technique or even basic public speaking skills. Students had few opportunities for intellectual conversation or socializing with peers, or for building collegial relationships with fellow clergy.

And, of course, putting one's career in the hands of one man had far graver implications. An ill-informed doctor or incompetent lawyer might damage the body or land an innocent man in prison — but an incompetent teacher in matters of salvation bore the threat of eternal consequences. As one worried Congregationalist warned, with every ordination of a new minister, "the purity, peace, and prosperity of the Church, [as] well as the honor of Christ, are at stake. When a man is once introduced into the ministry, who is corrupt in doctrine or immoral in practice, a deep wound is inflicted upon the Church." He is a "contaminating leaven" putting the "welfare of souls" at hazard. "The mouths of infidels and revilers are opened, and saints hang their harps upon the willows."[17] Indeed, another agreed, "the eternal state, not of one but of millions of our fellow beings, may, and probably does, in a very serious sense, depend upon the qualifications as well, as fidelity of the ministers of Christ."[18]

Leaving Cambridge

As Henry Ware's ascendance to the Hollis chair looked more and more inevitable, Eliphalet Pearson organized the opposition. A ponderous, emphatic man (nicknamed the "elephant" by Harvard students, an apparent pun on his name and a comment on his physical size), he was considered next in line to the presidency after Samuel Willard's death. But all of Pearson's pleading and threatening failed to move the laymen on Harvard's Board of Overseers. Ware became Hollis professor and Samuel Webber, a mathematician with a reputation for liberal views, became Harvard's next president.

17. "On the Necessity of Religious Experience, and a Fair Reputation in Ministers of the Gospel," *Panoplist* (November 1813): 408-409.

18. "Thoughts on the Importance of a Theological Seminary," *Panoplist* (December 1807): 307.

Pearson quickly resigned in protest and fled north to Andover, by then a familiar site of refuge. During the Revolutionary War, his wife's family had relocated to the town some twenty-five miles north of Boston; as the conflict raged he had grown close to the wealthy Phillips family, and encouraged their plans to establish an Academy for the education of young men. Phoebe Phillips, said to be a matriarch of uncommon spiritual ardor, became the primary benefactor. Under her conviction and Pearson's urging, the school took on a clear religious aim.[19] With Pearson as principal, the Academy's constitution declared that its "*first* and *principal* object" was "the promotion of true PIETY and VIRTUE" through instruction in the "great and important doctrines" of Christianity.[20] The original deed of Andover Academy, written in 1778, also stipulated the teaching of Christian theology within the larger curriculum. Under this arrangement, Jonathan French, the local Congregational pastor, regularly tutored a small number of Academy students aiming for ministerial careers.

When he returned in 1807, Pearson hoped only to expand this original charter, building a theological school onto the Andover Academy with a minimum of fuss. He already had an important ally on the board of trustees, Jedidiah Morse, a former Harvard Overseer who had resigned his post in the wake of the Ware nomination. In June, the Massachusetts legislature authorized its Andover Trustees to do just that under their original charter.[21]

Though legally a part of the undergraduate Academy, the divinity school was entirely distinct in faculty, infrastructure, and, of course, in purpose. Situated, in time-honored biblical fashion, on the top of a hill that commanded a lengthy view of its surrounding horizons, Andover did not look likely to capitulate to Unitarian rationalism. The Phillips family agreed to fund two facilities, one a three-story dormitory big enough to house fifty students, and the other a multi-purpose kitchen,

---

19. Richard D. Pierce, "The History of Andover Theological Seminary," *Andover Newton Bulletin* 49 (April 1957): 6; Sarah Loring Bailey, *Historical Sketches of Andover* (Boston: Houghton, Mifflin, and Co., 1880), p. 559.

20. Cited in Eliphalet Pearson, "Historic Sketch," in *Constitution and Associate Statutes of the Theological Seminary in Andover; With a Sketch of Its Rise and Progress. Published by Order of the Trustees* (Boston: Farrand, Mallory, and Co., 1808), p. 3.

21. On Morse's role see Joseph W. Phillips, *Jedidiah Morse and New England Congregationalism* (New Brunswick, NJ: Rutgers University Press, 1983), pp. 138-140.

dining hall, chapel, library, and lecture hall. A generous gift of $20,000 from businessman Samuel Abbot (originally intended for Harvard) funded a chair of Christian theology, the first such position ever established outside an American university.[22]

But before the Abbot professor ever uttered a word in an Andover classroom, the school took a new direction. Just a few miles distant from Andover, in the coastal town of Newburyport, Massachusetts, another group of Calvinists was pondering the future of orthodoxy in New England, with an even deeper sense of alarm. The two groups were, in many ways, natural allies — but the partnership would require many months of wary courtship before it could be fully brought to pass.

Newburyport

The Newburyport group was formidable. Its leading lights were Leonard Woods and Samuel Spring, prize students of Hopkins and Bellamy, and accomplished masters of theological debate. It also included some wealthy and ambitious laymen: William Bartlet, Moses Brown, and John Norris. Though none of these men were renowned for their piety — Norris was an alcohol distiller and Bartlet so hard on his debtors than even his eulogists were constrained to admit that "he did good in his own unpopular way" — they were prepared to be generous. In Norris's case, his wife's determination to fund evangelical causes clearly operated as the tipping point.[23] With an initial gift of $40,000 and promise of more, this well-funded group planned to establish a theological school in nearby West Newbury, with Woods as its first professor of theology.

Real theological differences impeded a quick alliance. The Andover men, sometimes referred to as "Old Calvinists," were content with the old Westminster Confession as a hedge against heretical teaching. For men like Pearson and Morse, the point of reference was the old Puritan Calvinism, including its various modifications over the course of the

22. On Abbot's original gift, see Woods, *History of Andover Theological Seminary,* pp. 55-62.

23. *Memorial of the Semi-Centennial of the Founding of the Theological Seminary at Andover* (Andover: Warren F. Draper, 1859), p. 20; "The Norris Gifts to the Associate Foundation in Andover Theological Seminary," *Andover Review* 1 (1884): 24-37.

seventeenth and eighteenth centuries. They placed great faith in the regular ordinances of the church — the sacraments of baptism and the Lord's Supper — as a means of bringing people to salvation. Accordingly, they accepted the allowances made under the so-called Halfway Covenant of 1662 for unconverted parents to present their children for baptism.[24]

Old Calvinists tended to view Jonathan Edwards and his disciples as dangerous innovators, hard-nosed divines immersed in endlessly speculative theories about Calvinist metaphysics. They referred to them, somewhat dismissively, as the "New Divinity," implying that old Puritan forms were an adequate standard in need of no modern revision; or, even more dismissively, they called them "Hopkinsians," after Samuel Hopkins, widely known as one of the most doctrinally controversial of Edwards' followers.

For their part, the New Divinity men preferred to call themselves "consistent Calvinists." They did in fact believe that a certain amount of metaphysics was helpful to true piety. Following Edwards, they walked a fine theological line between the absolute sovereignty of God and the validity of a sinner's emotional decision to accept the salvation provided by Christ's sacrifice. They insisted, again using Edwards' terms, that though human beings had a "natural ability" to do what is right, sin had eradicated their "moral ability" to do so. Like a prisoner sitting in an open cell, all human beings were technically free; all that remained was the choice to leave.[25]

New Divinity theology was complex and, as historian Douglas Sweeney aptly describes it, "multifarious"; but this key emphasis on the core responsibility of the human will set them apart from their Old Calvinist cousins.[26] New Divinity theologians objected, for example, to the Puritan doctrine of imputation, the idea that Adam's sinfulness was somehow directly passed on to the entire human race. Though encapsulated in the Westminster Confession, this model was in their view both logically unintelligible and borderline immoral, for it allowed human beings to evade full responsibility for their own fallen state. New Divinity

---

24. Sweeney, *Nathaniel Taylor*, pp. 29, 43.

25. See E. Brooks Holifield, *Theology in America: Christian Thought from the Age of the Puritans to the Civil War* (New Haven: Yale University Press, 2003), pp. 135-149.

26. Sweeney, *Nathaniel Taylor*, p. 31.

theologians argued that in some sense, all human sin was a personal choice, a path every infant takes in the earliest moments of life. To use Nathaniel William Taylor's famous phrase, "the sin is in the sinning." It was in some sense a function of the will.[27]

These deeply nuanced discussions also had significant practical implications. New Divinity theologians, like Edwards, believed in the necessity of an emotional, heartfelt experience of grace that would set the believer apart from the unsaved and uncaring. They had no truck with the elaborate Puritan schemes of halfway covenants and long-drawn-out conversions. As Sweeney writes, the Edwardseans "encouraged their flocks to quit wandering the barnyard and enter the sheepfold at once."[28] Unlike later generations, whose revivalistic zeal tended to drift toward anti-intellectualism and whose orthodoxy shaded into rationalism, the New Divinity men were determined to hold onto Edwards' delicate synthesis. In their view, both Unitarian rationalism and lukewarm Calvinism threatened the doctrinal purity and the piety of New England's founding generations.[29]

Not surprisingly, then, Spring and his backers were wary of any proposal coming from Andover. They worried that the Academy had too many close ties with Harvard, and that if challenged would not maintain an appropriate distance. Moreover, they were far from convinced that Andover's Old Calvinists had sufficient theological backbone or experiential piety to carry the cause for orthodoxy. But, as historian Leonard Bacon recalled fifty years later, the Unitarian threat drew them together. "[I]n the presence of a common adversary so powerful and so flushed with success," the two parties were "compelled to recognize each other's orthodoxy, and, suspending for a while their controversies with each other, to unite in measures for the defence and advancement of their common faith."[30]

In a deeper sense, however, it was not Unitarianism, but the fear of

---

27. H. Shelton Smith, *Changing Conceptions of Original Sin* (New York: Charles Scribner's Sons, 1955), pp. 106-108.

28. Sweeney, *Nathaniel Taylor,* p. 33.

29. For a helpful summary see Douglas A. Sweeney and Allen C. Guelzo, eds., *The New England Theology: From Jonathan Edwards to Edwards Amasa Park,* (Grand Rapids: Baker Academic, 2006).

30. Bacon, *A Commemorative Discourse, On the Completion of Fifty Years from the Founding of the Theological Seminary at Andover* (Andover: W. F. Draper, 1858), p. 22.

sectarianism that drew Andover's founders together. The idea of two theological schools north of Boston, each vying to compete with Harvard, was hardly good news to Calvinists of any stripe. Dividing their forces laid them open to charges of schism, and promised an open field to their Unitarian opponents. In his own version of the seminary's founding, Eliphalet Pearson took considerable pains to emphasize the "great system of revealed truth" underlying both schools of Calvinist thought. "Nor will any force or influence, but that of *truth,* be employed with the Students," he declared, "to gain their assent to any system of doctrine." If anyone was sectarian, Pearson argued, it was the Harvard Unitarians who had departed from the one true faith.[31]

It is worth pointing out, in fact, that many of Andover's founders were strong advocates of union and compromise. Morse played a major role in the organization of the General Association of Massachusetts Proper, now the Massachusetts Conference of the United Church of Christ. As chapter three lays out in more detail, Andover people would facilitate the formation of the American Board of Commissioners for Foreign Missions and the American Home Missionary Society, two of the most important interdenominational cooperative efforts of the early nineteenth century.

Andover's founders also reflected the spirit of the times. Fears of sectarian mischief in the new American nation grew apace as Europeans descended into decades of revolutionary turmoil. Leaders like Thomas Jefferson encouraged the growth of public, religiously neutral institutions to offset the rapid multiplication of Protestant denominations. He hoped that bringing theological schools under the aegis of state-funded universities would "liberalize and neutralize their prejudice, and make the general religion a religion of peace, reason and morality." Although Jefferson's dream fell short of reality, and independent denominationally based schools like Andover continued to multiply in the early nineteenth century, they knew better than to give free rein to prejudice. Education in the early American republic, whether religious or secular, had to have a firm civic mooring.[32]

31. Pearson, "Historic Sketch," pp. 7-8.
32. Jefferson quoted in Marsden, *Soul of the University,* p. 74.

Merger

Even so, all of Andover's founders felt the need for specificity. In the spring of 1807, Morse and Pearson approached the Newburyport group with news about their own proposed new seminary. As the months passed, the two groups hammered out an agreement — a process that no doubt wearied the determined Pearson, as he plied the roads between Andover and Newburyport, facing the arguments of "keen dialecticians" at either end of his twenty-mile journey.[33]

In the end Andover and Newburyport worked out a series of fateful compromises. The solution was as layered and complex as one might expect from a group of men gifted in the languages of biblical exegesis and philosophy, as well as business and commerce. In effect, Andover was a union of two schools with two working sets of doctrinal standards.

The seminary's constitution, completed August 31, 1807, left little room for doubt about its doctrinal rigor. Every professor at the school had to be "a man of sound and orthodox principles in divinity," as defined by the Scriptures, the Westminster Assembly, and the original constitution of the Phillips Academy. In the remote chance of misunderstanding, each professor also made a public declaration of his opposition not only to "Atheists and Infidels, but to Jews, Mahommetans, Arians, Pelagians, Antinomians, Arminians, Socinians, Unitarians, and Universalists, and to all other heresies and errors, ancient or modern, which may be opposed to the Gospel of Christ, or hazardous to the souls of men." And to remove any further source of doubt, every professor was required to reaffirm this Andover creed before the board of trustees every five years. If a majority found him wanting, he would be "forthwith removed."[34]

In March of 1808, the New Divinity men, now known as Associate Founders, added to these provisos their own set of statutes and a lengthy, much more explicit creedal statement.[35] Written by Leonard Woods and Samuel Spring, the so-called Associate Creed was, according to historian Glenn Miller, "one of the strangest documents in the history of theology." An amalgam of standard Reformed theology and

---

33. Description by Park quoted in Bailey, *Historical Sketches of Andover*, p. 561.
34. *Constitution and Associate Statutes*, pp. 19-20.
35. *Constitution and Associate Statutes*, p. 20.

New Divinity particularities, it was, as Miller argues, hazy about essentials and agonizingly specific on lesser matters. "At best, the Creed was a muddle," he writes; "at worst (as later history proved), an invitation to a theological debacle."[36]

The Associate Statutes also created a Board of Visitors, whose job it would be to regularly examine the orthodoxy of each faculty member, and to approve each new hire. The Visitors, designated as two laymen and one clergyman, were to be the "Guardians, Overseers, and Protectors" of the seminary, as well as a court of appeal for all cases of dispute between the Andover Trustees and the teaching faculty. As such they had the authority to "admonish or remove" an Andover professor, "either for misbehaviour, heterodoxy, incapacity, or neglect of the duties of his office." Even with this safeguard in place, however, the Associate Founders also included a proviso allowing them to opt out of the Andover experiment at any time during its first seven years. And to the eventual dismay of future generations, the Associate Statutes also provided for a final appeal to the Supreme Judicial Court of Massachusetts.[37]

In the end, Andover seminary incorporated the concerns, if not the spirit, of both groups. The final agreement, completed December 1, 1807, was ratified by the board of trustees in May 1808. Reputation was all. Worried that their small new school might invite scorn in comparison with an established college like Harvard, Nathaniel Emmons and Jedidiah Morse determined that it should be called a "theological seminary" — the first American use of that now-standard term.[38] The two-tiered system of liberal arts education and theological graduate study was common in Europe, among both Protestants and Catholics, but virtually unknown in North America. Indeed, in 1808 Andover Seminary was the first and only post-graduate school of any kind established in the United States.[39]

---

36. Glenn Miller, *Piety and Intellect: The Aims and Purposes of Ante-Bellum Theological Education* (Atlanta, GA: Scholars Press, 1990), p. 65.

37. *Constitution and Associate Statutes,* pp. 39-40. Miller notes that the Board of Visitors had no legal standing, as they were not provided for in the original charter. An act of the legislature finally settled the matter in 1820. See Miller, *Piety and Intellect,* p. 65.

38. Frasier, *Schooling the Preachers,* p. 34.

39. A good comparative overview is found in Natalie Naylor, "The Theological Seminary in the Configuration of American Higher Education: The Ante-Bellum Years," *History of Education Quarterly* 17 (Spring 1977): 17-30. An explanation of the broader back-

Evangelical Scholars

To outsiders, all of the wrangling over Calvinist theology at Andover's founding predicted nothing but disaster. The editors of the *Monthly Anthology* and their literary readership took a dim view of the new "Jesuit's College" in Andover, with its elaborate creeds and imprecations. Clearly, the New Divinity metaphysicians had won the day over their more moderate Calvinist allies. "It is a yoke too galling to be endured by any man," they declared. "In this age of religious light and liberty, to see an institution rising among us, which would have disgraced the bigotry of the dark ages," was too much to bear. "We devoutly pray," they concluded, "that the Being, who brings good out of evil, will make this institution an instrument to effect his purposes of benevolence and wisdom, and disappoint the forebodings, which, we confess, at present almost overwhelm our hopes."[40]

But Andover represented far more complex intellectual aspirations than this warning caricature allowed. It is important to remember, first of all, that the school was overtly nonsectarian, open to "Protestants of every denomination," though all of the professors were to be Congregationalists or Presbyterians, reflecting the recent Plan of Union between the two denominations.[41] Moreover, none of the Andover creeds were

---

ground in German university culture is found in H. George Anderson, "Challenge and Change within German Protestant Theological Education during the Nineteenth Century," *Church History* 39 (March 1970): 36-48.

40. M. A. DeWolfe Howe, *Journal of the Proceedings of the Society Which Conducts the Monthly Anthology and Boston Review, October 3, 1805, to July 2, 1811* (Boston: Boston Athenaeum, 1911), p. 160; *Review of the Constitution and Associate Statutes of the Theological Seminary in Andover; With a Sketch of Its Rise and Progress . . . From the Monthly Anthology of November, 1809* (Boston: Joshua Cushing, for William Wells, 1808), p. 35. See the vigorous rejoinder in "Further Remarks on the Theological Institution, in Andover, occasioned by the Review of its Constitution and Statutes, in the Monthly Anthology," *Panoplist* (March 1809): 471-481.

41. *Constitution and Associate Statutes,* p. 13. In 1801, Congregationalists and Presbyterians engaged in a cooperative plan aimed at pooling resources for church planting and evangelism in the western territories. Though New England churches were Congregationalist, they often adopted more Presbyterian forms of local church government, as these offered more oversight and direction to individual congregations. Indeed, out west, the majority of new churches sought the organizational advantages of Presbyterianism more than the freedom allowed by Congregationalism, and in 1837 the Plan of Union came to a rather unhappy end.

required of students. Andover's ministers in training were, as many would later attest, always invited to consider the evidences for Christianity with an open mind, at least within the constraints of their historical and cultural setting.[42]

Preaching at the opening of classes, on September 28, 1808, Yale president Timothy Dwight gave his own memorable description of the Andover ideal. As an elder statesman of sorts among New England's Edwardseans and a personal colleague of many Andover faculty, he was the perfect figure to articulate the new school's intellectual promise. While Yale was as yet a few years away from establishing its own divinity school, it had already produced not just the great Jonathan Edwards himself, but a string of revivals within its student body.

Dwight set the bar high for Andover's future. He described the "evangelical scribe" as one thoroughly versed in theology as well as Latin, Greek, and Hebrew. He needed to know ancient history both "civil" and "ecclesiastical," and he needed to be thoroughly acquainted with logic, "to reason with skill and success," and with rhetoric "to speak with propriety and force." "Generally, his mind ought to be variously, and extensively, furnished with useful knowledge," Dwight argued, "because, otherwise, his views will be contracted; his illustrations of divine truth inapposite, uninstructive, and unsatisfactory; and his images few, poor, and often low and disgusting." Against those who argued that spiritual leadership was simply a divine gift ruined by hard schooling, Dwight declared these "preachers in a moment" a danger to the churches. The same people who settled for untutored ministers were careful to hire trained lawyers to manage their property and to find "able physicians" when a child fell ill. What folly to "place their Religion, their souls, and their salvation, under the guidance of quackery."[43]

His audience needed no admonition, of course. The education Andover's founders had designed was both rigorous and thoroughly innovative for its time. Their school was the first in the United States to require a three-year curriculum of graded study, in effect a professional

42. On Congregationalists and creeds, see Roland Davis Gunn, "The Andover Case: A Study of the Role of Creeds in Nineteenth Century Congregationalism" (M.A. Thesis, 1983).

43. Dwight, *Sermon Preached at the Opening of the Theological Institution in Andover; and at the Ordination of Rev. Eliphalet Pearson, L.L.D. September 28th, 1808* (Boston: Farrand, Mallory, and Co., 1808), pp. 3, 4, 8.

degree for Protestant clergy. The Andover model, soon the standard form for theological education in every denomination across the country, came nearly a century before law and medicine required similar credentialing. Although other seminaries began to form in quick fashion — Bangor in 1816, Yale in 1822, and Harvard in 1815 — Andover was the first and the most famous. Even the University of Berlin, considered the world center of Protestant theological scholarship, was Andover's peer in the design of its three-year curriculum.[44]

Andover's founding class, some thirty-six students in all, came to the study of divinity with a college degree or its equivalent already in hand. Before they even opened a seminary text, they were required to produce a certificate of good character and to demonstrate knowledge of Greek and Latin, which they would put to use during the course of their education.

The original constitution called for instruction in five basic areas. The first, natural theology, offered a combination of what would now be taught as apologetics, philosophy, and ethics. It covered "the existence, attributes, and providence of God," the immortality of the soul, and "the great duties of social life." Sacred Literature dealt with the "formation, preservation, and transmission" of the Bible. Students were to study the text in its original languages and cover the "canons of biblical criticism," at the time mostly analysis of ancient texts and their origins. Ecclesiastical History began with "Jewish antiquities" and continued on through the "sects and heresies of early Christianity," and the "rise and progress of popery and mahometanism," ending with the Protestant Reformation. The fourth discipline laid out in the Andover constitution was Christian theology. This course of study included the "great doctrines and duties of our holy Christian religion, together with the objections made to them by unbelievers, and the refutation of such objections." Students would learn the classic doctrines of the Trinity, sin and salvation, the offices of the Holy Spirit, and the nature of "future rewards and punishments."

The founders also insisted on training in "Pulpit Eloquence," recognizing the central role of preaching in the minister's weekly duties. The course material included not just the organization of sermons but "the proper management of the voice and correct gesture" and "the immense importance of a natural manner." Students were to be instructed on

---

44. Miller, *Piety and Intellect*, p. 69.

"methods of strengthening the memory" and on the "character and style of the most eminent Divines and best models for imitation."[45]

Above all, Andover professors were to be friends and spiritual guides. They were to be available for private instruction on sermon preparation for all students, where "in a free, but friendly manner," they might "point out their defects and errors," "favoring them with candid remarks" about their subject matter and delivery. Faculty were also, when necessary, to help "solve cases of conscience," and to watch over their pupils' health and morals with "paternal solicitude."[46]

By 1829, the curriculum required students to take each subject in a particular sequential order. First-year students began with biblical studies, including Hebrew grammar and hermeneutics, New Testament Greek and exegesis of the four Gospels. They also received a basic introduction to theological arguments for biblical revelation and the divine inspiration of scripture. During their second year students met five days a week for instruction in theology, supplemented by more New Testament exegesis and topical lectures in "sacred literature" from the Professor of Sacred Literature. Only in the third year did students take on the study of homiletics and church history, supplemented by more work in Hebrew and Greek exegesis.

At the end of every school year, students stood for public examinations by the faculty. In 1818, for example, the Junior class translated Greek and Hebrew texts, and delivered orations on "the meaning of the 'Seven Spirits'" in Revelation 1:4, the "faults of our common Hebrew Lexicons," and the "dangers" posed by the critical study of the Scriptures and how these might be avoided. The Middle class displayed their knowledge of Christian theology with orations on "divine immutability" and "the duty of prayer," the different methods of justification, common objections to the doctrine of election, and "the obligations of a pardoned sinner to holiness." The Senior class, having spent their year studying sacred rhetoric, delivered orations on "industry in a preacher," "the power of moral painting in sermons," and "the defects of sermons addressed to impenitent sinners."[47]

45. *Constitution and Associate Statutes*, pp. 14-18.

46. *Constitution and Associate Statutes*, p. 18.

47. "Exercises at the Annual Examination of the Theological Seminary in Andover, Sept. 23, 1818," *Panoplist* (September 1818): 420-422.

Study at Andover was not for the faint of heart. Faculty began their day with a seven o'clock chapel and lectured twice daily, skipping only Monday mornings and Saturday afternoons, and of course, Sunday. Students also rose for morning chapel, and after breakfast, proceeded on to morning study, from eight till noon. Afternoon study began again at half past one and lasted till three, followed by recitation, prayer, and supper at six. They fell to their books again an hour later, and at nine they most likely dropped into bed, eager for rest. On Wednesday evenings, they met with Leonard Woods, who led them for an hour of prayer and instruction on topics conducive of personal piety.

But life at Andover always involved far more than just intellectual pursuit: recognizing the value of physical exercise as well as a means of cutting costs, Andover trustees encouraged one or two days of manual labor a week on seminary land. Students grew cafeteria fare in their garden, and formed their own Mechanical Association and ran a woodshop that, perhaps fittingly, supplied the local townspeople with sturdy wooden coffins. As one observer commented, "The students do not seem to have been miserable, perhaps because they were seldom idle."[48]

An ascetic tendency was a distinct advantage for one seeking an Andover degree. Thanks to a generous endowment, Andover students paid no tuition and only a small amount of board, around $2 to $4 a year. But they also chopped wood and paid for their own heat, as well as for the heating of the lecture hall and dining room. Cold food was, however, a staple for some of the more zealous, who complained vociferously when their bread came to the table warm from the oven.

Even so, Andover students also found time to cultivate the finer pleasures. Faculty encouraged the study of sacred music, and in 1812, students formed their own voluntary society, with the disarmingly serious title, the Lockhart Society for Improvement in Sacred Music. In honor of Ebenezer Porter, for twenty years the professor of sacred rhetoric, students also formed the Porter Rhetorical Society, "to improve themselves in sacred eloquence for the purpose of being useful to mankind," through debate, public lecture, and study. The Porter Society regularly sponsored Andover's commencement orations. Andover's library

48. Rowe, *History of Andover Theological Seminary* (Newton, MA: Thomas Todd, 1933), p. 36.

began with the formation of a Bartlet Athenaeum in 1818, which, after the fashion of the time, allowed members access to a reading room and a small collection of donated books and periodicals.

Founding Faculty

Andover's instructors were every bit as rigorous as the curriculum. The full story of their careers requires much longer treatment than this opening sketch allows — and in fact most of the founding generation will reappear in subsequent chapters. But perhaps a few descriptive sketches will provide enough for now.

Eliphalet Pearson and Leonard Woods were Andover's original faculty. Pearson, the Westminster Calvinist, taught natural theology and was the Bartlet Professor of Sacred Literature; Woods, the New Divinity man, was Abbot Professor of Christian Theology. A student of Nathaniel Emmons, and according to one description, an "able if unimaginative Edwardsean," Woods held his post at Andover for thirty-eight years, and proved himself a leading defender of Calvinist orthodoxy.[49]

Pearson and Woods were soon joined by Edward Dorr Griffin, appointed to the Chair of Public Eloquence in 1808. Griffin came with a considerable scholarly pedigree, a graduate of Yale and mentored by Jonathan Edwards, Jr. His reputation for orthodoxy earned him a founding role at Andover and also at Boston's Park Street Church, established in 1809 as a counterpoint to the Unitarian drift of the city's Congregational churches. Griffin's oratory is sometimes said to have been the reason why Park Street's address, at the corner of Park and Tremont Streets in Boston, was long known as "Brimstone corner." True or not, Griffin's reputation thoroughly endeared him to his fledgling congregation, and in 1811 he resigned the post at Andover to devote his full energy to the rapidly growing church.[50]

By mid-century, the true exemplar of Andover's aspirations was Moses Stuart. Appointed to the faculty to replace the ailing Pearson, Stuart

49. Bruce Kuklick, *Churchmen and Philosophers: From Jonathan Edwards to John Dewey* (New Haven: Yale University Press, 1985), p. 85.

50. H. Crosby Englizian, *Brimstone Corner: Park Street Church, Boston* (Chicago: Moody Press, 1968). Griffin finished his career as president of Williams College.

was a prodigious intellect and a tireless scholar. He came to Andover from his post as pastor of the First Congregational Church in New Haven, a Yale College graduate who had studied law, and then under the tutelage of Timothy Dwight, entered into ministry. When Stuart arrived at Andover to teach Sacred Literature, he could read neither Hebrew nor German. But he rapidly made up the loss, learning both languages well enough to produce authoritative dictionaries and commentaries. Over the course of his long career — he retired in 1848 — Stuart also became the primary conduit of German biblical scholarship into the United States, and as one historian writes, "his work represented the most careful and responsible biblical criticism in the English-speaking world."[51] Under Stuart's leadership, and that of his colleague Edward Robinson, Andover became a leading force in the academic study of biblical texts. Robinson, who later left for Union Seminary, established the field of biblical geography and founded Andover's venerable scholarly journal, the *Bibliotheca Sacra,* in 1843.

Prospects

Andover's early years boded well for the survival of Calvinist orthodoxy in New England. In short order the school amassed an endowment of $300,000 — a figure double that of Harvard's. Indeed, as one observer noted, "When Harvard was offering her professors $1,000 and a house, Andover was providing $1,200 and a house."[52] With such "ample funds" and "brilliant prospects both of honor and usefulness," another enthusiastic supporter declared Andover Seminary "the most important Institution, that ever arose in the United States," and quite possibility in the entire history of Christianity.[53]

Later events would of course temper such optimism, but by mid-century the Andover experiment was a clear success, a model for theological education across the country, and some would say, around the world. Indeed, over the following decades, as New England Congrega-

---

51. Kuklick, *Churchmen and Philosophers,* pp. 90-91.
52. Richard D. Pierce, "The History of Andover Theological Seminary," p. 5.
53. "Review of Reviews: The Constitution and Associate Statutes of the Theological Seminary in Andover," *Panoplist* (January 1809): 372.

tionalism moved into a variety of new forms, new seminaries arose in fairly rapid fashion, each carving out a particular theological niche. Thus, Harvard became home primarily to Unitarians, Andover to the orthodox Calvinists of the New Divinity, and Yale Divinity School, with its star scholar Nathaniel William Taylor, a rival to Andover. Bangor appeared shortly after Andover, advertising a special course for ministers already serving pulpits but desiring further education. Presbyterians could choose between the solid "Old School" Calvinism of Princeton — dominated by the conservative social and intellectual tradition of Charles Hodge and Benjamin Warfield — and the "New School" upstarts at Union Seminary in New York.

In fact, just a few years after Andover's founding and a few miles away in Newton, in a small village west of Boston, an important group of Baptist admirers set about to establish their own version of the original. Their story is the subject of the following chapter.

CHAPTER TWO

New England Baptists and the Cure of Souls: The Early Years of the Newton Theological Institution

———⁓⁓⁓———

"It is proverbial that we live at an eventful period of the world," Jonathan Going declared, as he pitched the idea of a theological seminary to his fellow Massachusetts Baptists in 1819. And indeed, later generations would remember the early decades of the nineteenth century as a "second great awakening," a wave of organizing zeal that would permanently alter the course of religion in the United States. Those years saw a rapid expansion of churches, schools, and moral and evangelistic societies of every kind, into what has been commonly called a "benevolent empire" of Protestant institutions. In real terms, organized religion had hardly flagged since the spiritual peak of the so-called First Great Awakening in the mid-eighteenth century, dominated by the intellectual shadow of Jonathan Edwards and the evangelistic feats of George Whitefield. But the public surge of activity that Going was witnessing in 1819 did seem like a genuinely new dispensation. It was time, he said, for Baptists to consider "the literary and theological education of the sons of Zion."[1]

During those luminous times, nothing seemed impossible and everything seemed worth doing. "The friends of God and men are making more spirited exertions for the promotion of his glory and their benefit than at any former time," Going declared. It is forgivable perhaps, that

---

1. Jonathan Going, "Outline of a Plan for Establishing a Baptist Literary and Theological Institution in a Central Situation in New-England. By a Friend to an Able Ministry," 1819, reprinted in *Andover Newton Quarterly* 16 (January 1976): 186.

his sense of the unprecedented gave way to millennial expectations. With a new wave of missionaries "running through the world," spreading the gospel in strange and distant lands, and with reports of revival regularly filling the pages of Baptist periodicals, God seemed clearly prepared to bless any able enterprise.[2]

Baptist optimism fueled the organization of the Newton Theological Institution in 1825. Though Newton pursued a path already set by Andover, the language of evangelical piety rather than theological controversy shaped its earliest years. While for many Congregationalists the early nineteenth century was a painful, defensive time, Baptists enthusiastically rode the crest of the spiritual wave. From their origins as a small breakaway sect within Puritan New England, American Baptists numbered around 125,000 by the opening of the nineteenth century. While Congregationalists thinned out beyond the Hudson River, Baptists were truly a national denomination, following the flow of western emigration and developing a vigorous wing in the South. The next several decades brought a complete transformation: by 1830, about one-quarter of all American Christians were Baptists, and by century's end, they would surpass Methodists to become the single largest denominational body in the United States.[3]

But this very success bred restlessness. In spite of their enormous success outside of New England, Massachusetts Baptists often felt they ran a distant second behind their Congregational cousins. They lacked the infrastructure of tax-supported parishes and Harvard-trained clergy that Congregationalists took for granted; even their numerical success did not immediately grant them the social influence many felt was their due. "While the denomination has increased with a rapidity which almost compels infidels to acknowledge the interposition of the hand of God," Going wrote, "it has generally kept in the background." Any future growth would be hindered by the "want of ability and influence in its ministers."[4]

Going's proposal for a theological seminary soon found backing and support. During its first half century it prospered, though in a fairly

2. Going, "Outline of a Plan," p. 186.

3. One good source of figures is Edwin Scott Gaustad and Philip L. Barlow, *New Historical Atlas of Religion in America* (New York: Oxford, 2001), pp. 20-22, 79-89; Appendix C.

4. Going, "Outline of a Plan," p. 186.

modest way, admittedly not along the intellectual and financial lines enjoyed by Andover. Newton's problematic, if it can be called such, was nearly the opposite of the older seminary. While Congregationalists considered the possibility of supporting two theological schools before deciding to end up with one, many Baptists were not sure if they wanted any school at all.

Baptists and Higher Education

In the minds of some, Baptist success was an argument against the need for graduate theological education. With souls perishing for want of a simple gospel, a course in biblical exegesis or training in the homiletical arts seemed an almost criminal waste. Everyone knew that some of the denomination's best frontier preachers and evangelists were the ordinary laymen, called to ministry by the urgings of the Holy Spirit, not by a duly formed ecclesiastical council. Thus one contributor to the *American Baptist Magazine* began a defense of theological training by conceding that "Knowledge, of whatever kind, is useless, unless it conduct us to some valuable result, unless it influence our practice as well as our opinions." In fact, he went on to admit, academic attainments could be a genuine hazard to the soul. "Whatever is purely intellectual, though it may furnish an inexhaustible fund of rational amusement," he wrote, "rarely proves a powerful incentive to noble and virtuous deeds." For the "poor and illiterate" who formed the majority of most Baptist congregations, learning was properly the "handmaid of religion," not its master.[5]

Remembering their origins as a small and often persecuted New England sect, Baptists did not take kindly to honorifics like "Reverend" or "Doctor." "I do not know where our ministers get the authority, to confer, or receive such titles," one "Baptist brother" muttered darkly in 1812, "unless from the cabinet of our opposers, or the power of the beast."[6]

The Baptist ideal was the "farmer-preacher," dividing his time be-

---

5. Observator, "The Advantages of Education," *American Baptist Magazine* (July 1817): 131-132.

6. "On Titles," *Massachusetts Baptist Missionary Magazine* 3 (September 1812): 210-211.

tween the hay mow and the pulpit. Not surprisingly perhaps, Going's proposal for a theological seminary included a hefty dose of farm labor as part of the curriculum. Not only would two hours a day spent cleaning stalls and baling hay help defray costs, it would offset the health risks of intellectual pursuits. As "intense study deranges and enervates the mind," Going warned, regular exercise would promote "brisk circulation of the fluids of the body" and "all the animal functions." And, of course, it would "greatly contribute to [the] future usefulness and comfort" of ministers in training. "It is desirable that ministers should have a competency of the goods of this world, that they be not diverted from their work, nor discouraged in it."[7]

Baptist churches had few formal prerequisites for ordination. A young man had to demonstrate a good moral life, knowledge of the English Bible and some ability to preach and teach, and, most important, a clear calling to the ministry. Baptists defined a "call" as both inward and outward: an individual had to have had an experience of being singled out by God for religious work and a local congregation had to affirm his conviction. After that, a formal education was perhaps helpful, but not entirely necessary.[8]

Baptists were slow, therefore, to begin the task of establishing denominational schools. The establishment of Rhode Island College, later Brown University, was a study in Baptist ambivalence: Ezra Stiles, a prominent Congregationalist, had helped get it under way, and perhaps partly for that reason it was never fully embraced by New England Baptist clergy. A few decades after its founding in 1764, twice as many graduates ended up in Congregational churches as in Baptist ones.[9]

But it would be wrong to overdraw the contrast between the Baptists and Congregationalists. Not only did the two denominations share the same Puritan roots, they followed a similar decentralized polity. Baptists were every bit as proud of their local independence as their Congregational cousins. Nor were New England Baptists merely anti-intellectual. By 1825, they had a solid record of establishing schools, including the Maine Literary and Theological Institute in Waterville,

---

7. Going, "Outline of a Plan," pp. 182-185.

8. Glenn Miller, *Piety and Intellect* (Atlanta, GA: Scholars Press, 2001), pp. 299-300.

9. William Warren Sweet, "The Rise of Theological Schools in America," *Church History* 6 (1937): 263.

Maine, in 1813 (later Colby College), and Hamilton Literary and Theological Institution in New York State in 1820. In 1817, enterprising Philadelphia Baptists had organized a "classical and theological seminary," eventually known as the Columbian College. Established by Luther Rice in Washington, D.C., the small school offered basic training in law, divinity, and medicine, as part of a rudimentary liberal arts curriculum. After it failed for want of funds, the school took a more secular path, and eventually ended up as George Washington University. But as Baptists expanded into Ohio, Michigan, and Illinois, the academy model proved generally successful, a useful and inexpensive combination of practical and academic instruction.[10]

Newton's founders were prepared to aim higher, however. Though they claimed to have begun without a clear plan in mind, they were certainly aware of the Andover model. Recently opened and generously funded, the seminary at Andover was clearly the highest standard of aspiration. Following in its wake, Newton became the first freestanding post-graduate Baptist seminary to be established in North America, the first Baptist graduate school of any kind.

Newton's Founding

Unlike Andover, which was chartered by the state legislature and governed by a board of trustees, Newton was the product of a voluntary society. In September 1814, a small group meeting at Boston's Second Baptist Church formed the Massachusetts Baptist Education Society, with the simple goal of affording educational support to pious and destitute young men aiming for the ministry. As one account later recalled, the fundraising campaign was "sufficiently modest" and undergirded by impeccable leadership, so that it aroused little opposition, and even a modicum of support from churches. By 1825, the Society had funded sixty-five young men, with somewhere between twenty and thirty going on to achieve full ordination. It was frustration, rather than satisfaction, with this somewhat limited success that led members to press for a free-

10. William H. Brackney, "The Development of Baptist Theological Education in Europe and North America: A Representative Overview," *American Baptist Quarterly* 18 (June 1999): 86-94.

standing theological school in Boston, "where the combined powers of two or three men of God, can be employed in instructing and forming the manners and habits and character of pious young men for the ministry." Accordingly, on May 25, 1825, a group meeting in Boston's First Baptist Church, on Salem Street in the city's North End, under the auspices of the Education Society, set out to create a seminary.[11]

The original Newton trustees purchased land for the school in Newton, Massachusetts, eight miles west of Boston. In 1825, the Baptist church there was barely half a century old; under the saintly "Father" Grafton, as their eccentric pastor was affectionately called, it had only just begun to prosper. The rough-hewn building on the shore of Newton's "Baptist pond" (later known as Crystal Lake) had bare wood walls and seats made out of planks laid across sawhorses. The congregation could not afford a wood stove until 1810.[12]

Like Andover, the Baptist school would be situated on a hill, with an inspiring view of the surrounding countryside. The old Peck estate had been built in 1798 by John Peck, who set out to create an English country house complete with emerald lawns and a long sloping driveway lined with tall trees. When his fortunes took a turn for the worse during the War of 1812, Peck grazed some five hundred sheep on his formerly elegant lawns, and when this failed to right his accounts, abruptly left for better prospects out west. As Newton president Everett Carlton Herrick described it, much later, "Familiarly and affectionately for all of us it is The Hill, our Hill, our Zion."[13] Alvah Hovey, a student in 1845 and later a Newton professor and president, remembered his view from

11. "Eleventh Annual Report of the Executive Committee of the Massachusetts Baptist Education Society, Sept. 1825," *American Baptist Magazine* (November 1825): 43-45; "Circular Respecting the Newton Theological Institution," *American Baptist Magazine* (July 1826): 217-219.

12. M. F. Sweetser, *King's Handbook of Newton, Massachusetts* (Boston: Moses King Corp., 1889), pp. 296-297. "Once, at a public dinner, being annoyed by the swearing of a young man near him, he rose straightway, and exclaimed: 'Mr. President, I move you that no person at this table have permission to utter a profane oath, except my friend, the Rev. Dr. Homer!' This playful allusion to the saintly old Congregationalist divine silenced for that day the ill-speaking youth." Pp. 288-289. Later pastors of the First Baptist Church included Samuel Smith, the author of "My Country 'Tis of Thee."

13. Everett Carlton Herrick, *Turns Again Home: Andover Newton Theological School and Reminiscences from an Unkempt Journal* (Boston: Pilgrim Press, 1949), p. 30. See also description in *King's Handbook of Newton*, p. 304.

room twenty-nine in Farwell Hall for many years: to the west he could see the "blue, rounded dome of Mount Wachusett, in the heart of the Commonwealth," and to the north "the faint gray peak of Mount Monadnock, in the borders of New Hampshire." The southeast view commanded a panorama of the Blue Hills of Milton, and the east, a glimpse of Boston with its Bunker Hill monument, gilded State House dome, and the red brick buildings of Harvard University.[14]

But the resemblance between the two institutions ended there. Newton had few of Andover's financial resources: in 1825 the eighty-five acre Peck estate included only a single residential building which had to be refitted to accommodate classroom space. The entire cost of the transaction, around $8,000, was quickly underwritten by a few generous friends. But the cost of a new brick building, originally called the Farwell Athenaeum (later Farwell Hall), built in 1829 with student apartments, reading room, chapel, and library space, added $5,000 to the negative side of the ledger. Rarely free of financial worries, Newton struggled financially almost from its inception. Support from the Baptist Education Society ended by 1830, and a newly formed board of trustees depended on smaller gifts from Baptist churches and a long list of individual supporters.

The Baptist seminary's institutional structure was also relatively slight. In contrast to the weighty admonitions in Andover's constitution, Newton's articles of incorporation, passed on February 22, 1826, simply provided for a moderately sized group of trustees (fewer than twenty-five and more than nine), and established a few procedures for recruiting and maintaining them.[15] Newton had no constitution, and its leaders made no attempt to set forth a faculty creed, course curricula, or any means of doctrinal oversight of the school.

The nearest attempt at imposing standards came from the Northern Baptist Education Society, which in 1849 requested representation on the board of trustees. Recognizing the pecuniary advantages of a "more direct and intimate connection with the Baptist churches of New England," the Newton trustees assented to the creation of a Board of Visitors, selected by the boards of the Baptist educational societies across

---

14. George Rice Hovey, *Alvah Hovey: His Life and Letters* (Philadelphia: Judson Press, 1928), p. 30.

15. "Newton Theological Institution," *American Baptist Magazine* 6 (1826): 128-129.

New England. The design, ratified in 1850, allowed the Board of Visitors to attend student examinations at the end of the school year, and make "inquiries" about the "courses and manner of instruction and study," as long as they did not interfere with the ordinary round of study.[16]

Newton's founding faculty was small, but their ambitions were considerable. Irah Chase, lately of the failing Columbian College in Washington, was the first faculty member, engaged to teach first-year students in Biblical Theology. A native of Vermont and graduate of Middlebury College, Chase was himself an Andover alumnus, graduating in 1817. By the time he finished, he was thoroughly impressed by its intensely purposeful atmosphere. "There seemed to be, on that consecrated hill," he later reminisced, ". . . a wakeful spirit of Christian enterprise and energy" that Baptists would do well to replicate. "I resolved to do what I could; and looked to God for guidance and success."[17] In 1826 Henry Ripley, of Riceborough, Georgia, joined Chase as Professor of Biblical Literature and Pastoral Duties.

The two professors immediately introduced a three-year curriculum following the Andover model, though with a significant difference. The course of study emphasized biblical theology, rather than systematics, giving more prominence, as one description later put it, "to the study of 'God's Word Written' than was assigned that study in any theological seminary in existence at that time."[18] The basic program included Biblical Literature, Ecclesiastical History, Biblical Theology, and Pastoral Duties, a regimen of study which was deemed "appropriate to a theological institution, designed to assist those who would understand the Bible clearly, and as faithful ministers of Christ, inculcate its divine lessons the most usefully." The bare-bones course of study encouraged students to study sacred music "as voice and health will permit," and to labor in the fields of the Peck estate, "for the purposes of salutary exercise."[19] But it took almost fourteen years before the Newton faculty grew large enough to meet the demand of the curriculum, designed for

16. "Book of Records of the Newton Theological Institution," 1826-1859, ANTS archives.

17. "Rev. Irah Chase, D.D.: An Autobiographical Sketch," *Baptist Memorial and Missionary Record* 9 (1850): 74.

18. Albion Small, "New England Theological Institutions: Newton Theological Institution," *New England Magazine* 6 (August 1888): 359.

19. *Rules and Regulations*, pp. 4, 10.

four full-time professors. Barnas Sears was hired in 1835 as Professor of Christian Theology, and in 1839 Andover graduate Horatio Hackett joined the faculty as Professor of Biblical Literature and Interpretation.

In the classroom, instructors labored to balance the demands of piety and scholarship. Barnas Sears, for example, opened his theology course with a lecture on the "Hindrances to an acquisition of the knowledge of God," including indifference, "pride of opinion and love of originality," "idle casuistry," a "supposed necessity of appearing well informed on every subject," and an "over active imagination." But, like any good heir of the commonsense tradition, Sears also insisted that the Bible "must not only be interpreted by reason, but its genuineness and inspiration must be established by arguments addressed to human reason."[20] His pedagogical approach was equally rigorous, employing a mix of reading, class discussion, and Socratic question and answer. A distinguished academic in his own right, Sears was "careful to imply that there was a right or wrong position."[21]

Student life was also challenging. Blessed with eighty-five acres of arable land, the seminary exchanged tuition and housing fees for manual labor in the garden, weather permitting. During the winter months, students worked in a carpenter's shop that had been erected on campus. They also seemed to have created some share of fun, judging from the new section added to the *Rules and Regulations* in 1836, admonishing against the use of tobacco and levying charges for broken furniture and damaged wallpaper.[22]

Yet entrance requirements, especially in the early years, were not imposing. The "Rules and Regulations," first published in 1826, asked only that each student declare his conviction "to devote myself to the work of the gospel ministry," to act in a "faithful and christian manner," "to pay due respect and obedience to the guardians, professors, and teachers, and to conduct myself towards my fellow-students as brethren, and towards all men as becomes the gospel of Christ."[23] New-

---

20. Theological Lectures by Barnas Sears, 1846-1847, Alvah Hovey papers, Box 20, ANTS archives.

21. Miller, *Piety and Intellect,* p. 326.

22. *Rules and Regulations of the Newton Theological Institution* (Boston: Gould, Kendall and Lincoln, 1836), pp. 8, 9.

23. *Rules and Regulations of the Newton Theological Institution* (Boston: Lincoln and Edmans, 1826), pp. 3-4.

ton admitted college graduates and "others, whose attainments enable them . . . to proceed profitably in theological studies." Students were required to demonstrate "genuine piety, with suitable gifts and attainments," "proper motives" for pursuing theological education, and a certificate of endorsement from their local church. Though the school soon added a requirement for basic knowledge of Hebrew, it also established a preparatory class (known as the English class), enabling students without a college education to begin the path to seminary.[24]

The first three students stood for examination on September 14, 1826, reported as "a day of deep interest, of devout gratitude, and joyous anticipation." After an examination in Hebrew and biblical literature, the young men read essays on "The History of the Hebrew Language," "The Greek of the New Testament," and the "Common English Version of the Bible," all of which, it was generally agreed, "gave evidence of careful research, sound thought, and warm piety." Two senior students, both matriculating from Andover, presented papers on "Preaching Christ Crucified" and "The Connexion between a Preacher's Private Life and His Official Ministration," efforts deemed of "uncommon value," demonstrating "just views and elevated piety."[25]

In 1829, with pardonable pride, the Baptist *Watchman* reprinted the comments of a Unitarian visitor who had witnessed commencement exercises at both Andover Seminary and Newton Theological Institution — and pronounced the Baptist students better pastors. He commended the Andover men for the "direct, business-like manner" of their presentations, and the presence of "strong religious feeling." But, he said, from a purely literary point of view, "preference must be given to the exercises at Newton." There, "the young men spoke with clearness and perspicuity," in contrast to Andover, where, he conceded, "they spoke in not so clear and perspicuous a style." All told, however, the Unitarian visitor found little to complain about. "If all denominations will take this course," the *Unitarian Register* announced, "we have no fears for the result."[26]

24. "Anniversary of the Newton Theological Institute," *American Baptist Magazine* 9 (September 1828): 358; "Newton Lyceum: Or Preparatory Department of the Newton Theological Institution," *American Baptist Magazine* 12 (1832): 199-201.

25. "Newton Theological Institution," *Baptist Missionary Magazine* (October 1826): 308.

26. "Andover and Newton," *Christian Watchman*, 9 October 1829, p. 162.

Yet challenges lay ahead. Though the school climbed out of the deficits of its early years, reporting an excess of $6,000 in the budget by 1835, the stability did not last long. In the late 1850s, trying times returned and by 1852 the shortfall was around $16,000. By then, Newton had built three homes for its faculty and was sustaining three scholarships of $1,000 each; in 1856 it admitted its largest entering class of twenty-three students. Within months, the financial Panic of 1857 threw the Newton campus into crisis. The trustees began cutting faculty salaries, dismissing instructors, and, by the end of the decade, selling property. The number of graduates fell sharply, hitting bottom with only three in the class of 1859.

Alvah Hovey

The career of Alvah Hovey, as Newton student, professor, and president, demonstrates all of the institution's strengths and weaknesses in the mid-nineteenth century. Somewhat puckishly, Everett Herrick, who had known Hovey in his declining years, described him as "sound and judicious." "He was sound because he did not deviate from the conventional and theological pattern of his time. He was judicious because he was big, wore side whiskers, and was deliberate in all his utterances. When he started out to weigh the evidence," Herrick recalled, "you could not help being impressed with his learning, and sometimes, after a while, you could not help getting a bit drowsy."[27]

While Hovey might not have possessed the polish of a European-trained theologian, he was a defining presence during Newton's most difficult years. Arriving at the school in 1845 and graduating in 1848, he came back to teach Hebrew the following year. Hovey must have been an obvious choice, even though the graduating class included only five students. In a letter home during his senior year, he reported that he had read the entire Old Testament in Hebrew, as far as the sixty-fifth chapter of Isaiah. "I sometimes spend an hour on a single word," Hovey wrote, "looking, by aid of a Hebrew concordance, every place where it occurs, and striving to form an independent judgment of its meaning."

27. Herrick, *Turns Again Home*, p. 31.

As Barnas Sears reportedly boasted to Andover's Edwards Park, "I have a student named Alvah Hovey. He is a lion."[28]

With the faculty down to only three overworked members, Hovey also pitched in as school librarian. The job was not onerous, he later recalled, because the school had relatively few books. When a professor sent back an unexpected package from Europe, Hovey nearly swooned. "I shall never forget the almost choking sensation of delight with which I opened the boxes. . . . Never again will the sight of a few hundred foreign books move my spirit as it did on that occasion."[29] Despite these limitations, Hovey was not idle; in 1854 he introduced a card catalog system into the library, using the Smithsonian methods introduced by the Massachusetts State Library. He also perfected his German, and began reading German theology. While boarding with a Methodist family in Newton and teaching Latin and German at a local finishing school, he began tutoring the two daughters in "mental and moral philosophy." He married the eldest, Augusta Maria Rice, in 1852.

By that time Hovey was also Newton's professor of church history. He prepared for teaching in his typically intense and systematic fashion: as his son and biographer later related, in two years Hovey had read all of the Apostolic Fathers, including Justin Martyr, Athenagoras, Theophilus of Antioch, Tatian, the whole of Irenaeus, nearly all of Clement of Alexandria, Tertullian, and Cyprian, some parts of Origen, and considerable parts of Augustine. "It was his fashion," the younger Hovey noted, somewhat superfluously, "to know thoroughly what he taught."[30]

Even during the depths of Newton's struggles during the 1850s, Hovey continued to expand his scholarly output. In 1855, following a sudden resignation, he became professor of Christian theology, but continued to teach church history and to contribute scholarly books and articles, including a translation of a German work on John Chrysostom and a biography of Baptist notable Isaac Backus. Hovey also preached regularly in Baptist pulpits, and served on the Newton school committee. Even after he became president of Newton in 1868, his teaching responsibilities continued with Theology and Christian Ethics in 1870 and New Testament from 1892 to 1894.

28. Hovey, *Alvah Hovey*, pp. 32, 33.
29. Hovey, *Alvah Hovey*, p. 40.
30. Hovey, *Alvah Hovey*, p. 49.

Hovey traveled to Europe in 1861, sitting in on lectures by famous German biblical scholars and touring famous sights. His diary recorded his awe and intellectual satisfaction, and his Vermont Baptist discomfort with the pipe smoking and snuff dipping he witnessed among the German professors. He worried about their want of piety, the lack of private and family prayer, and believed "as never before the importance of deep and earnest love to God in all who preach the gospel." "Knowledge and faith," Hovey confided in his journal, "should grow up together in the soul. If some men have zeal without knowledge, it is equally true that some have knowledge without love or zeal."[31]

Not surprisingly, Hovey's students remembered him much this same way. "Dr. Hovey's influence over his students was not inspirational," a graduation speaker reminisced grandly in 1903. "He did not have the flash of the diamond, but rather the luster and weight of the ingot of gold."[32] In 1858, a young man, George Gow, confessed to the Newton admissions committee that he had no "dogmatic faith," except to believe in God and in his love as the "only source of right character." It was a very "meager faith," he admitted, and wondered aloud if he should even think of attending seminary. Hovey was the first to reply, welcoming him to Newton and over the next several years befriending the young skeptic and tolerating his questions. In later life, Gow credited Hovey with bringing him to back to faith. "[H]ere at Newton," he wrote, "I found a teacher, as orthodox as need be and certainly as learned in Scripture, who not only asked but cared to give the reason why. This genuine rationalism, coupled with his kindliness of manner made me almost forget my skepticism. . . . He lead me through reason to faith."[33]

Back from the Brink

Alvah Hovey's career aptly sums up the legacy of Newton's early years, a dogged combination of personal piety and scholarly toil. Within its first fifty years, the school had weathered consistent challenges in student

---

31. Hovey, *Alvah Hovey,* p. 83.
32. D. T. Magill, "Reminiscences of Dr. Hovey," *The Newtonian* 2 (December 1903): 4.
33. Hovey, *Alvah Hovey,* p. 70.

enrollment and financial support; discouragements were common. In 1850, the faculty issued a polite but strongly worded complaint to the board of trustees of "circumstances in our present condition which materially diminish the pleasure which we should otherwise experience." "This is the oldest theological school of a high character which the Denomination in this country established," they declared. "The location is one at which, if anywhere, such an Institution can be liberally sustained." But their experience of life in Boston, with its stellar array of colleges and theological schools, only rendered Newton's deficiencies "more conspicuous and humiliating." The library, which in any other city would be an "ornament," was "wholly inadequate, not to say disreputable" in comparison to Andover and to Harvard. Indeed, the faculty took special pains to point out that Andover's library was four times the size of Newton's, and contained all of the *particular works* needed for successful instruction." They demanded not just new additions to the library, but more faculty — even a few entire new departments — to do full justice to the students and to the churches who depended on Newton for the denomination's future.[34]

The complaint registered. In 1852, facing a shortfall of $16,000, the board of trustees voted to raise the astonishing sum of $100,000 to lay the foundation for a permanent endowment. They subscribed over a third of that sum at the very same meeting. In 1854, the board enlarged its numbers to forty-eight, to allow more participation across the denomination. They also appointed the aptly named Horace T. Love as a fundraiser, and by 1867 he had brought in $117,298.38 in amounts ranging from just a dollar to one donation of $18,000. The funds went toward the erection of a new building, later dedicated as Colby Hall, in honor of Gardner Colby, who had served as board treasurer from 1844 until 1868. This was a considerable achievement: not only did Newton pursue ambitious goals during wartime, but in the face of wrenching denominational turmoil over slavery, with the entire southern branch departing in 1844.

At the building dedication in 1866, Alvah Hovey praised its finely appointed reading room, with its electric wiring and ready supply of current newspapers, allowing the students fuller understanding of "the hopes and fears and perturbations of living hearts in every nation under

34. "Report of Faculty, 1850," ANTS archives.

heaven." "Never, I am sure," Hovey declared, "will students who have access to that reading-room be justly accused of indifference to the great questions which agitate society." The lecture rooms on the second floor were devoted, one each, to biblical instruction and Christian theology, with church history and pastoral duties sharing space. The entire third floor provided space for the library.[35]

With a brighter future ahead, Newton's supporters pointed with pride to the fact that never once, during their hardest times, had they suspended the work of the seminary, even for an hour. In 1865 Gardner Colby noted joyfully that "for the first time in twenty years the several accounts are free from indebtedness" and the school's financial base had been "liberally increased by skillful management."[36]

Gentlemen Theologians

This was no small achievement. Throughout the early and mid nineteenth century, Newton was struggling to keep pace not just with its own institutional priorities, but with fundamental changes in the clerical profession itself, and in American society. As the economy shifted from trade and agriculture to vigorous capitalist competition, social patterns followed suit. Young men could no longer assume that they would follow their father's trade — in the open spaces of the United States, each man stood alone to make his own fortune. Reality, of course, rarely matched the fervor of the rhetoric of choice and freedom; inherited wealth and privilege still determined the ground rules for success even in democratic America. But the entrepreneurial spirit of striving and achievement sifted through every level of society, including the churches.

During the early years of Newton's founding, the ministry was becoming a career, with its own scale of status and achievement. Even among Congregationalists, the old ideal of a lifetime "settled pastorate" was giving way to an assumption of upward mobility. Particularly in

35. "Address by Alvah Hovey, Jr.," in *Newton Theological Institution: A Sketch of Its History, and an Account of the Services at the Dedication of the New Building, September 10, 1866* (Boston: Gould and Lincoln, 1866), pp. 44-51.

36. "Book of Records of the Newton Theological Institution, 1865," ANTS archives.

urban centers like Boston, middle-class congregations began to demand more than just a resident scholar or a spiritual guide — they wanted a bit of polish. The mid-century Protestant pastor was a "gentleman theologian," equally at home in the pulpit or a parishioner's tastefully appointed parlor.[37]

Guidebooks on proper clerical conduct began to multiply, advising young men on the formation of "proper habits." In careful detail they told the aspiring pastor how long to spend on a visit to the sick, how to choose appropriate clothes and furniture, how to spit, sneeze, or belch without attracting undue attention. ("Rather than once allow yourself, on any occasion, to spit on the floor in company, you ought to walk a hundred yards, or more, to find a door or window.")[38]

The new attention to pastoral gentility reflected the demographic reality that most Protestant pastors spent the majority of their time conversing with women, who were, of course, the primary constituency of American religious institutions. The market economy took middle-class men out of the home for long stretches of time; instead of going to the barn or shop to work, they commuted to stores and businesses. Ministers thus fought the perception that they were insufficiently manly — a "third sex" that was neither male nor female.

Still, respectability was an achievement that few Baptists, especially in Puritan Boston, were prepared to reject. In 1836, when Newton Baptists banded together to build a new church nearer to the seminary, they still felt compelled to build in a plain style "demanded by Christian frugality and good taste." But over the next several decades, they remodeled their old building twice, alleviating the "positively grim simplicity" of the original structure. In 1886 they would start anew, in a grand style reminiscent of the Romanesque structure housing the First Baptist Church in Boston's wealthy Back Bay neighborhood.[39]

In their early years, Andover and Newton symbolized the social and intellectual disparities among American Protestants. Congregational clergy, the so-called "standing order" of New England and agents of its legally established faith, enjoyed pride of place. They drew from their

37. E. Brooks Holifield, *History of Pastoral Care in America: From Salvation to Self-Realization* (Nashville: Abingdon Press, 1983), pp. 116-119.

38. Samuel Miller, *Letters on Clerical Manners and Habits* (Princeton, NJ: Moore Baker, 1835), pp. 55-56.

39. *King's Handbook of Newton*, p. 297.

Puritan roots a sense of cultural ownership, an often unstated belief that the local Congregational clergyman would set the moral and social tone within his community.[40] As one contemporary account put it, "He is identified with his people in all that concerns their welfare."[41] In contrast, Baptists and other historically "disestablished" sects tended to look toward their own. They took pride in their humble origins, and in the simple honesty of physical toil. They insisted on the separation of church and state not just to preserve the integrity of religious institutions, but to ensure their own protection against an outside world they assumed was at best indifferent.

But as the century progressed, the social distance between Baptists and Congregationalists, at least in New England, began to narrow. Within a few years of Newton's founding, both denominations were heavily involved in the ambitious task of "Christianizing" the frontier regions of the United States, and in sending missionaries abroad to Asia, Africa, and the Pacific Islands. Newton was very quickly realizing the ambitious scope of Jonathan Going's design for a "literary and theological institution"; Andover too was fulfilling the broader mission its founders had imagined. In the years ahead, in the great nineteenth-century surge of missionary enthusiasm, both Andover Seminary and Newton Theological Institution would play a leading, and at times legendary, role.

At mid-century, however, the two schools were still worlds apart. Andover marched through its early years with relative confidence, financially secure and intellectually strong. Its faculty was, in many instances, world-renowned and its students came from the top layers of an already well-educated and influential Congregational world. Newton traveled a more difficult path, but toward a destination set by Andover. In its early years, it struggled not just with the financial realities of maintaining a working theological institution, but with the ingrained suspicions of Baptist laypeople, worried that a preacher with too much education would lose spiritual fervor. Measured against those chal-

---

40. Peter Field, *The Crisis of the Standing Order: Clerical Intellectuals and Cultural Authority in Massachusetts, 1780-1833* (Amherst, MA: University of Massachusetts Press, 1998).

41. John Mitchell, *A Guide to the Principles and Practice of the Congregational Churches of New England; With a Brief History of the Denomination* (Northampton: J. H. Butler, 1838), p. 146.

lenges, the achievements of the first fifty years — a solid core of faculty, a working library, new buildings furnished with the most up-to-date classroom facilities, and a regular flow of students — generated well-deserved Baptist pride.

CHAPTER THREE

Andover, Newton, and the Benevolent Empire

———✺———

U ndeniably, both Andover and Newton seminaries owed their early
success to the American Protestant world into which they were
born. The first half of the nineteenth century was a time of vigorous economic and geographic expansion, propelled by an enormous wave of religious zeal. As New England's trade and industry blossomed, the region's emerging wealth endowed Protestant endeavors with a broad
base of financial support — and in Andover's case, considerable largesse. The early nineteenth century also saw unprecedented ease in
mass communication, as an expanding American market economy
opened up new roads, canals, rail systems, and produced a seemingly
endless supply of printed books and pamphlets.

It was, in a word, a good time to open up a school for preachers. During their early years, Andover and Newton prospered under favorable
circumstances: a growing market for trained clergy, an opening continent, and a rising sense of spiritual urgency. But as they matured they
took a central role in realizing the hopes and dreams of the evangelical
Protestant communities that brought them into being. Their stories
document an obvious but important truth, that theological education,
at its best, is a reciprocal endeavor. Seminaries are more than just intellectual think tanks, reservoirs of theological purity, or vocational training schools cranking out a steady supply of religious professionals.
They also introduce the wider church to new ideas and new people,
sometimes in deeply challenging ways. In the early nineteenth century,
when evangelical Protestants were poised to expand their reach beyond

their own shores into the wide world, Andover and Newton seminaries played an indispensable part in that significant, and at times morally ambiguous, task.

The Benevolent Empire

Economic expansion was key to the pious goals of both seminaries' founders. In the late eighteenth and early nineteenth centuries, New England's livelihood shifted from trade to manufacturing. The emerging "cotton kingdom" in the South, supported by the labor of African slaves, produced a ready supply of raw materials for the textile mills of Lawrence and Lowell — and a moral evil that later generations would be forced to confront.

But in practical terms, for many rural families the textile economy meant opportunity. A young man with a particular zeal and a curious mind no longer had to combine his studies with a long day of farm work. The textile mills in Lowell and Lawrence, Providence and Fall River, employed thousands of young women from rural Massachusetts, Maine, and New Hampshire, who sent their paychecks home to support the family economy. Thanks to the often unrecognized labors of sisters and daughters, increasing numbers of pious New England families realized they could afford to send their sons not only to college, but on to seminary.[1]

The emerging Protestant world also fed the flow of new students. The century opened nervously, as church leaders contemplated the formal disestablishment of religion, mandated by the federal constitution. One by one, state constitutions took up the question of separation between church and state, recognizing it as both a problem and an opportunity. New England Congregationalists faced the loss of a spiritual monopoly they had enjoyed for almost two centuries. Baptists and other sects once outlawed by that monopoly greeted the new arrangement with unmixed joy. Baptist optimism eventually overtook Congre-

---

1. See for example, Sean Wilentz, "Society, Politics, and the Market Revolution," in *The New American History*, ed. Eric Foner (Philadelphia: Temple University Press, 1990), pp. 51-68; Steven Mintz and Susan Kellogg, *Domestic Revolutions: A Social History of American Family Life* (New York: Free Press, 1988), pp. 43-65.

gational gloom: the separation of religious institutions from government funding meant that all evangelical Protestants would have to cultivate a network of voluntary support to succeed. And they had before them an urgent and ambitious task. The possibility of "Christianizing" a now secular nation quickly galvanized people from all denominations toward a common purpose.

Evangelical Protestants discovered a genius for organizing. In the early nineteenth century, they created what historians have labeled a "benevolent empire" of missionary, moral reform, and humanitarian efforts. This vast international movement spanned the Atlantic Ocean, joining Americans and Europeans in a common cause. It was supported by an enormous network of local societies, many composed of pious women. The ever expanding array of Christian causes included moral reform societies, temperance organizations, and assistance to the poor, the prisoner, and the mentally disturbed. From New York's notorious "Five Points" neighborhood to the wilds of California and the shores of far-off India, zealous Protestants traveled everywhere their vigorous imaginations could conceive.[2]

Education was at the heart of their task. In the decades before the United States had a functioning school system, Sunday schools accompanied biblical and moral instruction with rudimentary skills in literacy. In many isolated rural communities and inner-city slums, these schools provided the only opportunity for poor children to read and write.[3] For their part, foreign missionaries traveled to other lands not simply to preach, but to translate the Bible and set up schools so the sacred word could be properly understood. Indeed, enthusiasm for the classroom soon threatened to overshadow the primacy of preaching. At the end of the nineteenth century, American, Canadian, and European missionaries had established over 20,000 schools of every description, from universities to kindergartens, with over a million students.[4]

2. The phrase comes from Frank I. Foster, *The Evangelical United Front, 1790-1837* (Chapel Hill: University of North Carolina Press, 1960).

3. William Bean Kennedy, *The Shaping of Protestant Education: An Interpretation of the Sunday School and the Development of Protestant Educational Strategy in the United States, 1789-1860* (New York: Association Press, 1966); Ann M. Boylan, *Sunday School: The Formation of an American Institution, 1790-1880* (New Haven: Yale University Press, 1988).

4. James S. Dennis, *Centennial Survey of Foreign Missions* (New York: Fleming H. Revell, 1902), p. 267.

This new era in American Protestant history created an enormous demand for well-trained clergy. Pioneers moving west out of settled East Coast communities, new immigrants arriving from Europe, and growing urban populations all needed churches and pastors. By 1850, even in a relatively "churched" area like Massachusetts, the ratio of clergy to the general population was only 1.7 per 1,000; in frontier areas and in the South, the proportion was far wider. Few seminary graduates encountered any difficulty in locating a suitable post.[5]

But Andover and Newton were not just the passive beneficiaries of good times; in many practical ways, the "benevolent empire" owed them both a fundamental debt. Simply put, all of the great causes of the nineteenth century, foreign missions, social reform, and benevolence, would not have succeeded without the infusion of trained leaders coming from Andover and from Newton, as well as a host of other theological seminaries. Newton's earliest supporters — Thomas Baldwin, Jonathan Going, Lucius Bolles, Daniel Sharp, and Nathaniel Cobb, to name only a few — were well-known figures in the ongoing story of Baptist home and foreign missions. The two great Congregational missionary arms, the American Board of Commissioners for Foreign Missions and the American Home Missionary Society, began within the entrepreneurial visions of Andover students and faculty.

The historical narrative of both schools makes the most sense, therefore, within the broader tale of evangelical Protestant growth and organization. The key story for our purposes, of course, deals with foreign and home missions, as these both exerted a powerful pull on young men training for service to the church. But that story itself points toward a larger truth, the powerful reciprocal relationship between these two theological schools, their American Protestant world, and in fact a larger global context. "Globalization," the popular buzzword of the late twentieth century, is not new; already some two centuries ago, the ambitious dreams formed in seminary classrooms forever changed the shape of Protestant Christianity. No longer a solitary enterprise contracted with a busy mentor and his dense theological library, ministerial education introduced students to a vast network of

5. Roger Finke and Rodney Starke, *The Churching of America, 1776-1990: Winners and Losers in Our Religious Economy* (New Brunswick, NJ: Rutgers University Press, 1992), pp. 66-71.

pressing spiritual and social concerns. From their vantage point on two separate hills looking out over the New England countryside and a world beyond, students at both Andover and Newton had much to contemplate.

The Missionary Call

By the time Andover reached its semi-centennial in 1858, its graduates were scattered all across the globe. Over 150 served in Asia, Africa, Europe, the Pacific Islands, and the United States.[6] Only a third of the students who had died during those first fifty years were buried in New England; the rest were scattered across the world: seventeen in Asia, six in Africa, six in Europe, and ten in the Pacific Islands. Four had been buried at sea.[7]

Many of the Andover men were justly famous as pioneers whose careers shaped the religious and political future of entire societies. Levi Parsons ('17) and Pliny Fiske ('18) were the first American Protestant missionaries in Palestine, arriving there in 1821. Hiram Bingham and Asa Thurston, who both graduated from Andover in 1819, sailed to the Sandwich Islands that same year, along with their families, seventeen persons in all. The story of the Hawaii mission has not fared well over time: novelist James Michener memorably described his main character Abner Hale as a "stringy-haired" and "pasty-faced" model of Protestant repression. But in fact, both Bingham and Thurston were vigorous, almost charismatic figures who initiated a long and successful missionary effort in Hawaii. Just a few decades after their arrival, in 1837, the mission station employed ninety Americans and several hundred Hawaiian converts. The church itself had grown to 18,000 — almost a fifth of the island's population — and the constitution of the Hawaiian kingdom forbade the passage of any laws "at variance with the word of the Lord Jehovah."[8]

6. *General Catalogue of the Theological Seminary, Andover, Massachusetts, 1808-1908* (Boston: Thomas Todd, 1908), pp. 512-513.

7. *Memorial of the Semi-Centennial Celebration of the Founding of the Theological Seminary at Andover* (Andover, MA: Warren F. Draper, 1859), pp. 8-9.

8. William R. Hutchison, *Errand to the World: American Protestant Thought and Foreign Missions* (Chicago: University of Chicago Press, 1987), pp. 70, 71.

Other examples abound. Elijah Coleman Bridgman, from the class of 1829, was the first American missionary to China, arriving in 1830 after receiving additional medical training to work with the Scots Presbyterian Robert Morrison. By the beginning of the Civil War, some 120 Andover students had followed in their wake. As Henry Rowe wrote in 1933, the early history of the American Board "is the story of Andover men and their sacrificial service."[9] By the time of Andover's centennial in 1908, the school had sent out some 248 foreign missionaries, a figure that did not even begin to include all those who had served in frontier parishes in North America, or in urban missions.[10]

Newton posted similar numbers. Half of its first graduating class — admittedly one of two men receiving degrees — set off immediately for the west. Elijah Burnham Smith made it only as far as the wilds of Buffalo, New York, but other alumni would go much farther. Within its first half century, the Baptist school had sent 54 young men abroad as "missionaries of the cross." By 1925 their number had reached 300; by the time of its centennial, Newton counted seven graduating classes in which half of the number had gone overseas.[11]

To be sure, the missionary rhetoric of the nineteenth century held little of the nuance that modern sensibilities expect. Entire native populations became simply "the heathen" in need of Christian salvation; while many missionaries took great pains to learn local languages and to recruit native clergy, they rarely questioned the need for adopting western ways. They assumed that Christianity and "civilization" were merely different sides of the same beneficial coin. While acknowledging the good intentions of most nineteenth-century missionaries, many people in the present day also point to the harm caused by the imperialistic forces that so often followed in their wake. But, in the nineteenth-century heyday of missions, few disputed its social and intellectual impact, as missionaries established schools, hospitals, and a generation of trained leaders. Bible translators introduced literacy and missionary

---

9. Henry K. Rowe, *History of Andover Theological Seminary* (Newton, MA: Thomas Todd, 1933), p. 111.

10. *General Catalogue of the Theological Seminary,* pp. 512-514.

11. L. Call Barnes, "Newton Men and Missions: Historical Addresses Delivered at the Newton Centennial, June 1925," *Institution Bulletin* 18 (1925): 28-41; *The Baptists and the National Centenary: A Record of Christian Work, 1776-1876* (Philadelphia: American Baptist Publication Society, 1876), p. 138.

doctors brought down the death rate from famine and disease. In that sense, both Andover and Newton played a significant role in shaping the political and intellectual course of their own nation, and other societies all around the globe

But the nineteenth-century missionary movement was not just a one-way conversation. Considered in all its complexity, the missionary cause had a deep and permanent effect on American institutions, both religious and secular. This was especially true of seminary life, where tales of missionary labors captured the imagination, instilling the tedium of study with a lively purpose. At both Andover and Newton, and at other seminaries across the country, student-run Societies of Inquiry attracted the ablest and most ambitious scholars. The schools' public identification with prominent missionary names like Adoniram Judson, Frances Mason, and Samuel Mills brightened their aura within the churches; no doubt that for many a young Congregationalist or Baptist, tales of the Haystack prayer meeting or the exploits of the "Andover band" made a far deeper impression than even the deepest theological utterances of Leonard Woods or Irah Chase.

Most important in the long run, missionary enthusiasm brought new people onto seminary campuses. This chapter includes the stories of Henry Opukaha'ia, a young Hawaiian, and Niijima Jo (also known as Joseph Hardy Neesima), who traveled to New England from Japan. Both of them arrived on Andover's campus under the sponsorship of evangelical Protestant friends, and both would become influential figures on their own native soil. It is also important to point out that the first women to attend Newton Theological Institution were training for evangelistic careers overseas, sponsored by the Women's Foreign Missionary Society in 1894. That is a story that is best told more fully in a later chapter — but clearly, it illustrates the same point: missions introduced diversity onto both seminary campuses.

It would be impossible and probably inadvisable to name all of the missionaries who trained at Andover or at Newton. Earlier historians of both institutions never seemed to tire of constructing lists and tables, and all of these are readily available in every semi-centennial, centennial, and bi-centennial volume published over the last two hundred years. Perhaps a few good stories will suffice.

The Haystack Legacy

Sometime in the late summer of 1806 — the exact date was never re-corded — a group of students from Williams College met in a field to pray. The weather in Massachusetts' Berkshire hills, always unpredict-able, was ominously hot and humid that day. Without warning the looming clouds emptied into a deluge. The five students ran from the driving thunderstorm to the lee of a haystack, and being both pious and practical sorts, they decided to continue their prayers as they huddled together under the straw.

All five of the young men — Samuel Mills, Harvey Loomis, James Rich-ards, Francis Robbins, and Byram Green — had serious matters on their minds. Before the rainstorm, their conversation had turned to the "moral darkness" of Asia, their information drawn from startling reports coming from the recently formed London Missionary Society. Like many college students of their day, the Williams men were deeply influenced by the reli-gious revivals sweeping up and down the Atlantic coast and far into the western backcountry. Some were already referring to a Second Great Awakening, a renewal of that first wave of religious excitement that had forever transformed the waning Puritan piety of New England's churches. Already by 1806, the revival had awoken the lackadaisical student body at Yale, and in the following years it would bring forth countless organiza-tions, both local and national, dedicated to the spread of the Christian gospel around the world and into every corner of the United States.

As the rain spattered across their makeshift shelter, one of the young men made a momentous suggestion. Why not, said Samuel Mills, take the gospel to Asia ourselves? Why pray for God to act when they themselves were perfectly able to do the job on God's behalf? "We could do it if we would," Mills pleaded. As Byram Green later remem-bered, only Harvey Loomis objected, arguing that the plan was simply too dangerous. But the rest immediately warmed to Mills' ambitious ideal; their petitions turned into promises that as soon as they could find a way, they would devote their lives to missionary service.[12]

---

12. See for example, Thomas C. Richards, *The Haystack Prayer Meeting: An Account of Its Origin and Spirit* (New York: The De Vinne Press, 1906); Thomas C. Richards, *Samuel J. Mills: Missionary Pathfinder, Pioneer and Promoter* (Boston, 1906). I am indebted to Sharon Taylor for the research and background material for this section.

Over the course of the next half century, the events of that summer afternoon drifted into legend, marking the birth of the American Protestant foreign missionary movement and the great "age of missions" in the nineteenth century. According to one tally published in 1900, American and European Protestants had organized 588 missionary societies, and were supporting over 18,000 missionaries and nearly 80,000 "native workers." The total income for that year was estimated at twenty million dollars. Through the efforts of many local women's societies and an enthusiastic wave of young men and women propelled by the Student Volunteer Movement, missionary work continued to attract a regular stream of college and seminary graduates.[13]

In the weeks and months after that famous summer thunderstorm, the Williams students continued to pray for revival and to study the news from abroad. They met regularly, sharing reports from the London Missionary Society and drawing new members, even as their ranks ebbed and rose with the rhythms of the school year. In 1808 they organized themselves into a Society of the Brethren to, as they said, "effect a mission to the heathen in the persons of its members." The original group included some, though not all, of the original Haystack group — Samuel Mills, James Richards, Ezra Fiske, John Seward, and Luther Rice. Not content just to support the missionary cause with money or prayer, they were determined to go abroad themselves.[14]

The idea seemed so outrageous that the Brethren took an oath "to solemnly promise to keep inviolably secret the existence of this society." They recorded their proceedings in an elaborate code, perhaps hoping to avoid criticism for over-reaching if their ambitious plan ended in failure. As Ezra Fiske later recalled, "*modesty* required us to conceal our association lest we should be thought rashly imprudent and should injure the cause we wished to promote."[15]

The Haystack legacy persisted, to a large degree, because of Andover Seminary. In early 1810, Samuel Mills, James Richards, and Harvey

---

13. Dennis, *Centennial Survey*, p. 263.

14. Society of the Brethren, Minutes. ANTS archives.

15. Society of the Brethren, Constitution, Article 5, ANTS archives. Fiske is quoted in Richard D. Pierce, "A History of the Society of Inquiry in the Andover Theological Seminary, 1811-1920, Together with Some Account of Missions in America Before 1810 and a Brief History of the Brethren, 1808-1873" (B.D. Thesis: Andover Theological Seminary 1938), p. 15.

Loomis enrolled at Andover to prepare themselves for future careers as missionaries. Sometime during that year Ezra Fiske brought the Brethren records over from Williamstown, and the small group reestablished themselves on Andover Hill. They recruited cautiously, investigating the character and fervor of each potential recruit before admitting him to the group. Eventually they added three important new members, Adoniram Judson, Samuel Newell, and Samuel Nott.

In June 1810, six students and several of the Andover faculty met at the home of Moses Stuart to discuss the possibility of a missionary trip. Costs and logistics seemed prohibitive, especially for young men still in school. But the students proposed an innovative plan: they would devote themselves to evangelistic work overseas on behalf of fellow Christians at home, and those Christians would provide the funds for their labors. Two days later, on June 28, 1810, four of the students — Adoniram Judson, Samuel Nott, Samuel Mills, and Samuel Newell — met with the General Association of Massachusetts Proper on the campus of Bradford Academy to offer themselves for work abroad. Carried by their enthusiasm, an influential group of leading Congregationalists quickly agreed to act as sponsors. On September 7, 1810, they formed the American Board of Commissioners for Foreign Missions, the first but definitely not the last of national foreign missionary societies formed over the course of the nineteenth century.

Buoyed by that success, in January 1811, the eight seminarians, together with their friends back at Williams, established a new organization, the Society of Inquiry on the Subject of Missions. Unlike the close-knit secret Society of the Brethren, this group was open to all Andover students. In fact, over the next twenty-five years, 827 of them would sign on, including many who later traveled to India, the Sandwich Islands, Syria, and to Native American tribes.[16]

During the group's heyday, up through the early 1870s, its members met monthly to pray and to collect information about missionary work being done overseas. They created their own library of missionary information and collected a museum full of curios from abroad. Society of Inquiry members corresponded regularly with seminarians in other

16. *Memoirs of American Missionaries Formerly Connected with the Society of Inquiry Respecting Missions, in the Andover Theological Seminary* (Boston: Pierce and Parker, 1833), pp. 13-29.

schools, where the Andover model was widely copied. In fact, within a few decades, similarly named groups had already sprung up at Yale (1818), Union Theological Seminary in Virginia (1818), New Brunswick Seminary (1820), and the Protestant Episcopal Seminary in Virginia (1824). Most important of all, Society of Inquiry members urged each other to go abroad to evangelize, bolstering their zeal with regular correspondence from missionaries in the field, an increasing number of whom were Andover graduates.[17]

All of these efforts came to fruition on February 6, 1812, when five Andover students stood for ordination as foreign missionaries. Their names would become staples of Protestant missionary lore: Adoniram Judson and his young wife Ann Hasseltine Judson, Samuel Newell and his bride Harriet Atwood Newell, as well as Gordon Hall, Samuel Nott, and Luther Rice. All five were commissioned by the American Board at the Tabernacle Church in Salem, Massachusetts, in a solemn ceremony led by Leonard Woods, the Abbot Professor of Theology at Andover.

In his sermon, Woods laid out, really for the first time, a theological rationale for global Christianity. Although like most other American Protestants of his time and place, Woods believed in the duty of western Christians to convert the "heathen," he also saw missions in much grander terms, a labor of "love for souls." "Of what consideration is their nation, climate, color, language, government, education, manners?" Woods demanded. "Learned and ignorant, refined and rude, honorable and base, are all on a level in point of accountableness to God and immortality of soul." Christians of different denominations, he argued, had focused far too long on the matters that divided them. The remedy was to focus on "some great and common cause" in which they might find a "grave for all their jealousies and animosities." In its purest form, Woods declared, Christianity was a faith for all people in every part of the world, and in urgent millennial terms he lifted up the responsibility of American Protestants to reach the world with their gospel message.[18]

17. Clarence Shedd, *Two Centuries of Student Christian Movements*, vol. 1 (New York: Association Press, 1934), pp. 68, 73.

18. Leonard Woods, *A Sermon Delivered at the Tabernacle in Salem, February 6, 1812, On Occasion of the Ordination of the Rev. Messrs. Samuel Newell, A.M., Adoniram Judson, A.M., Samuel Nott, A.M., Gordon Hall, A.M. and Luther Rice, A.M., Missionaries to the Heathen in Asia, Under the Direction of the Board of Commissioners for Foreign Missions* (Boston: Samuel T. Armstrong, 1812), pp. 11, 24.

Difficult days lay ahead, however. The Judsons and the Newells sailed from Salem on February 19, 1812, reaching Calcutta by mid-June. The British East India Company gave them a cool welcome, however, fearing missionary interference in their growing business interests. The Newells traveled on to the island of Mauritius, but by the time they reached port in October, Harriet was gravely ill, having lost her prematurely born daughter on the voyage. She died two months later, at the age of nineteen. Samuel eventually joined his two other Andover colleagues Luther Rice and Samuel Nott in Bombay, but he too died a few years later in 1821.

Adoniram Judson

The Judsons traveled on to Burma, but no longer as Congregationalists. During the long days of the sea voyage to India, as Judson later related, he had read the scriptures and become convinced that adult baptism was the true form of the sacrament; they underwent immersion soon after the ship docked. Jokes persisted about the psychological effect of many months with little to do besides staring at the watery depths of the ocean, but other evidence suggests that Judson was a skeptical pedobaptist at best during his days at Andover. The change of theology led to a formal disassociation from the American Board and, now joined in Baptist sympathies by Luther Rice, Judson immediately appealed to Thomas Baldwin, pastor of Boston's Second Baptist Church, suggesting the formation of a national Baptist Missionary Society. The letter reached Boston in early 1813 and "spread with electric rapidity." A small group convened in Baldwin's home and formed the Baptist Society for Propagating the Gospel in India and Other Foreign Parts, which became the immediate predecessor of a national denominational group in 1914. Baldwin was a guiding spirit behind the American Baptist Missionary Union, subsequently formed in Philadelphia.[19]

Over the course of his long missionary career, Judson's name be-

19. The story goes that in a theology class debate Judson was assigned to play the part of the Baptist, and studied so hard that he convinced himself of the rightness of that position. See J. Leslie Dunstan, "Andover Newton and Missions," *Andover Newton Bulletin* 49 (April 1957): 19. On early Baptist missions see William Gammell, *A History of American Baptist Missions in Asia, Africa, Europe, and North America* (Boston: Gould, Kendall and Lincoln, 1849), pp. 14-21.

came revered in Baptist circles. By the time he died in 1850, he had established a church of some 7,000 members and 100 native clergy in Burma. All the while Judson suffered imprisonment, illness, and bereavement; but his trials, including the untimely deaths of his three wives, only added to his legend. Ann Hasseltine Judson died in 1826, shortly after his release from prison. Judson married Sarah Boardman, the widow of a colleague, in 1834, but she died eleven years later in 1845. In 1846 he married Emily Chubbock, who survived him only by a few years. During a time when few white, middle-class American women traveled much beyond their own homes, the story of the Judson wives was simply remarkable. As models of Christian faithfulness and feminine piety, they quickly inspired an entire genre of missionary hagiography.[20]

News of Ann Hasseltine Judson's death reached Newton Theological Institution on April 16, 1827, and students formed a Society of Inquiry that very same day. Instead of being "discouraged by the loss of . . . the lamented Mrs. Judson," the young seminarians determined to commit themselves to "the cause for which she unwearingly and successfully toiled, and in which she prematurely died." Following the Andover model, the object of the society was "to gain information on all subjects connected with the advancement of missions," including "the literature, morals, and religion of different countries, and the causes which operate on the moral improvement of mankind."[21]

The students' commitment reflected a surge of missionary interest among New England Baptists that was well under way before Judson's shipboard change of heart. Massachusetts Baptists had organized their own missionary society in 1802 to "furnish occasional preaching, and to promote the knowledge of evangelistic truth in new settlements within these United States."[22] Not surprisingly, missionary interest created a rising demand for ministerial training: the leaders of the missionary society figured prominently in Newton's formation a few years

20. Joan Jacobs Brumberg, *Mission for Life: The Story of the Family of Adoniram Judson, the Dramatic Events of the First American Foreign Mission, and the Course of Evangelical Religion in the Nineteenth Century* (New York: Free Press, 1980).

21. "Constitution of the Society of Inquiry in the Newton Theological Institution, April 16, 1827," ANTS archives.

22. W. H. Eaton, *Historical Sketch of the Massachusetts Baptist Missionary Society and Convention, 1802-1902* (Boston: Massachusetts Baptist Convention, 1903).

later. And in fact, one of the first acts of the American Baptist Missionary Union was to press for the organization of the Columbian College in Washington, D.C., the short-lived seminary that preceded Newton.

In its early days, the Newton group met the third Wednesday of every term, assigned themselves to committees, and read "dissertations" to each other about foreign missions, the work of Bible and tract societies, Sabbath schools, temperance organizations, slavery, and evangelistic work being done among sailors and soldiers — in short, the full sweep of the benevolent empire in which Baptists played a prominent role. Like most student groups, the Society of Inquiry (renamed in 1836 the Society of Missionary Inquiry) battled with the inconsistent zeal of members toward the end of each semester, when assigned written reports tended to become extemporaneous ones. But there was no doubting their seriousness of purpose. In 1838 the group held an impromptu debate on the question, "Ought missionaries to devote any portion of their time to the gratification of literary tastes?" After a "spirited" exchange, the students decided in the negative.[23]

The first famous name to emerge from the Newton Brethren was Francis Mason, who arrived in Burma in 1830. Born in England in 1799 as the son of a shoemaker, Mason came to Newton with relatively little formal education but convinced of his calling after a profound conversion experience. After graduating in 1830, he promptly left for Burma, and in his first two years baptized 6,000 converts and founded 126 churches. During his forty-year career Mason also mastered two Karen dialects, translating the entire Bible into one and parts of it into another. The determined autodidact also prepared grammars in both languages. He became a well-known naturalist and eventually a member of the Royal Asiatic Society. Mason's book, *Burma, Its People and Natural Productions,* was for a long time the definitive work on the subject.[24]

It is not difficult to imagine the effect of Mason's correspondence to the Society of Inquiry. Writing in 1842, he reminisced about his own admittedly short years in Newton classrooms, and he held out the example of other alumni who were laboring against irreligion in the wilds of

---

23. Minutes for November 1838, Society of Missionary Inquiry of the Newton Theological Institution, ANTS archives.

24. On Mason's Newton years see Francis Mason, *The Story of a Working Man's Life: With Sketches of Travel in Europe, Asia, Africa, and America, As Related by Himself* (New York: Oakley, Mason, and Co., 1870), pp. 206-211.

Michigan and Ohio, preaching to African slaves in the South, or dying prematurely in the service of the gospel. "Is there not *one* among the next graduating class, and another in the middle, and a third in the junior class," Mason pleaded, "whose duty it is to give himself to this specific work? I wish each of you," he insisted, "to post the question distinctly to God, 'Lord is it I?'"[25]

Many others did follow in Mason's wake. Josiah Goddard left for Bangkok within a few months of graduating from Newton in 1838, and finished his career in China. He had been a member of the so-called "conscientious class" of Brown University, who had refused to receive their diplomas at the graduation ceremony because they felt the academic honor detracted from the pure pursuit of godly study. Over the years his children, grandchildren, and great-grandchildren continued the missionary tradition in China. His son and namesake graduated from Newton in 1867 and revised and completed his father's translation of the New Testament into the Chinese dialect at Ningpo.[26] Nathan Brown, who translated the Bible into both Assamese and Japanese, left from Newton in 1832.[27] Josiah Cushing graduated from Newton in 1866 and sailed for Burma that same year. A brilliant scholar and linguist, he had been a Hebrew tutor at Newton and according to legend, occupied the same dormitory room as C. H. Carpenter, who had left for Burma a few years earlier. Cushing quickly mastered the Shan dialect, printing a grammar in 1873 and a full translation of the Bible in 1885.[28]

The Reciprocal Effect

The list of able, sometimes brilliant, linguists and translators from both schools could go on almost indefinitely; clearly, foreign missions

---

25. Correspondence to NTI Society of Inquiry from Francis Mason, October 17, 1842, ANTS archives.

26. Francis Wayland Goddard, *Called to Cathay* (New York: Baptist Literature Bureau, 1948), pp. 47-49.

27. Walter Sinclair Stewart, *Early Baptist Missionaries and Pioneers* (Philadelphia: Judson Press, 1926), pp. 55-77.

28. Stewart, *Early Baptist Missionaries and Pioneers*, pp. 204-229. On his Newton years, see Wallace St. John, *Josiah Nelson Cushing: Missionary and Scholar, Burma* (Rangoon: American Baptist Mission Press, 1912), pp. 23-31.

attracted some of the brightest and most capable students. As Newton professor James Knowles declared, "The revival of the missionary spirit, in all its diversified yet kindred forms of benevolence, has created an urgent demand for increased mental cultivation and resources in the ministers of Christ." Even the clergyman who chose to stay behind would have to learn how to manage "complicated benevolent operations," a duty which "severely tasks the intellect" and "leaves him very little leisure for study." Missionary work in all of its many forms created "a stern necessity for previous and thorough training."[29]

Even Andover saw no contradiction between academic rigor and missionary zeal. "It is vain for ministers to think of limiting their studies to theology, regarded mainly as a *science*," declared American Board secretary Rufus Anderson, "in neglect of their own and of their people's relation to the great surrounding world." In his charge to Thomas Laurie, an Andover graduate headed to Syria, Anderson reminded his studious audience that "Nothing can prevent that world from knocking continually at the door of their study. The set time for sending the gospel to the nations has come; and ministers, whether at home among the churches, or abroad among the heathen, will feel themselves more and more constrained to cultivate religion . . . as an art having a sublime purpose — *the only art of reconciling this revolted world to God*." An Andover graduate and one of the most famous missionary spokesmen of his day, Anderson insisted that the "sublime studies" of a seminary curriculum would produce "a delightful confidence in the gospel, and a happiness in studying and preaching it, approaching to that which angels may be supposed to have in their ministries of love."[30]

The missionary movement also opened both campuses to the wider world. Every month Society of Inquiry students at both Andover and Newton researched and presented talks to each other about places far away from New England, from Madagascar to China. For many students, these meetings became a consistent source of information about current events and even a few looming social issues. In the decades before the Civil War, members of the Newton Society periodically dis-

29. James D. Knowles, *Importance of Theological Institutions: An Address, Delivered Before the Trustees, Students and Friends of the Newton Theological Institution, November 14, 1832* (Boston: Lincoln and Edmands, 1832), p. 9

30. Rufus Anderson, "Charge to Rev. Thomas Laurie," 1848, Congregational Library Small Collections, Boston, MA.

cussed slavery and abolition, and eventually began holding their meetings as public events in the Newton Baptist Church. Throughout the 1870s the group supported an African American student preparing for the ministry.

Henry Opukaha'ia

Missions also internationalized seminary campuses. Andover in fact was host to two of the century's most famous Christian converts, Henry Opukaha'ia and Joseph Hardy Neesima, both of whose stories are significant within the longer history of Andover Newton seminary.

Opukaha'ia, a native of Hawaii (then the Sandwich Islands), arrived at Andover in 1810.[31] Orphaned by war, he had taken passage on board a ship bound for New York, and after his arrival, traveled on with the ship's captain to his home in New Haven, Connecticut, in 1809. Only sixteen years old and possessed of very little English, Opukaha'ia's prospects looked dim. In his loneliness he took to walking the streets of the city, though when he was offered a chance to return to Hawaii he refused. Opukaha'ia's deepest wish was to learn to read and write.

A chance meeting soon turned his fortunes. Edwin Wright, a student at Yale, noticed the young man weeping and in an inspired moment walked over to him and asked "Do you wish to learn?" Opukaha'ia immediately brightened; he quickly proved himself an unusually able student and within a short time was taken in by Yale's president Timothy Dwight. The next key encounter was with Samuel Mills, who was temporarily studying at Yale. Recognizing the young Hawaiian's intellectual gift, he determined to continue Opukaha'ia's schooling. The two went to Mills' home in Torringford, Connecticut, where Opukaha'ia learned to swing a scythe, write a letter, and recite the catechism — though at this point by his own account uninterested in Christianity.

In 1810 Mills and Opukaha'ia went to Andover. While Mills pursued his studies, Opukaha'ia honed his English, roaming the dormitory and taking "much satisfaction" in conversing with anyone who would spare

---

31. The standard account is Edwin W. Dwight, *Memoirs of Henry Obookiah* (New Haven, CT: Religious Intelligencer, 1818). See also *Narrative of Five Youth from the Sandwich Islands Now Receiving an Education in This Country* (New York, 1816).

him a moment. It was during this time that he said his first Christian prayer, expressing his desire to some day return to Hawaii with his new faith. But full understanding took time. In 1811 Opukaha'ia went to study at nearby Bradford Academy, where he lived with the Hasseltine family, whose daughter Ann had recently left for missionary work in Burma. After a bout of aimlessness, the lonely young man began to experience a new zeal and began to make "rapid progress in religious knowledge." When Mills left for missionary work in Africa in 1814, Opukaha'ia returned to Connecticut, reconnected with his old friend Edwin Dwight, and became one of the first students in a Foreign Mission School that the American Board had organized in nearby Cornwall. The remarkable school, aimed at educating Native Americans, soon numbered eleven students, seven of whom were from Hawaii. By the time the missionary school closed in 1826, seventeen alumni had gone there as evangelists.[32]

Opukaha'ia yearned to return as well, but his remaining days were short. He died of typhoid in 1818 at the age of twenty six, at the verge of a voyage back to Hawaii. By then his story was known across New England; historian William Hutchison describes him as an early-nineteenth-century "matinee idol." The famous revivalist Lyman Beecher preached his funeral oration, and the citizens of Cornwall raised funds to erect a tomb in his memory, testifying to his powerful example of "piety and missionary Zeal."[33]

Niijima Jo

Niijima Jo, or Joseph Hardy Neesima, first arrived at Andover to study at the Phillips Academy in 1865. Like Opukaha'ia, he had left his native country under difficult circumstances, and was taken in by pious Christians who recognized his gift. Niijima departed from Japan in 1864, when it was still closed to most communication with the western world. An ambitious and well-educated son of a samurai, or minor aristocrat,

32. Paul H. Chamberlain, *The Foreign Mission School* (Cornwall, CT: Cornwall Historical Society, 1968).

33. Hutchison, *Errand to the World,* p. 67; Lyman Beecher, *A Sermon Delivered at the Funeral of Henry Obookiah, A Native of Owhyhee, and a Member of the Foreign Mission School in Cornwall, Connecticut* (Elizabethtown, NJ: Edson Hart, 1819).

he was by then already acquainted with Christianity, having served as translator to the chaplain at the Russian consulate in the northern city of Hakodate. Traveling abroad was a capital offense, but Niijima was determined to learn more about the United States and about Christianity. He escaped to Hong Kong, where he found a ship bound for Boston. The owner of the ship, a devout Congregationalist named Alpheus Hardy, became convinced that his intense young cabin boy (who had been dubbed "Joe" by the ship's crew) had a special calling, and he became Niijima's patron.

With Hardy's help, the young man, who renamed himself Joseph Hardy Neesima, undertook a rigorous educational regime and continued to progress in Christianity. At the Phillips Academy he was baptized in the seminary chapel; after finishing his program there he went on to Amherst College where he received his B.S. in mathematics. Niijima then entered Andover Seminary and began to prepare himself for a missionary career.

But by then the young man was becoming restless. In Japan the political winds had shifted decisively; the new Meiji government had brought an end to the old feudalism and set the country on a vigorous program of modernization. Under the new regime, Japan would become a major competitor with the United States and Europe, adopting a western calendar, postal system, railroads, and military infrastructure. Niijima recognized in this new enthusiasm for western ways a unique opportunity to present the Christian faith to Japan's ambitious samurai classes. In 1874, having finished his course of study at Andover and having received his ordination credentials, he returned to Japan to open a school.

In June 1875 Niijima purchased land in Kyoto adjacent to the imperial palace grounds, and established the Doshisha or "one purpose" school. With the aid of only a handful of American Board missionaries, Niijima and a local company of Japanese converts set about to create an institution that would be renowned for its high intellectual standards. The Meiji vision of modernization did not, of course, include an embrace of Christianity; recognizing the deep skepticism of Japanese intelligentsia toward western religion, Niijima insisted that Christians "must not be charged with being ignoramuses."[34] The

---

34. Neesima quoted in Kenneth Scott Latourette, *These Sought a Country: Being the Tipple Lectures in Drew University, 1950* (New York: Harper and Brothers 1950), p. 123.

Doshisha eventually included a theological seminary as well as a full university curriculum designed, in Niijima's words, to "raise up Christian statesmen, Christian lawyers, Christian editors, and Christian merchants, as well as Christian preachers and teachers." Japan's embrace of Christianity was selective and temporary, however; when Niijima died in 1890 the theological school numbered 85 students, but the other programs (which included a nursing course and a "Science School") reached 485.[35]

Home Missions and the Haystack Legacy

One more set of stories remains, about the evangelization of the American interior. Home missions was a cause dear to the men of both seminaries; it is no accident that Jonathan Going, who helped found Newton seminary, also started the American Baptist Home Missionary Society. Over the years, many other Newton students followed the example of the first graduate, Eli Burnham Smith, who had left New England's confines for a missionary tour in Buffalo, then a frontier settlement. George Leonard in Ohio, Thomas Ward Merrill in Michigan, and Timothy Horton Hall in Indiana were only 3 of the 124 Newton men who served in western churches during the school's first hundred years.[36]

The Andover Bands, those groups of determined young seminarians who set up schools and colleges in the western territories, achieved the greatest fame among nineteenth-century Protestants. With the equally well-known Yale Bands, they laid the first groundwork for Congregationalism in the central Midwest, including the establishment of Illinois College. They braved physical hardship of an unforgiving climate and, during the years before the Civil War, continual threats of violence for their antislavery stand.

Like the scores of alumni who became foreign missionaries, the Andover Bands also traced their beginnings to the five young men who prayed together under a haystack during that famous thunderstorm. In 1816, when Samuel Mills finished his studies at Andover, he did not fol-

35. Arthur Sherburne Hardy, *Life and Letters of Joseph Hardy Neesima* (Boston: Houghton, Mifflin, and Co, 1891), pp. 288, 349.

36. L. Call Barnes, "Newton Men and Missions," pp. 28-29.

low other Society of the Brethren members abroad. Instead he joined up with the Missionary Society of Connecticut and undertook two long tours of the American south and west, reaching New Orleans not long after the famous battle of 1815.

Even while a student at Williams he had confided in his diary his concern for Africa, a determination that only grew as he witnessed the evils of slavery on his travels. Mills was instrumental in beginning an African school in Newark, New Jersey, and attended the first meeting of the American Colonization Society (ACS) in December 1816. The goal of the Society was ambitious: recognizing the deep entrenchment of slavery in American economic and social institutions, the ACS proposed to redeem and resettle southern slaves in Africa. It was a daunting and ultimately controversial goal. Later generations of abolitionists would argue that the Society did little to eradicate the institution on American soil or to offer the survivors of slavery a stake in their own native land — by the early nineteenth century, African American family lines went back much further than those of the average European immigrant. But Mills, like many social reformers of his day, believed deeply that resettlement was the best and perhaps only moral option. In 1817 he set off as an agent for the American Colonization Society to explore the coast of Africa. With Dedham pastor Ebenezer Burgess he arrived there in March 1818 and began a "laborious inspection" for a proper site for a settlement. The two left for home in May, but Mills took a fever within the month; he died in June and was buried at sea.[37]

Mills' example was not lost on his Andover colleagues; over the next century, the school played a pivotal role in the organization of the "domestic mission" movement, a diverse effort that involved church planting in the wilds of the American interior, and later on the evangelization of Native Americans, foreign immigrants, Roman Catholics, and Mormons. After the Civil War, home missionaries were some of the first to provide education and material aid to freed slaves. The enormous, complex movement drew from many sources and took many forms, but in many ways, it owes its origin to Andover.

---

37. *Memoirs of American Missionaries Formerly Connected with the Society of Inquiry Respecting Missions,* pp. 66-70.

Home Missions and the Andover Bands

In Andover seminary's early days, anything seemed possible. Talk of a national home missionary organization, as New Hampshire pastor and historian Nathaniel Bouton later remembered, began during a stage-coach ride between Andover and Newburyport. He and another gradu-ating senior, Aaron Foster, were on their way to the funeral of Phoebe Bartlet in late January 1825, when the conversation turned to "the need of enlarged operations" in the country's western territories. Though the hinterlands of Ohio, Michigan, Indiana, and Illinois had their share of itinerating preachers — many of them Methodists and Baptists — few churches sat under the care of a permanent, "settled" pastor. The idea of forming a national society to place frontier ministers "flashed on my mind with great force," Bouton recalled, and as the talk became more and more animated, he and Foster determined to take action. Joined that evening by their friend Hiram Chamberlain, they sat in the living room of Ebenezer Porter, Andover's Professor of Sacred Rhetoric, and formed a plan.[38]

At the next meeting of the Porter Rhetorical Society, Aaron Foster laid out the crying need for "domestic missions"; his fervent oratory persuaded Andover's Society of Inquiry to take up the cause. In April 1825, the group set aside a permanent committee to plan for the evangelization of the American West — Wakefield Gale, Lucius Alden, Hiram Chamberlain, George Beckwith, Luther Bingham, George Howe, John Maltby, and Aaron Foster. In the fall of 1825, Ezra Porter, who had assisted in the ordination of the first foreign missionaries in Salem, traveled across New England to support the students' ambi-tious plan.

The ordination of these new "home missionaries," all Andover stu-dents, followed soon after. On September 29, 1825, in Boston's Old South Church, six young men declared their intent to devote their lives to "labors in the west." All but two signed on with what was at the time the largest organization supporting ministerial placements outside

---

38. Nathaniel Bouton, *History of the Origin and Organization of the American Home Mis-sionary Society* (New York: John A. Gray, 1860), pp. 4-5. The story is also told in Colin Goodykoontz, *Home Missions on the American Frontier, with Particular Reference to the American Home Missionary Society* (Caldwell, ID: Caxton Printers, Ltd., 1939), pp. 176-179.

New England, the United Domestic Missionary Society of New York. Within weeks they were dispersed to Illinois, Indiana, Missouri, and Ohio. The American Home Missionary Society (AHMS) was formed on the day following the ordination, on September 30, 1825. The organizing committee included many of New England's leading lights: Andover professors Porter and Justin Edwards, Park Street Church pastor Sereno Dwight and Old South's Benjamin Wisner, Nathaniel W. Taylor from Yale, and the presidents of Bowdoin and Amherst Colleges. Their idea was to create one new organization to guide and encompass all of the smaller works being done by more locally based missionary societies, including the United Domestic Missionary Society of New York (UDMS). In March 1826, the UDMS, which was by far the largest on the field, officially endorsed the new society's constitution.

The new organization was an immediate success. Within ten years of its founding, the AHMS was sponsoring over 750 missionaries, with annual revenues over $100,000. By the end of the nineteenth century, the effort involved the five largest Protestant denominations and amounted to over seventy million dollars toward the establishment of hundreds of new churches. Congregationalists estimated that four-fifths of their new churches in the west were the direct result of home missionary outreach.[39]

The ripples generated by that stagecoach conversation continued to spread for a generation or more. John Ellis, one of the original six ordained at Old South, journeyed to Illinois, and within months was already looking for a place to situate a school. In 1828 he purchased a plot of land near Jacksonville, Illinois. The news quickly traveled east, and within a year a group of students from Yale — known as the "Yale Band" — had trekked out to join Ellis. Together the seminarians organized Illinois College, which opened for classes in 1830.

The Iowa Band, composed of eleven Andover students, left New England in 1843.[40] They were greeted by a somewhat skeptical Asa Turner, the AHMS agent, and a rudimentary infrastructure of Congregational churches. "Lay aside all your dandy whims boys learn in college,"

---

39. Goodykoontz, *Home Missions on the American Frontier,* pp. 406-407.

40. For a list and description see P. Adelstein Johnson, *The First Century of Congregationalism in Iowa, 1840-1940* (Cedar Rapids, IA: Congregational Christian Conference of Iowa, 1945), pp. 97-106.

Turner had warned the group before their departure. "and take a few lessons of your grandmothers, before you come. Get clothes, firm, durable, something that will go through the hazel brush without tearing. Don't be afraid of a good, hard hand, or of a tanned face." Turner also warned the young men not to try and go it alone. "Get wives of the old Puritan stamp," he advised, "such as honored the distaff and the loom, those who can pail a cow, and churn the butter, and be proud of a jean dress or a checked apron." In other words, as Turner admonished, "Don't come here expecting a paradise."[41]

The young men arrived in Iowa in the dead of November. The local Congregational clergy sat them down in a simple log house and with a map of the territory on the table, the seminarians assigned themselves to isolated posts. The hardships of the years ahead no doubt proved Asa Turner right any number of times, but all but one or two of the original Iowa Band stayed on for many years. Horace Hutchinson died after two years of service, the only loss by death for the next twenty-one years. William Salter, who was only twenty-two when he left New England, the youngest of the group of eleven, pastored churches in Muscatine and Burlington for the next sixty-seven years.[42]

No doubt, a sense of humor helped steel determination. One of the young men, preaching before a group of Baptists, recorded in his diary that as the sermon progressed, he became "vexed as I noticed two ladies smiling at some holes in my coat sleeve, revealed by my gesturing." He lowered his gestures and preached "straight at" the bemused women, in his irritation delivering "with more point and earnestness than usual." After the meeting, an Old School Presbyterian came over to remark that "he would give five dollars if I would stop and preach a year in the place." It was, the young preacher admitted, "quite a compliment, considering the source."[43]

Andover Bands also appeared in Maine, with five graduates arriving in the 1890s, and in Kansas during the height of the abolitionist excitement of the 1850s. The four men who formed the Kansas Band — Richard Cordley, Grosvernor Morse, Sylvester Storrs, and Roswell Parker —

41. Turner quoted in Goodykoontz, *Home Missions on the American Frontier*, p. 250.
42. Johnson, *First Century of Congregationalism in Iowa*, pp. 106-105; William Salter, *The Old People's Psalm, With Reminiscences of Deceased Members of the Iowa Band* (Burlington, IA: E. C. Gnahn and Mauro and Wilson, 1895), pp. 9-21.
43. Quoted in Goodykoontz, *Home Missions on the American Frontier*, p. 252.

were drawn by the example of the Iowa Band as well as the passionate controversy over the territory's future, during those difficult years when it was known simply as "Bloody Kansas." Cordley, born in Great Britain and raised in Michigan, arrived in Lawrence just as the Civil War was beginning and violence over the previous years escalating even further. He narrowly escaped death when William Clarke Quantrill, a notorious proslavery guerilla, burned the young preacher's house and all his possessions, hoping to get rid of "that damned abolitionist preacher."[44] Parker, who organized churches in Leavenworth and Wyandotte, kept guard over them with his Sharp's rifle in hand. By 1865, however, the number of Congregational churches had grown from just one in 1854 to thirty-two, with nearly 800 members.[45]

Prospect

"No more compelling is the call of the South to the waterfowl when the summer wanes," Andover's historian Henry Rowe rhapsodized in 1933, "than was the Macedonian call from heathendom to the dormitories and classrooms on Andover Hill." The same was clearly true of Newton. Both schools owed much, and contributed much, to the great century of missions a hundred years ago. Missionary work enlivened and complicated life on both the Newton and Andover campuses, especially for the young men who came there hoping for a simple career path. It tended to attract disparate people with unusual dreams: Samuel Mills, Henry Opukaha'ia, Niijima Jo, Adoniram Judson, and Frances Mason.[46]

Indeed, the missionary legacy of both schools, and Andover in particular, was so broad that it defies easy generalization. In the early nineteenth century, they provided crucial leadership and a regular supply of recruits for the missionary agencies that they helped envision and organize. Andover played a central role in the formation of the two great ecu-

---

44. See his account in Richard Cordley, *A History of Lawrence, Kansas, From the Earliest Settlement to the Close of the Rebellion* (Lawrence, KS: Lawrence Journal Press, 1895).

45. Edward D. Porter, *The Andover Band in Maine* (Cambridge, MA: Riverside Press, 1893), pp. 3-12; Charles M. Correll, *A Century of Congregationalism in Kansas, 1854-1954* (Topeka: Kansas Congregational Conference, 1953), pp. 23-28; "Sketch of Congregationalism in Kansas," *Congregational Record* 7 (March 1866): 145-151.

46. Rowe, *History of Andover*, p. 111.

menical arms of the early-nineteenth-century movement, the American Board of Commissioners for Foreign Missions and the American Home Missionary Society. Newton's leaders presided at the birth of Baptist foreign missions as well. Certainly by the end of the nineteenth century, the movement had grown far beyond its New England beginnings, especially as, after the Civil War, women's organizations assumed greater leadership. By then, virtually every denomination in the United States — and Roman Catholic churches as well — boasted its own array of overseas schools and churches, and the Christian faithful from every corner of the country donated their individual "missionary mites" to the fulfillment of that single cause. A movement that large grows from many sources, but it is still fair to say that the memory of the Haystack prayer meeting, and the young men who honed their vision at Andover, has captured Protestant imaginations ever since.

Difficult tests lay ahead, however. The last half of the nineteenth century would bring a new set of challenges to the Protestant cause, and over time these would erode the earlier confidence in Christianity and western civilization that energized the first generation of students and faculty. The passage of the Andover and Newton story into the modern era is, like many other stories of the past, fraught with irony. As old theological assumptions began to falter, the very creeds once raised to protect against heresy became a painful source of division. The missionary devotion which had contributed so profoundly to the unity of both schools would, especially in Andover's case, prove the biggest stumbling block of all.

CHAPTER FOUR

The New Theology Comes to Andover:
The Story of the Future Probation Controversy

——◁◦◦▷——

I f Andover had an "original sin," it was one of imprecision. Like Adam and Eve's first bite of the apple in the Garden of Eden, an act long viewed by many Christian theologians as a fatal flaw introduced into human history, Andover's founding documents set a course for future trouble. Almost from the school's inception, the two standards of orthodoxy demanded by the two sets of founders sowed confusion and, in a few cases, outright conflict. To the theologically trained eye, the Westminster catechism and the Associate Creed were logically incompatible, upholding two different views of original sin. More practically minded sorts wondered which creed was the school's bottom line of orthodoxy. Those versed in Massachusetts law found the role of the Board of Visitors a true puzzle. Strictly speaking, as a last-minute addition to the Andover constitution by the Associate Founders, it had no legal standing until the state legislature approved an amendment in 1820. Even after that, the extent of their power was unknown and, for a short while, untested.

The famous Andover Controversy, a series of doctrinal and legal disputes in the 1880s and early 1890s, marked the public phase of this ongoing internal debate. The occasion for the uproar was the so-called "Andover theory," the suggestion that non-Christians might receive a second opportunity to repent and accept salvation after death. This somewhat arcane set of ideas, normally allocated to a drowsy afternoon seminar, became a matter of hot public debate when the Board of Visitors refused to approve Andover's newly appointed Abbot Professor, fearing that he would bring this controversial idea to his Andover classrooms. In 1885, after placing five Andover professors on trial for various transgressions against the original Andover creeds, they convicted the faculty president, Egbert Smyth, of teaching the doctrine of second probation. Smyth would not depart quietly, however. The school's private matter became a thoroughly public issue when the Supreme Judicial Court of Massachusetts heard Smyth's appeal and vacated his conviction in 1893.[1]

The controversy was, in many ways, a classic confrontation between new theology and old, between liberal progressivism and the New England Calvinism Andover had been founded to protect. But in a deeper sense the Andover controversy was about governance. Who owned Andover, and who could set its standards for orthodoxy? The three men on the Board of Visitors? The board of trustees? The Congregational churches? Through all the charges and countercharges lurked a suspicion as old as Andover itself, that the school was at bottom a merely sectarian institution, the property of a few who could determine its doctrinal standards and set its future course.

The full story is very long and complicated, defying easy summary. Most simply, it falls into a series of battles involving several generations of Andover professors and unfolding across several decades. The school's early skirmishes over slavery and abolition provide an instructive prelude to an ongoing series of debates over the meaning and scope of the Andover creeds. For clarity's sake, these are laid out as three separate "rounds," beginning in the 1820s and ending in 1893. Through all of the public upheaval, life in the classroom continued unabated. The full story of the Andover controversy, therefore, also involves some important innovations in pedagogy and curriculum, which played an important role in the world of theological education.

---

1. I am indebted to Sharon Taylor for much of the material in this chapter, and to her willingness to share work from her dissertation, "That Obnoxious Doctrine: Future Probation and the Struggle to Construct an American Congregationalist Identity" (Ph.D. diss.: Boston College, 2004).

Andover and Slavery

Controversy was, of course, nothing new on Andover's campus. In the decades before the Civil War, temperance and antislavery sentiment found ready adherents among both students and faculty. Indeed, in 1853, when Calvin Stowe arrived as Bartlet Professor of Sacred Rhetoric, his wife Harriet Beecher Stowe was an international celebrity, having just published *Uncle Tom's Cabin* in 1852. Mrs. Stowe's Andover years coincided with the peak of her international fame, with trips to Europe in 1853 and 1856, and a regular flow of best-selling novels. The family's "Stone Cabin" in Andover provided a welcome retreat during this time, when Andover's reputation as a center of moral reform spread, along with Mrs. Stowe's personal fame, across the Atlantic and across the country.[2]

Many Andover students shared her convictions. In 1832 Leonard Woods complained to the board of trustees about a "few individuals, heated by the subject of abolition" who were challenging the authority of professors in the classroom.[3] Radical sentiment was also causing friction in the Society of Inquiry, whose Committee on Colonization came under bitter attack by students committed to an immediate end to slavery.

Andover became the center of public controversy in 1835, when fiery English abolitionist George Thompson came through the town on a lecture tour. In his view the Andover professors were little better than proslavery apologists, and he attempted to organize an event right in the seminary chapel. His request denied, Thompson gave his address in a local hall, with several students from Andover present. When he heard that Thompson was planning on a second lecture the following week, Moses Stuart warned the students in a Sunday evening chapel service, "on the peril of your souls, not to go to that meeting tonight."[4]

All of Andover's faculty, not just Stuart, worried that abolitionist doctrine would divide and distract their students, and harm their fu-

2. Events of these years are found in Annie Fields, ed., *Life and Letters of Harriet Beecher Stowe* (Boston: Houghton, Mifflin and Co., 1898), pp. 162-179.

3. Woods, "To the Reverend and Honorable Trustees of Phillips Academy, "1835, Faculty Reports, ANTS archives.

4. Stuart quoted in John H. Giltner, "Moses Stuart and the Slavery Controversy: A Study in the Failure of Moderation," *Journal of Religious Thought* 18 (1961): 29.

ture usefulness. In the wake of Thompson's visit, the professors issued a plea for a disbanding of the abolitionist society on campus, a powerfully worded argument that the students found unable to resist. A flurry of visits by leading radicals — William Lloyd Garrison, Henry B. Stanton, Theodore Weld, James G. Birney, and Angelina and Sarah Grimké — did not dissuade the seminary from its moderate public course.[5]

During the 1850s, when the Fugitive Slave Law brought religious debates over slavery to their peak, Moses Stuart waded into the fray once more with a closely reasoned treatise opposing the popular abolitionist claim that the Bible condemned slavery. While Scripture did not specifically sanction slavery, he argued, it certainly did not condemn it as a *malum in se,* an evil in itself, as the radicals routinely insisted. After all, most of the Old Testament patriarchs had bondservants, and Christ himself never took the opportunity to teach against the ancient institution. Stuart advocated a form of gradual abolition, a moderate position that, in the overheated political climate, branded him guilty of "foul dishonor" to the sacred text and a blot on Andover's antislavery record.[6]

Indeed, despite its well-known concern for creedal standards, Andover was an intellectually lively place. In the classroom, both Woods and Stuart encouraged — even demanded — free-ranging inquiry. "Although I endeavor to impress on the minds of the students due respect for the learning and piety of illustrious Divines," Woods reported to the trustees at the beginning of his career in 1811, "at the same time I remind them of the direction of Christ, *to call no man master.*" The young professor encouraged his students to "call into question sentiments held by the best inspired men, and sanctioned by the faith of ages." When some of the more "daring" pushed this freedom too far, Woods said that he "let the evil cure itself"; "instead of forbidding or stopping

---

5. The full story is told in J. Earl Thompson, Jr., "Abolitionism and Theological Education at Andover," *New England Quarterly* 47 (1974): 238-261. In 1835 the trustees instituted a ban on student antislavery societies.

6. Moses Stuart, *Conscience and the Constitution, With Remarks on the Recent Speech of the Hon. Daniel Webster in the Senate of the United States on the Subject of Slavery* (Boston: Crocker and Brewster, 1850); William Jay, *Reply to Remarks of Rev. Moses Stuart on Hon. John Jay and an Examination of His Scriptural Exegesis Contained in his Recent Pamphlet Entitled 'Conscience and Constitution'* (New York: John A. Gray, 1850); Giltner, "Moses Stuart and the Slavery Controversy: A Study in the Failure of Moderation," pp. 27-39.

them, I have urged them on still farther and farther, til they have been made to feel that they are *beyond their line,* and are willing to return to sober sense and modesty." The remedy, Woods declared, was all but universally successful. Even in his later years, beset by criticisms that his classroom was dull and stodgy compared to the brilliant success of Nathaniel William Taylor down at Yale, Woods countered that he at least was willing to say "I don't know" and confess honest ignorance — a trait he found notably absent in his Connecticut rival.[7]

Moses Stuart similarly assured the board of trustees that his classroom was intellectually challenging. The European fashion, he said, was to simply read a lecture; most American teachers demanded rote recitation by students. He did neither. "When in the lecture-room I take the helm," Stuart explained, "work myself, and keep all hands on board busy also. I lecture mostly without notes, but not strictly *ex tempore;* I call on students to recite; I push them with questions; I endeavor to explain what is dark to them." Stuart's classroom was, in his words, "a scene of severe effort, keeping all wide awake; for no one knows who will next be called upon to show what he knows." In his class on Galatians, for example, Stuart required his students to read the epistle through at least ten times, and come to class with their own analysis, written independently of published commentaries. After reviewing and examining this work, the class pursued their own "minute critical inventory" of the epistle word by word.[8]

The Creed: Early Rounds

Not everyone was pleased with this methodology. Already in 1825, the trustees fielded accusations that Stuart was introducing infidelity into his classroom. "It was whispered," he later recalled, "that I was not only secretly gone over to the Germans, but was leading the seminary over with me, and bringing up, or at least encouraging, our young men to deistical rationalism." It was all the other professors

---

7. Leonard Woods, Reports to the Trustees for 1811 and 1845, ANTS archives.

8. Moses Stuart, "To the Honorable S. T. Armstrong, Chairman of the Committee of Inquiry into the State of the Seminary, Etc," 18 April 1845; Stuart, "Plan of Study for the Last Summer Term in Sacred Literature, 1810," Faculty Reports, ANTS archives.

could do, so the rumor mill had it, "to keep the seminary from going over into Unitarianism."[9]

Admittedly, Stuart pressed the edges of Protestant orthodoxy. Though always "careful and responsible," he approached the Bible like his German peers, as an historical document in need of modern reinterpretation. Though Stuart shared the supernatural presuppositions of the biblical writers, he also strove to understand them as people working within the limitations of a specific place and time. His reverence for the biblical text therefore stopped short of affirming the full verbal inspiration of each word.[10]

But Stuart stoutly resisted the suggestion that his scholarship violated Andover standards. The original creeds were hardly designed "to extend to all the supposed or believed minutiae of doctrine and practice," he declared. Their purpose was to state the fundamentals of belief, not to nail down every point; creeds were meant to be "platforms for unity and not mechanisms for division."[11] From his earliest days at Andover, Stuart insisted that the school's scholarly agenda and its commitment to orthodoxy required a unique brand of courage. Even the Founders had realized that "the acquisition of knowledge is attended with danger. They were by no means ignorant how easily ambition and a secular spirit might creep in, and pervert the young and unwary heart of the Student." But, he declared, ignorance was a far greater danger to the church than scholarly inquiry; at bottom, most objections to learning drew from ignorance and sloth, not genuine piety.[12]

If Stuart's scrape with the trustees affirmed the positive aim of creedal subscription, Leonard Woods' experience revealed the Andover system's incipient flaws. When Woods was first hired, Daniel Dana, a

---

9. Quoted in "Professor Park on Pioneering in Theology," *Christian Union*, 31 May 1883, p. 427.

10. Bruce Kuklick, *Churchmen and Philosophers: From Jonathan Edwards to John Dewey* (New Haven: Yale University Press, 1985), pp. 90f.

11. Moses Stuart, "Have the Sacred Writers anywhere asserted that the Sin or Righteousness of One is imputed to Another?" *Biblical Repository and Quarterly Observer* 7 (April 1836): 326; Taylor, "That Obnoxious Doctrine: Future Probation and the Struggle to Construct an American Congregationalist Identity," p. 194.

12. Moses Stuart, *A Sermon Occasioned By the Completion of the New College Edifice for the Use of the Theological Seminary at Andover, And Delivered Sept. 13, 1821* (Andover, MA: Flagg and Gould, 1821), pp. 17, 18.

conservative trustee who had no use for the New Divinity creed (and had in fact been absent for the vote which united Newburyport and Andover in 1807), opposed him on the grounds that he had not subscribed to the Westminster Confession. Woods argued in turn that Andover professors might assent to the Catechism *"generally* as containing a summary of the principles of Christianity," not line by line.[13] The trustees agreed and let the matter go — but failed to ask a few key questions: When it came to specific areas of content, might one creed supersede the other? Were Andover professors allowed to choose which standard they would affirm?[14]

Confusion deepened in 1826, when the trustees decided to remove church history professor James Murdock, in this case more for general cantankerousness than for heterodoxy.[15] They took the occasion to study the subscription process, and came up with a standard statement that all Andover professors would be required to recite. Each man was to declare his faith in the "fundamental and distinguishing doctrines of the Gospel of Christ as summarily expressed in the Westminster Assembly's shorter catechism."[16] Was the Associate Creed then unnecessary? Leonard Woods later attributed this wording to a scribal error, assuming that the trustees could not possibly have meant to privilege one standard over the other.

Just a few years later, in 1839, when another church history professor, Ralph Emerson, refused to subscribe to the Westminster standard, the trustees were forced to revisit their error. But the ensuing discussion did little to clear up the confusion. Leonard Woods argued that Andover's founders had intended a form of dual subscription, that is, that all professors would be answerable to Westminster, but those faculty members whose chairs were funded by the Associate Founders —

---

13. Woods, *Letters to Unitarians* (Andover, 1820), p. 134.

14. The main point of contention between the two creeds was the doctrine of imputation. As described in chapter one, the Westminster standard of the "Old Calvinists" stated that Adam's guilt was passed down directly to each individual person born subsequently. The New Divinity Associate Creed emphasized the primary responsibility of each individual for his or her own sin, to the point of implying an element of choice in human error.

15. For the full story of this episode, see J. Earl Thompson, "Church History Comes to Andover: The Persecution of James Murdock," *Andover Newton Quarterly* 15 (1975): 213-227.

16. Minutes of the Trustees, ATS, 26 September 1826.

the Bartlet Chairs of Sacred Literature and Sacred Rhetoric, and the Moses Brown Chair of Ecclesiastical History — were *also* required to repeat the Associate Creed. Further inspection revealed that, even before the 1826 ruling, no Andover professor had ever recited both creeds. Throwing up their hands, the trustees decided to split the difference: in 1842 they ruled that all faculty on the Associate Foundation were responsible that creed alone; the others would answer to Westminster. Woods objected strenuously, pointing out that the trustees' ruling had in effect created two schools on separate theological foundations. Even Daniel Dana's fervent appeal to the Board of Visitors was voted down.[17]

Disputes over the creeds were far from over, however. Another round opened in 1847 when Edwards Amasa Park, previously the Bartlet Professor of Sacred Rhetoric, succeeded Leonard Woods in the Abbot Chair. According to seminary rules, he was also moving from the Associate foundation to the Westminster one. Would he then have to change his creedal subscription? Once again Daniel Dana used the occasion to argue for a single Westminster standard, and to chastise Park for his views on original sin.[18] When the Board of Visitors duly examined Park, they discovered that Dana was in fact correct: the ascending Abbot Professor did not hold to the Westminster catechism, specifically its statement on the imputation of Adam's sin. In this case, however, Park's willingness to subscribe to the Associate Creed was deemed sufficient; he would not be required to resubscribe to Westminster. The affair rumbled to a close and ended in usual fashion: over Daniel Dana's vociferous protests, the board of trustees approved Park's election.[19]

Edwards Park, Newman Smyth, and the New Theology

Perhaps no stranger to controversy, Andover was still an unlikely candidate for theological controversy. In comparison to New School Presbyte-

17. Leonard Woods to Trustees of the Theological Seminary, 6 September 1842; Board of Visitors File re Subscription to Creed, ATS archives. For a full treatment of the subscription issue, see Taylor, "That Obnoxious Doctrine," pp. 193-196.

18. Daniel Dana, "To the Honorable Board of Visitors of the Theological Seminary," 6 April 1847, ANTS archives.

19. Minutes of the Examination of Professor Park by the Board of Visitors, 15 April 1857, Board of Visitors folder 1857, Mid-March to April 15, ANTS archives.

rian upstart Union Seminary in New York and the squarely Old School Princeton, Andover was a solid Yankee alternative, with a well-deserved reputation for pioneering but judicious scholarship. Out to the west Oberlin Seminary was upholding the banner of revivalism and social reform, and down in New Haven, Nathaniel William Taylor was rattling the cages of Connecticut conservatives. Andover, however, stood slightly apart and above the fray, rarely swayed by the latest theological fad.[20]

But seismic rumbles in the larger intellectual world, rippling across the disciplines of theology and biblical studies, soon made separate peace impossible. The decline of the so-called New England Theology has been told often and well — and perhaps most famously by Oliver Wendell Holmes in his poem "The Deacon's Masterpiece, or the 'Wonderful One-Hoss Shay.'" Built to last on the eve of the American Revolution, the solid wooden transport served the deacon well for decades; but by the 1850s it was giving off "a general flavor of mild decay." "First a shiver, and then a thrill,/Then something decidedly like a spill," and the old cart "went to pieces all at once, — All at once, and nothing first, — Just as bubbles do when they burst."

Orthodoxy hardly endured a sudden collapse in the middle of the nineteenth century, but as Holmes' metaphor suggests, decades of slow changes in the early nineteenth century certainly concluded with a dramatic flourish after the Civil War. Indeed, the difficulties Andover faced in the late nineteenth century went far beyond a mere faculty squabble over the wordings of creeds. They were embedded in the logic of American Protestant theology.

Holmes' figurative horsecart encountered its first real difficulty at Andover under Edwards Park. In one sense, he represented the seminary's "old guard," caring little for the latest word in biblical criticism or German theology. "He challenged them," as one historian writes, "but they were not his chief concern." A dominating figure in the classroom, Park taught Calvinist theology as a finely hewn system and over the course of his thirty-seven years exercised a remarkable influence over the hundreds of students under his purview.[21]

---

20. Allen Guelzo and Douglas A. Sweeney, eds., *The New England Theology: From Jonathan Edwards to Edwards Amasa Park* (Grand Rapids: Baker Academic, 2006).

21. Rowe, *History of Andover Theological Seminary* (Newton: Thomas Todd, 1933), p. 160.

But Park was also a mediator whose theology bridged the incipient rationalism of the New England Theology with more intuitive approaches to faith. This was a strain within liberal thought introduced at Andover in two lectures by Horace Bushnell, the innovative Connecticut theologian. In an 1839 address on "Revelation," Bushnell had argued that theological language offered only a figurative rendering of otherworldly realities; in effect, he was rejecting the old "common-sense" assumption that the truth of a biblical text was plainly evident to all.[22] Park's famous sermon of 1850, "The Theology of the Intellect and That of the Feelings," argued subtly but provocatively that Bushnell was right in asserting the "poetical" intent of Scripture, and that intuition was a valuable means of appropriating Christian truth. I know the truth of the Westminster catechism, Park declared, not just with my mind but with my heart. Park did not believe that biblical texts were merely metaphorical, however; even a poetic image contained propositional truth.[23] This assertion prompted alarm from Princeton Seminary's redoubtable conservative Charles Hodge, who took his Andover colleague to task for wandering from the solid ground of common sense. In his view, Park played with theological terms "like juggler's balls, until no man can tell what they mean, or whether they have any meaning at all."[24]

But Andover's real test came when Park retired in 1881. His appointed successor was Newman Smyth, an Andover alumnus and pastor of the First Presbyterian Church in Quincy, Illinois. Smyth was well versed in German critical thought, having gone on to study under Friedrich Tholuck and Isaac Dorner after leaving Andover. A thoughtful, well-read scholar-pastor, he was openly critical of the New England Theology's syllogistic certainties. "The history of doctrine," he argued, "shows that one work which is required, every generation or two, of Christian thought, is to rearrange its faith in new lights." "Our age

22. E. Brooks Holifield, *Theology in America: Christian Thought from the Age of the Puritans to the Civil War* (New Haven: Yale University Press, 2003), pp. 346-347, 452-460.

23. Harold Young Vanderpool, "The Andover Conservatives: Apologetics, Biblical Criticism and Theological Change at the ATS, 1808-1880" (Ph.D. diss.: Harvard 1971), pp. 28, 29; Holifield, *Theology in America*, pp. 346-347.

24. Charles Hodge, "Professor Park and the Princeton Review," *Biblical Repertory and Princeton Review* 23 (October 1851): 687. On Park, see also Kenneth E. Rowe, "Nestor of Orthodoxy, New England Style" (Ph.D. diss.: Drew University, 1969).

comes speaking new tongues, which our fathers knew not of," he insisted; though modern Christians had every reason to be initially fear-
ful, that new language contained "the best words the human reason has
ever found in which to declare the ways of the Spirit."[25]

Smyth's approach to Protestant orthodoxy placed him securely
within the ranks of what was popularly called the "New Theology."
Late-nineteenth-century liberalism was not so much a set of specific
doctrines as it was a set of attitudes about doctrine. Its proponents
held that "truth can be attained only through a never-ending process of
criticism and experiment." Their characteristic stance was a "willingness to understand many points of view."[26] Rejecting the common-
sense assumption that the truths of the Bible were self-evident to the
pious mind, and taking up the thread of new argument from Bushnell,
Smyth and his generation of German-trained theologians stressed the
role of intuition, feeling, and mystery. Emphasizing the presence of
the divine within the everyday material world, they argued that God
was the object of a continuing spiritual quest, not the final line of a syllogistic proof.[27]

From this point, all of the old categories of belief took on a different
cast. If God was to be found not beyond but within the created order,
then human activity itself bore the marks of redemption. The world was
an opening arena for spiritual discovery, its once-fixed certainties always giving way to new understanding. During the late nineteenth century, evolution became a popular metaphor for theologians endorsing
God's progressive revelation in and through the natural world. Progress
was the central idea and ethics the focus of discussion. In all of its own
constantly evolving forms, late-nineteenth-century Protestant liberalism emphasized the incarnated Christ as the highest, most compelling
moral standard for human society.

Smyth's candidacy as Park's replacement may have startled a few of
Andover's old guard, but in many ways it made perfect sense. The New
Theology clearly drew from Edwards Park's "theology of feeling," and
his insistence that human "moral sense" was the true arbiter of correct

25. Smyth, *Old Faiths in New Light* (New York: Charles Scribner's Sons, 1879), p. 16.

26. Daniel Day Williams, *The Andover Liberals: A Study in American Theology* (1941; re-
print, New York: Octagon Books, 1970), p. 64.

27. On the new theology, see William R. Hutchison, *The Modernist Impulse in American Protestantism* (Cambridge, MA: Harvard University Press, 1976), pp. 76-110.

doctrine. And in a larger sense, Smyth's skepticism about propositional truth, reflecting his scholarly studies in Germany, followed a trail of inquiry already blazed by Moses Stuart. If Andover was truly committed to educating the best and the brightest students, as Stuart and his colleagues frequently reminded the board of trustees, it could not afford to ignore scholarly challenges from abroad. As historian Daniel Day Williams observes, "In the very act of founding a theological seminary with opportunities for wide acquaintances with theological literature the founders of Andover sowed the seeds of revolt from orthodoxy."[28]

But Newman Smyth would never become a professor at Andover. Though approved by the board of trustees, he failed to pass muster with two of the three men on the Board of Visitors. In April 1882, Julius Seelye, the president of Amherst College and of the American Missionary Association, and Rev. Dr. William T. Eustis, pastor of the Memorial Church in Springfield, Massachusetts, voted against Smyth, over the objections of Charles Russell, a Boston law professor. All three agreed that Smyth was in substantial agreement with the Andover creed. But they objected that he tended to "conceive of truth poetically rather than speculatively," and this "rhetorical quality would interfere with his precision as a teacher." In effect Smyth was too much of a poet and not enough of a philosopher to teach at Andover.[29]

The Board of Visitors' verdict marked the first time they had ever negated a decision of the board of trustees, signaling many more difficulties to come. The trustees registered their dismay over the loss of Smyth by appointing him as a guest lecturer, a post that did not require subscription to the creed or a vote by the Visitors. While Smyth eventually moved on to become the celebrated pastor of the Center Church in New Haven, Andover's faculty and trustees found themselves increasingly mired in a public relations crisis with no end in sight.

At the height of the controversy over Smyth's candidacy, critics in the denominational press charged that he had held to a theory of second probation, the idea that those who died before accepting Christian salvation would have another opportunity after death. The evidence

28. Williams, *The Andover Liberals*, p. 16.

29. Minutes of the Board of Visitors 22 April 1882. See also William Jewett Tucker, *My Generation: An Autobiographical Interpretation* (Boston: Houghton Mifflin, 1919), pp. 115, 116.

was slim, largely a few offhand remarks from a sermon and fragments from some of his public works, but the accusation created a sensation. Not only was Newman Smyth questionable on standard doctrinal matters, but he was also espousing a heretical, slightly exotic theory that those who had died unsaved would be given a second opportunity beyond the grave.[30] And indeed Smyth later concluded that the future probation charge was the real reason for his failed candidacy.[31]

The doctrine did not originate with Smyth — its earliest Christian reference is a passage in the New Testament book of First Peter, describing Christ's post-crucifixion descent into hell, where he preached to the souls of the damned. Throughout the history of the Christian church, the possibility of a future probation was a periodic topic of discussion; Smyth himself had likely received it from his German mentor Isaac Dorner. The attractiveness of the doctrine is obvious, especially alongside normative Christian teachings about the endless punishment awaiting anyone who died outside of Christian salvation. But its slender biblical justification meant that it would never become a majority view.[32]

By the time the Andover Board of Visitors negated Smyth's appointment in April 1882, school business had become a matter of vigorous public debate. The *Congregationalist* charged that the theology taught at Andover was "not essentially out of harmony with that taught at Harvard."[33] All the prominent pastors of Boston, and Congregational pulpits across the country, issued public doubts about Andover's orthodoxy. In April 1882, just a few days before the Visitors ruled against Smyth, the *Congregationalist* announced that it had tallied 118 different editorials in the religious press, with only 28 of them in his defense.[34]

Life at Andover was becoming difficult. Smyth's departure provoked a new wave of discussion about the faculty creed, and issued forth a

30. "Dr. Newman Smyth and the Doctrine of Eternal Punishment," *Congregationalist*, 22 March 1882, p. 1. For a fuller description of this and related episodes see Tucker, *My Generation: An Autobiographical Interpretation*, pp. 101-247.

31. Smyth, *Recollections and Reflections* (Boston: Charles Scribner's Sons, 1926), pp. 104, 105.

32. Sharon Taylor, "That Obnoxious Doctrine," pp. 40-83.

33. "Another Bad Move," *Congregationalist*, 10 May 1882, p. 4.

34. "More Testimony," *Congregationalist*, 19 April 1882, p. 5.

round of resignations. Both Hebrew professor Charles Mead and Joseph Henry Thayer, the Bartlet Professor of Sacred Literature, chose to leave Andover rather than stand for the five-year renewal of their original subscription. One public statement was enough, they insisted; being forced to repeat the creed under an air of suspicion was, in their view, "not only superfluous, but in a degree humiliating." It did not help matters, however, that Thayer left his post of eighteen years to teach at Harvard, launching his parting shot from the pages of the Unitarian *Christian Register*.[35]

The Creed: Round Two

The selection of George Harris to fill the Abbot chair did little to stem the bleeding. An Andover graduate and pastor of a church in Providence, Rhode Island, Harris was a worthy candidate for the position; but from start to finish, the process of installing the new professor was almost more than Andover's beleaguered public image could take. By that time, with the retirements of Austin Phelps and Edwards Park, the school was in the midst of heavy faculty turnover; indeed, during the 1882-1883 school year, the few remaining overworked professors voted not to admit a junior class. The arrival of five new men — Harris, Edward Hincks (Biblical Theology), John Phelps Taylor (Biblical History and Oriental Archaeology), Frank Woodruff (Sacred Literature), and George F. Moore (Hebrew Language and Literature) — raised sagging spirits, but of course, also promised a new round of wrangling about the Andover creed.[36] All of the new faculty were elected without a dissenting vote from the trustees or the Board of Visitors; they avowed their belief in Christian doctrine as it was "expressed in the Creed," but did not recite it line by line.[37]

The rest of the inaugural festivities proved more difficult. In his ad-

35. Tucker, *My Generation*, p. 121. J. H. Thayer, "The Broad Church," *Christian Register,* 22 February 1883, p. 116

36. The other faculty at this time were Egbert Smyth, the Brown Professor of Ecclesiastical History; John Wesley Churchill, Jones Professor of Elocution; John P. Gulliver, Stone Professor of Relations of Christianity and Science; and William Jewett Tucker, Bartlet Professor of Sacred Rhetoric.

37. Taylor, "That Obnoxious Doctrine," pp. 208-209 n. 81.

dress as incoming Abbot Professor, Harris pointedly declared the need for a new Andover creed. "Truth for the individual," he said, "must be found in other than merely historical or theoretical forms. It must be found in relation to his own needs. It must be worked out in life, through faith and love." "Experience," he said, "is the ground of certainty." Though "evidences give a high degree of probability," "personal experience gives absolute certainty."[38]

Already by the afternoon, a few alumni were rumbling about Harris's remarks, and by the time of their formal dinner the next day, discontent was palpable. Following a series of remarks by invited dignitaries, popular lecturer Joseph Cook turned the proceedings upside down. Dubbed "the great Goliath" by the local press, Cook was well known for his outspoken fervor on a wide range of topics. That evening he strode to the podium waving a pile of paper — testimonies, he said, from leading pastors and professors who were refusing to send any more young men to Andover. The heretical teaching of probation after death had made the school a theological pariah among other doctrinally "sound" Congregational seminaries.[39]

The audience rumbled with displeasure. Several students rose to defend their teachers, testifying to their piety in chapel prayers and denying that they had ever heard the "noxious doctrine" taught in a classroom. Egbert Smyth, president of the faculty, stood up to declare that he had just assented to the creed for the fifth time, and "without any mental reservations whatsoever." The crowd broke out into long applause. But Cook was not finished. He sprang to his feet, "looking like a maniac and acting like a savage" according to one account, and insisted that Smyth answer him there and then about the possibility of a future probation. "How do you reconcile probation after death with loyalty to the creed?" he demanded. The startled professor never had a chance to answer, as the quick-thinking moderator ordered Cook to be seated and hastily concluded the evening with the singing of the doxology. But the larger controversy was only just beginning.[40]

---

38. George Harris, "The Rational and Spiritual Verification of Christian Doctrine," *Independent*, 14 June 1883, p. 5.

39. "Andover Alumni Dinner," *Congregationalist*, 21 June 1883, p. 5.

40. "Andover Triumph," *Boston Herald*, 15 June 1883, p. 1.

The New Theology in the Classroom

In the meantime, life in Andover's lecture halls and classrooms continued on, at first hardly troubled by the looming controversy outside. The curriculum blossomed and grew, adding to its traditional strengths and reflecting the best of new currents of thought in the international seminary world. In 1867 Edwards Park had helped found the Smith Professorship, a course of study that did not require Greek or Hebrew and was designed for older men already in the ministry. He also helped establish a series of popular lectures on "Foreign Missions, Congregationalism, Home Missions, Revivals of Religion, and Popular Infidelity."[41] In 1878, the school endowed its first chair devoted to "The Relation of Christianity to the Secular Sciences," held by John P. Gulliver.

Major curriculum changes began in the 1870s and gathered steam under the new faculty. For many years, founding faculty like Moses Stuart and Leonard Woods had complained bitterly about Andover's three-tiered program of instruction. Stuart, for example, had sole care of incoming juniors, teaching them all that was humanly possible about biblical languages and the rules of exegesis. But just as the students were beginning to grasp these complicated subjects, they moved on to study theology in their second year. "It is an evil which I deeply feel, and greatly deplore," Stuart wrote back in 1818, "that at the very time the junior class have fairly made a beginning in the exegetical study of the Hebrew and Greek testaments, they are obliged to desist from their studies and go into another department. . . . I can hardly endure the mortification of quitting them," he told the Andover trustees, "when I have just begun the satisfaction of having them make substantial progress in their studies, and turning them off, half formed, from my department."[42]

The new system offered a series of graded courses, following the fashion of the day but also responding to many years of faculty frustration. Thus, students received instruction in two traditional subjects, systematic theology and biblical exegesis, throughout their seminary careers. The curriculum also introduced them to a new range of topics now deemed essential to the professional education of ministers: ar-

---

41. J. Earl Thompson, "The Andover Liberals as Theological Educators," *Andover Newton Quarterly* 8 (March 1968): 209.

42. Stuart, "Plan of Study," 1818, ANTS archives.

chaeology, science and religion, and the field of "biblical theology." Under Egbert Smyth, church history took on an increasing prominence, expanding beyond the traditional final course at the end of the third year to 13 percent of the students' classroom time.[43]

Andover also began to experiment with advanced courses and electives, one of the first American seminaries to follow the German model. The 1881-1882 school year introduced a fourth year Advanced Class, designed to follow the research-oriented approach that was popular in German university education. Generously underwritten by a Philadelphia businessman, Andover's innovative program allowed a small group of handpicked students the opportunity to pursue a research topic and participate in a monthly faculty-led seminar. With the expansion of Andover's elective system in the 1890s, all students received greater freedom to follow special academic interests. Andover faculty defended the change as a perfect balance between the "foundation work" required in traditional seminary courses and the "specialization" increasingly demanded of a modern pastor.[44]

Under William Jewett Tucker, the Bartlet Professor of Sacred Rhetoric, Andover students learned about the social problems of the Gilded Age firsthand. Tucker was an open critic of the popular Protestant "gospel of wealth," the idea that material reward is a sign of God's favor. This popular philosophy was touted by both secular and religious figures, including philanthropist Andrew Carnegie and by Baptist pastor Russell Conwell, famous on the lecture circuit for his "Acres of Diamonds" speech. Tucker introduced a course at Andover in Social Economics, a wide-ranging overview of all the inequities of the day: the exploitation of workers, the mistreatment of criminals, the deepening poverty of the nation's cities. Tucker's solution was a modified form of socialism, based on profit sharing. Hardly a wild, left-wing theory, in the late nineteenth century, similar ideas were widely discussed among some of the nation's more cutting-edge social reformers, including Henry George and Edward Bellamy. In 1890, Robert Woods, one of Tucker's students in the Advanced Class, went to London to live at Toynbee Hall, an experimental community deep in the heart of the city's poorest neighborhood. The settlement house model introduced middle-class reformers to the com-

43. Thompson, "The Andover Liberals as Theological Educators," p. 215.
44. Thompson, "The Andover Liberals as Theological Educators," pp. 215-217.

plexities of city life and offered practical services to the poor; as an alternative to older, more moralistic approaches to poverty, it was rapidly gaining adherents in the United States. Jane Addams' Hull House in Chicago was the most famous of many to follow.[45]

In Boston, Woods and Tucker established Andover House, a settlement situated in the city's dense South End neighborhood. Students came to live and study social issues on a street lined by saloons and boarding houses, pursuing their analysis through friendly visits door to door. "Each resident is encouraged to take up for particular investigation some of the larger phases of the city's life," Woods reported in 1893, "such as popular amusements, evening schools, [and] cheap lodging houses." Students got to know leaders of local trade unions, and pushed the city to provide better streetlights and cleaner streets, all the while deepening their own theological understanding of social sin. Though in 1895, with Tucker departing for the presidency of Dartmouth College, Andover House took on a more generic designation as the South End House, its founding marked one of the first academically related settlement houses in the United States.[46]

The Creed: Round Three

Intellectual life at Andover was strong on a number of fronts during the 1880s. The first issue of the *Andover Review* appeared in January 1884. The brilliant successor to the dependable *Bibliotheca Sacra,* lately removed to safer quarters at Oberlin after Park's retirement, the *Review* quickly became a leading voice for the New Theology. Edited by Egbert Smyth, William Jewett Tucker, John W. Churchill, George Harris, and Edward Y. Hincks, it called for a "profounder, clearer, more practical apprehension of revealed truth than has yet been gained, to a larger charity, to a higher unity." "We desire especially to do what we may to confirm the faith of believers in the essential truths of the gospel," Smyth declared in his opening editorial, "and to unite them in intelli-

45. Tucker, *My Generation,* pp. 172-185; Williams, *The Andover Liberals,* Chapter 7. Tucker's influential article "The Institutional Church," in the *Andover Review* (1889) articulated an urban ideal that was widely adopted in the wake of the turn-of-the-century Social Gospel movement.

46. "The Andover House Association, Circular No. 8, January 2, 1893," ANTS archives.

gent and effective Christian work." Yet still, he insisted, "there is a . . . demand for better statements of Christianity doctrine in the religious life of our time."[47]

In 1886, the editors issued a provocative volume of essays, drawn from the pages of the *Review* but published anonymously. *Progressive Orthodoxy: A Contribution to the Christian Interpretation of Christian Doctrines,* with chapters on the incarnation and atonement, the Bible and the work of the Holy Spirit, had much to discomfort the orthodox. One by one, the essays offered reinterpretations of key doctrines around sin and salvation, emphasizing human moral capacity instead of depravity and helplessness. "The whole structure of New England theology," Daniel Day Williams writes, "was being pushed to one side by a theology of universal salvation through moral improvement."[48] But the final sticking point was future probation, discussed in the chapter on eschatology as a matter of divine justice. "We are unable to discover," declared the author (later revealed to be George Harris), "any more piety in representing God as a Being who creates millions of men to whom He never offers the means of salvation, than in representing God as a Being who will bring all men to the knowledge of the truth as it is in Jesus."[49]

On October 25, 1886, the Visitors issued a formal complaint against the editors of the *Andover Review.* Though all five stood accused, the complaint singled out Egbert Smyth for holding doctrines "antagonistic to, the Constitution and Statutes of the Seminary, and the true intention of its Founders as expressed in those statutes." The Visitors' statement outlined sixteen different departures from orthodox doctrine, including heterodox teachings about biblical infallibility and the atonement. The most sensational and potentially damaging charge, however, was that Smyth had advocated the theory of future probation, and that as a result he had undermined support for Christian missions.[50] A formal hearing was set for the end of the year.

---

47. "The Theological Purpose of the Review," *Andover Review* 1 (January 1884): 12.

48. Williams, *The Andover Liberals,* p. 72.

49. *Progressive Orthodoxy: A Contribution to the Christian Interpretation of Christian Doctrines, By the Editors of "The Andover Review"* (Boston: Houghton, Mifflin and Co., 1892), p. 109. See also Tucker, *My Generation,* p. 142.

50. *In the Matter of the Complaint Against Egbert C. Smyth and other Professors in the Theological Institution in Phillips Academy in Andover* (n.p., 1886), p. 2. Box 2, Legal cases, ATS archives.

In the months that followed, the Andover case, quickly billed as "the great heresy trial," caused a national sensation.[51] Though by the 1880s, public trials of eminent theologians were becoming somewhat of a commonplace, Boston's Congregationalists had yet to experience one in full. In 1875, prominent Chicago pastor David Swing withdrew from the Presbyterian church under charges of heresy; in New York Henry Ward Beecher had contended with accusations of sexual impropriety. Now Boston would have its chance, though of course the Andover case hardly matched the others for public drama. The hearing before the Board of Visitors was open to the public, and as reported in the daily press, encompassed reams of closely reasoned theological arguments.[52]

Fairly quickly, however, the Andover case took on a more humorous angle. Already in 1883, the Unitarian *Christian Register* had published an irreverent version of the Andover creed, set in the style of a Gregorian chant.[53] In December 1886, the British periodical *Puck* ran a cartoon depicting the Andover men fanning the flames while a heretic burned at the stake. Behind them spread all the splendors of modern art and culture, symbolized by Greek temples and Gothic university spires. "When some new century brings the perfect hour/When Art shall open her consummate flower," the caption ran, ". . . What then, poor victim of an outworn vow,/What then, O narrow Andover, art thou?"[54] Though the cartoon somewhat missed the point of the Andover trial, it captured accurately the growing public perception that, at bottom, the Andover case pitted modern free inquiry against a dry and rigid orthodoxy.

The verdict, issued on June 3, 1887, did little to change that image. The Visitors cleared Harris, Churchill, Hincks, and Tucker on technicalities, and focused their wrath on Egbert Smyth, the president of the faculty. Though all of the five had contributed to the offending volume, *Progressive Orthodoxy,* only Smyth was declared guilty of beliefs "inconsistent with and repugnant to the [Andover] creed." Not only had he denied the infallibility of the Bible, the Visitors ruled, he had suggested that repentance was possible without a knowledge of Christ and, even

51. "A Question of Creed," *Boston Daily Advertiser,* 1 January 1887, p. 3.

52. The published accounts of the trial are found in *The Andover Case* (Boston: Stanley and Usher, 1887) and *The Andover Defence* (Boston: Cupples, Upham and Co., 1887).

53. The cartoon was published in the *Christian Register* on June 21, 1883.

54. Taylor, "That Obnoxious Doctrine," pp. 225-226; *Puck,* 1 December 1886, pp. 224-225.

worse, advocated a "probation after death for all men who do not deci-sively reject Christ during earthly life." Smyth was removed from the Brown professorship — but, in an odd and controversial twist, on the basis of articles written by four others whom the Visitors had decided to acquit.[55]

The board of trustees immediately issued a protest: not only were the Visitors overstepping their bounds, but their case for heresy was thin at best. Praising the professors for their "industry, their zeal, their scholarship, and their piety," they found little to suggest that the Andover creed was in any danger, especially from an "appended in-quiry" like the theory of future probation. The real issue was becoming very clear: two different judicatories, the Board of Visitors and the trust-ees, were each vying for ultimate control of Andover Seminary. Recog-nizing the matter at stake, the trustees encouraged Smyth to take his case to the Massachusetts Supreme Judicial Court, where it was heard before the full bench in October 1890.[56]

After many more hours of argument by counsel, and briefs submit-ted by professors from Harvard, Yale, and Columbia law schools, the Andover case came to its merciful conclusion a year later. With one dis-senting vote, the court ruled to set aside Smyth's dismissal, agreeing with the trustees' complaint that the Visitors had overstepped their le-gal bounds in pursuing the heresy case on their own.

Aftermath

Smyth and the trustees had wrested control of the seminary from the Board of Visitors, but their victory would be only temporary and it came at considerable cost. In the years that followed, Andover's reputation and its enrollment steadily declined; by 1890, the number of graduates had dropped to thirteen, far below the forty-one students in Yale's se-nior class. By the late 1880s, attendance at Andover decisively trailed prestigious institutions like Union, Yale, and the University of Chicago

---

55. Minutes of the Board of Visitors, 3 June 1887, ANTS archives. The technicality had to do with the fact that one of the Visitors, Eustis, had not been present to hear their testi-mony at the trial.

56. *The Andover Controversy: Judgment of the Trustees* (n.p., 1886), p. 6.

Divinity School. Even worse, statistics showed that a high number of Andover men were finishing their work at other seminaries. Of the fifteen who graduated in 1885, for example, only two had attended the school for all three years, and another seven had gone to Andover for only a year.[57]

Even worse, the Andover case proved financially costly. In 1892, the trustees authorized a sum of $36,779.35 to cover court costs, as well as expense payments of $6,000 to Smyth and $1,000 to each of the other four professors. During a time of already straitened circumstances, the burden was considerable. The trustees called for an immediate campaign to raise $400,000 to rejuvenate the school property as well as its academic fortunes, but the effort failed.

The most public rupture following the Andover case pitted the seminary against its old ally, the American Board of Commissioners for Foreign Missions (ABCFM). In 1885, at the height of the future probation debate, Joseph Hardy Neesima addressed the ABCFM at its annual meeting in Boston, asking support for eleven Andover students who had pledged to work at his Doshisha College in Japan. But when two of those students, William H. Noyes and Daniel Temple Torrey, presented themselves for service, the American Board's Prudential Committee voted to defer. In yet another lengthy public episode, the Andover students were accused of harboring beliefs in future probation, a belief that would "cut the nerve of missions" by offering the unrepentant heathen a second chance.

Once again Andover was in the news. A second *Puck* cartoon, published in October 1886, depicted Andover professors thrashing around in a small rowboat with heavy theological tomes while the "heathen" looked on with bemused patience. "Why do the Heathen Rage?" the caption ran. "They don't Gentle Reader. They are Taking Things very Peacefully and Pleasantly, while the Andover Missionaries are Settling their little Theological Differences among Themselves."[58]

Andover slowly disappeared from newspaper headlines in the 1890s, but the wrestling match for control of the seminary was far from over. Both the Board of Visitors and the trustees had remaining scores

---

57. Owen H. Gates, comp., *General Catalogue of Andover Theological School, 1927* (Boston: Fort Hill Press, 1927), p. iv; Taylor, "That Obnoxious Doctrine," pp. 234-235.

58. The full story is laid out in Taylor, "That Obnoxious Doctrine," pp. 286-365.

to settle, each side convinced that they had Andover's best interests at heart. Meanwhile, faculty were left wondering exactly what standard of orthodoxy they would be held to, and by whom. Not surprisingly, perhaps, in just a few years Andover's Visitors and trustees would head back to the courtroom for another round of battle, and Andover's professors would face yet another wearying round of disputes about the creed.

What did the Andover controversy mean? It is tempting to see the Andover debacle as a cautionary tale about the inherent dangers of theological education. The clash between Andover's trustees and Visitors might be seen as a microcosm of a larger battle between intellectual freedom and doctrinal orthodoxy, an inevitable conflict that was played out in all of the major Protestant seminaries of the late nineteenth century. Others might see the Andover controversy as a simple battle of truth against error, pitting the true defenders of the faith against those who took the easier path, accommodating doctrine to the demands of the age.

In many ways, however, Andover's struggle was unique. At a fundamental level, it had more to do with institutional struggles encoded into its founding documents than it had to do with epic battles for truth or heresy. Andover originated as part of a defensive strategy by Congregationalists, set on their heels by the inroads of Unitarian liberalism at Harvard. Unlike other seminaries brought into being to foster the upwardly mobile dreams of denominational founders, Andover was created to prove a point. For many years, even with all of their defects, Andover's creeds effectively symbolized the seminary's unyielding commitment to its original aim.

But Andover's brittle underpinnings did not age well. Once controversy moved outside of seminary walls into broader theological realms, and once the grounds of theological debate themselves began to shift, deep and difficult questions of institutional identity proved impossible to ignore. Indeed, the round of debate that concluded in the 1890s was only the first stage of a much longer and ultimately more destructive battle that Andover would wage with itself in the opening years of the twentieth century.

CHAPTER FIVE

Newton and the Fundamentalist-Modernist Debate

———~~~———

D uring the late nineteenth century, rumors of theological conflict made their way up Newton's hill with ominous regularity, but they never flared into the turmoil endured at Andover. Theological controversy was perhaps an institutional luxury beyond the reach of the Baptist school's small faculty and limited financial resources. The school survived two relatively brief skirmishes, and escaped without serious consequences.

Newton's supporters still harbored significant aspirations. By the early twentieth century, Boston's Baptists were entering a heyday of sorts, shedding the social insecurities instilled by generations of Unitarian and Congregational superiority. The First Baptist Church, established in 1665, boasted one of the most majestic buildings in the wealthy Back Bay; down by the business district, Tremont Temple garnered national fame for its lively revivalistic program and steady stream of new members at the door. The Boston Baptist Social Union, amply endowed by layman Daniel Sharp Ford, sponsored one of the city's most vibrant lecture series, the Ford Hall Forum.

Even out in Boston's growing suburban areas, Newton's Baptist Church moved into finer quarters in 1886, a red sandstone and granite Romanesque structure at the foot of Institution Hill. Its elegant Byzantine carvings, green damask upholstery, and enormous memorial windows brought the cost of the new Baptist edifice to near $90,000. "Truth is," the *Watchman-Examiner* declared in 1916, "Baptists are doing a large part of the redemptive work of Boston and its surrounding cities." The denomination's "striking unity" and broad appeal to "rich and poor, cultured and uncultured," boded well for a successful future.[1]

In 1912, Boston Baptists conducted a rigorous door-to-door survey and set out a carefully constructed strategic plan of church merging and planting. As Boston neighborhoods became more and more Roman Catholic, and as "streetcar suburbs" sprang up along the expanding trolley lines, Baptists wanted to make sure they were holding their own. To their disappointment, they found the wealthier regions of the city almost completely inhabited by Unitarians and Episcopalians, but took comfort in the knowledge that in terms of total membership, they were at least level with their old Congregational rivals.[2]

Shifting from their old defensive posture but retaining their characteristic pragmatism, twentieth-century Baptist congregations demanded a more professional ministry. "The Christian life is a business!" one Baptist layman declared with staccato intensity in 1920. "Not a pastime; not an avocation; not a temporary employment; not a chance job; not a last resort; but a calling, vocation, profession, business." The "amateur Christian," he warned, "if not a contradiction of terms, implies miserable failure."[3] Ordination standards rose, and with the help of wealthy Baptist layman John D. Rockefeller, denominational seminaries began to modernize curricula and offer a variety of specialized courses. The old farmer-preacher who had once dominated Baptist ministerial leadership stepped aside for the credentialed professional with a seminary degree.[4]

On a national level, Baptists took the lead in establishing university-level standards for theological education. The University of Chicago, boasting one of the most innovative and theologically liberal divinity schools in the country, was originally a Baptist institution. By the 1920s, Chicago was the epicenter of theological modernism and a pioneer in

1. George W. Coleman, "The Contribution of the Open Forum to Democracy in Religion," *Journal of Religion* 22 (January 1922): 1-15; M. F. Sweetser, *King's Handbook of Newton Massachusetts* (Boston: Moses King Corp., 1889), pp. 297-298; James S. Kirtley, "Browsing around Boston," *Watchman-Examiner*, 8 June 1916, p. 731.

2. Arthur Warren Smith, *The Baptist Situation of Boston Proper: A Survey of Historical and Present Conditions* (Boston: Griffith-Stillings Press, 1912).

3. Mitchell Bronk, "The Christian Business," *Watchman-Examiner*, 4 February 1920, p. 172.

4. Hugh Hartshorne and Milton C. Froyd, *Theological Education in the Northern Baptist Convention: A Survey* (Philadelphia: Judson Press, 1945), pp. 30-33.

the emerging field of sociology — with two Newton alumni, Shailer Mathews and Albion Small, at the helm.[5]

But innovation and success did not require cutting-edge liberal theology. Some of the most important "modernizing" trends in theological education came from conservative sources, in schools that hewed the most closely to the practical demands of local church life.[6] In fact, by the time of its merger with Andover in 1931, Newton's curriculum was at least as comprehensive as its Congregational partner's. While Andover struggled with the competing demands of its ancient creed and the New Theology, a battle that would only intensify in the early years of the twentieth century, Newton enlarged its offerings in sociology, psychology, and practical theology. Newton admitted women into classes and established a program in religious education that was specifically designed to equip them for work in local churches, more than half a century before Andover finally allowed female students to receive a B.D. degree. But not even Newton could match the energy of Boston's newest upstart, the Gordon Bible and Missionary Training School, with whom it briefly aligned in 1907. All of those stories are part of Newton's coming of age in the late nineteenth and early twentieth centuries.

The Gould Affair

Meeting in the winter of 1881, the Boston Baptist Convention of Ministers took extra time to question the Newton professor who stood before them. They had appreciated his informal remarks about New Testament scholarship, but the subject worried them. It was, to be sure, a relevant topic, but not necessarily a safe one, given the events lately transpiring up in Andover. How might he harmonize his views with a certain "confession," they wondered, with everyone in the room alert to the question's intent. The young man did not hesitate. "Name the verse of Scripture that contains the doctrine," he responded stoutly, "and I will tell you what I take to be its meaning."

---

5. Former Newton professor Rush Rhees became president of the University of Rochester in 1900.

6. Glenn Miller, *Piety and Profession: American Protestant Theological Education, 1870-1970* (Grand Rapids, MI: Eerdmans, 2007), p. xiii.

What a "welcome relief," the Baptist *Watchman* declared with a sigh, to find a scholar uninterested in "creed-terms" and endless disputes about the meanings of words. While their Congregational cousins battled noisily over the latest theological fad, Baptists "narrow[ed] the field of contention" by simply turning to the divinely inspired pages of scripture. Shaking his head over the sad "waste of energy" on Andover Hill, the *Watchman*'s editor congratulated his fellow Baptists for busying themselves with more important matters.[7]

One year later, that same young professor would find himself embroiled in controversy and out of a job. In 1882, just as the Andover affair began to reach its zenith in the pages of the national press, the Baptist school summarily fired its young New Testament professor Ezra Gould. The Newton drama garnered few headlines and never came close to replicating the painful theatrics over on Andover Hill; indeed, the utterly low-key tone of the entire dispute demonstrates something of Newton's position relative to Andover's in the 1880s. The charge against Gould was not heresy, but a much hazier accusation of unauthorized discussions in his classroom, and a claim that his open-ended teaching methods had "unsettle[ed] the faith of some of his pupils."[8]

Momentum built slowly. In June of 1882, the trustees appointed a Committee of Five, all but one of them Baptist clergymen, to conduct a thorough investigation. They duly gathered what evidence they could find from students, faculty, and of course from Gould himself. When they finished, the results were almost painfully inconclusive. Two members of the Committee were ready to oust Gould on the spot, but the other three were reluctant to disrupt the harmony of the faculty. All agreed that every one of Gould's responses, both his written statements of doctrine and his answers during oral questioning, was "fairly within the limits of a reasonable orthodoxy."[9]

The affair concluded oddly but quietly. Though the Committee of Five had been given a full year to make their inquiry, they were ready to report in just a few months. In September, they announced that they could not sustain a charge against Gould's orthodoxy. But unfortu-

7. "Watch-Notes," *Watchman*, 20 January 1881, p. 17.

8. C. B. Crane, "The Removal of Professor Gould," *Independent*, 12 October 1882, p. 2.

9. Crane, "The Removal of Professor Gould," p. 2. The paper also ran an article by Gould, "The Supernatural Element in Christianity," which offered a thoroughly orthodox defense of miracles.

nately for the embattled professor, that same summer one of his supporters on the Committee, J. M. English, left to take a post on the faculty. Without majority support, the young New Testament professor was dismissed by the board of trustees, by a vote of thirteen to nine.

Gould was clearly not a threat to Baptist orthodoxy. One of his most emphatic supporters was A. J. Gordon, pastor of the Clarendon Street church in Boston, and a man known for his deep piety and moral rigor. As one commentator observed, Gould's detractors on the board of trustees were all laymen, likely influenced more by financial fears than by the specter of heterodoxy.[10]

Anxiously watching the turmoil on Andover Hill, Boston Baptists gave a long collective exhale as they watched Gould's retreating form. Even a disquieting rumor that Gould was headed to Andover proved mercifully untrue.[11] Newton's defenders took that moment to reemphasize their commitment to the school's primary mission of training young men for Baptist pulpits. The school did not, as one observer commented, "welcome 'all comers' for the study of theology as 'a science,' or a philosophy, like the university schools of Germany, or the theological school at Cambridge in our vicinity." Newton was a safe and solid alternative that Baptist churches would do well to support.[12]

Newton and the New Theology

The Gould affair was an apt parable of Newton's growing pains in the late nineteenth century. The larger story of financial challenges and faculty upheaval, scholarly advances and internecine institutional conflict, demonstrates some of the complexities of religious life in the Gilded Age — and the tenacity of people determined to move forward in spite of deep disagreements.

Even as financial matters began to smooth out in the 1860s, the board found itself constantly scrambling to fill vacancies on the faculty as professors left, often in pursuit of more stable positions. In 1865, the

10. "Removal of Professor Gould from Newton Seminary," *Independent,* 12 October 1882, p. 16.

11. *Christian Union,* 5 October 1882, p. 1; *Nation,* 5 October 1882, p. 277.

12. "Watch-Notes," *Watchman,* 23 November 1882.

board of trustees received their worst news yet: the stalwart Alvah Hovey was planning to resign his post as chair of Christian theology to become president of Madison University. And just as quickly they learned that Horatio Hackett was retiring as chair of Biblical Studies.

A well-connected and well-traveled scholar, Hackett was frequently absent from Newton Hill, and his departure may well have come as good news to the self-sacrificing Hovey. Indeed, in December 1867 Hovey took the moment to press his advantage as one of the school's only remaining full-time instructors. He gave the board of trustees a list of demands, presumably conditional to an agreement not to go to Madison. The board agreed to expand the department of Biblical Studies and Interpretation with an instructor in Hebrew, and to make Hovey the new chair, replacing Hackett. To further sweeten the offer, the board appointed Hovey president of the institution, a new position coming into wide use in the late nineteenth century, roughly equivalent to a present-day academic dean. Even better, they promised to raise another $150,000 for the school's endowment. Always a willing servant of Newton, Hovey finally appeared to have won a measure of power.

Just as suddenly the board rescinded the offer. In 1868 Old Testament scholar Oakman Stearns came to Newton as chair of Biblical Literature and Interpretation, and Hovey marched back to his post in Christian theology, now saddled with additional responsibilities as president but little in the way of extra funding. At the same time, the board appointed a star member of the school's senior class — one Ezra Gould, who would one day defend his orthodoxy before the Newton board of trustees — to teach Greek and New Testament exegesis. By 1870 Gould had requested and received a salary increase and had been made a full professor in the department of Biblical Interpretation and New Testament.

After Gould's ouster in 1882, a few insiders saw Hovey's hand in the affair, and criticized him for removing a promising scholar over what appeared to be, in the end, a matter of personal dislike. Hovey's biographer, his son, denied the charges, crediting Gould as "an original thinker," "a masterly interpreter," and a "stimulating teacher." He fell below the standard set by his predecessor, the saintly Horatio Hackett, "only in the matter of cautious and well-considered statement of opinion."[13] But Hovey

13. George Rice Hovey, *Alvah Hovey, His Life and Letters* (Philadelphia: Judson Press, 1928), p. 168.

apparently made no effort to defend Gould against public attacks, and it is certainly possible that he was the source of the charge that the New Testament professor was allowing his classroom discussion to roam beyond exegetical matters into theological speculation. Hovey was, after all, the chair of Christian theology at Newton.

In all fairness, Hovey could not have enjoyed his double burden as seminary president and professor of theology. The student body began to grow again in the 1880s, with twenty graduates in the class of 1880-1881. That meant that Hovey was responsible to raise additional money for scholarships as well as $30,000 for a new chair of oratory recently added by the board of trustees.

During that same time Hovey also agreed to undertake an extensive scholarly project. His American Commentary took on the controversial project of Bible translation, coordinating the best work of Baptist scholars in a way that the denominational public could trust. Hovey's reference tool placed the new American Standard Version of the King James Bible side by side with the old text, providing explanation and evaluation. Hovey's work was "an important indicator that Baptist scholarship had acquired equality with that of the wealthier denominations."[14] The effort took fourteen years to complete, during which Hovey hewed a careful line between his scholarly peers and a restive Baptist public. By virtue of his post at Newton and his sturdy work ethic, the aging professor was an established denominational authority on a daunting range of difficult topics; he spoke and wrote regularly about divorce, temperance, racial issues, and even the mode and timing of the Second Coming.[15]

German theology was not, of course, unknown at Newton. Horatio Hackett, a student of Moses Stuart's, traveled regularly to Europe, as did Irah Chase and Barnas Sears and indeed Hovey himself. But, perhaps because scholars like Hovey continued to cultivate ties with Baptist congregations — and perhaps as well because they never faced arguments over even one faculty creed — the New Theology did not make a particularly dramatic entrance at Newton.

Shailer Mathews, who later became one of the University of Chicago's leading modernist theologians, entered Newton in 1884, and re-

14. Miller, *Piety and Profession*, p. 52.
15. Hovey, *Alva Hovey*, pp. 185-186.

membered his years there with a certain fondness, as the "Indian summer" of his life between Colby College and the beginning of his teaching career. "Without any particular sense of mission I did my class work, played tennis, learned to ride a high-wheeled bicycle, made social calls and on Sundays listened to Phillips Brooks preach," he recalled. Up on Newton Hill the simmering Andover controversy seemed far away — "we heard little about it except that such views 'cut the nerve of missions'" — and the overall outlook one of "orthodox evangelicalism." "Occasionally students would raise questions in the theology classroom," Mathews wrote, "but they were answered from a point of view of an authoritative scripture. Such a method made me theologically restless," he admitted. A theological school like Newton existed to train, as he said, "private chaplains" for Baptist churches, not to raise unanswerable questions that might shake a student's faith. "Our God was not under investigation," Mathews wrote. "He cared for us and could be trusted to direct our lives."

Mathews also remembered particular intellectual opportunities at Newton. Its historic emphasis on biblical studies opened students to pioneering scholarship in archaeology and Hebrew grammar. Some faculty members were genuinely inspiring: Ernest DeWitt Burton, for example, would later become an internationally respected New Testament scholar, S. S. Curry, the professor of "elocution," was "not only a fine teacher of public speaking but . . . alive to literary and philosophical questions. If he did not make us great preachers," said Mathews, "he did extend the horizon for those of us who like myself, were unaccountably developing an attitude of dissent."

In fact, Mathews recalled, it was under Alvah Hovey that he wrote his first independent research paper. The brilliant young student pressed his harried professor with so many difficult questions that Hovey pronounced him a "nuisance in the classroom," and sent him to the library to figure out matters for himself. Half a century after attending Newton, Mathews remembered his experience with wry fondness. The study of Hebrew "induced accuracy in detail" and theology "taught caution as well as open-mindedness." "Orthodoxy, of course, was regnant," the noted iconoclast recalled, "but it was not tinged with intolerance."[16]

16. Shailer Mathews, *New Faith for Old: An Autobiography* (New York: Macmillan Co., 1936), pp. 24-33.

Academic standards were often a vexed issue at Newton. Galusha Anderson, who taught homiletics from 1866 to 1873 and is credited with introducing the first blackboards to classroom instruction, always emphasized practice over theory. Though he "studied profoundly" in Aristotle's works on rhetoric, he never wrote a textbook and devoted only one semester to the philosophy of preaching. He spent the bulk of his time poring over the sermons of every individual student with a large vial of red ink by his side, marking each error with painstaking care. Guarding his reputation for being kindly but "severe," Anderson then conducted personal conferences with each of his young charges, insisting that they learn to preach without notes.[17]

New Standards

In the late 1880s, however, academic requirements grew more explicit, following the general trends toward standardization among theological seminaries. A curriculum revision in 1886 allowed students to take elective courses for the first time, dividing the school year into semesters with set hours for coursework. The new system allowed more room for classes in church history and theology, though the bulk of study still centered around the biblical text. In 1889 the board added a new requirement for a senior thesis, to be selected from an approved list of topics created by the faculty. Two years later, the trustees petitioned the Massachusetts state legislature for permission to grant a Bachelor of Divinity degree, and issued the first in 1900.

The range of course offerings also expanded, though unevenly. In 1891 Newton added a professor of missions, reflecting the growing Protestant enthusiasm for world evangelization at the turn of the century. But the school's chronic shortage of funds did not allow for too much specialization among the faculty. Through a cooperative arrangement with the Northern Baptist Education Society, the mission professor was also a part-time fundraiser, whose job it was to raise interest among New England's Baptist churches, superintend Newton students heading for missionary careers, and carry a regular teaching load. Not

17. Frederick L. Anderson, *Galusha Anderson: Preacher and Educator, 1832-1918* (n.p., 1933), pp. 26-29.

surprisingly, George Bullen, the Pawtucket pastor who took the job, found the competing responsibilities almost impossible to manage. In 1896 he implored the board of trustees for a telephone, which would allow him to contact area churches without making every trip by car. All of the time spent fundraising and supervising students had prevented him from teaching any of the courses he had been hired to cover. "It seems unfortunate, and it is somewhat embarrassing," Bullen told the board of trustees, "to be catalogued Professor of Christian Missions, when all my teaching work is in other departments."[18]

A similar mixture of good intentions and political necessity drove the organization of Newton's French course in 1889. The avowed purpose of instruction was to facilitate the evangelization of French-Catholic "Romanists" in New England. Like most American Protestants of their day, Newton's Baptists saw little good in the Roman Catholic church. Protestants in general could not avoid the uncomfortable reality that they were fast becoming a minority in the city of Boston, where the first Irish Catholic mayor, Hugh O'Brien, took his seat in City Hall in 1885. Indeed, the 1880s marked the height of anti-Catholic agitation in the city, a movement in which Baptists, especially those connected with Tremont Temple, played a leading role.[19] Newton's French course offered an openly partisan survey of Catholic doctrine, including of transubstantiation, purgatory, "saint and angel worship," "image worship," and "persecution as taught and practiced by the Roman Catholic Church." Many of the students, though they demonstrated "piety, talent and eminent natural qualities for Christian service," came with relatively little additional academic preparation. A few even lacked a common school education. After years of up-and-down struggle, the French department discontinued in 1898.[20]

Newton did, however, provide limited educational opportunities for African American and women students, far earlier than Andover. School records do not provide systematic evidence about the relative number of black students during the nineteenth century. It is likely that their numbers were small, that most hailed from the South, and that

18. "Report of the Faculty, 1896," in Records of the Board of Trustees, Newton Theological Institution, ANTS archives.

19. The full story is in Bendroth, *Fundamentalists in the City: Conflict and Division in Boston's Churches, 1885-1950* (New York: Oxford University Press, 2005), pp. 57-83.

20. "Report of the Faculty of the NTI to the Trustees, 13 May 1891," ANTS archives.

they did not always feel at home on a northern white seminary campus. The most remarkable African American graduate during this period was George Washington Williams ('74). Arriving at Newton as a seasoned war veteran, he went on to become the pastor of Boston's influential Twelfth Baptist Church, and after receiving his law degree in Cincinnati, he was the first African American elected to the Ohio state senate, serving one term, from 1880 to 1881. An influential author — his *History of the Negro Race in America, 1618-1880* was the first history of African Americans ever written — he earned his greatest fame as an international diplomat. Williams played a central role in publicizing the "crimes against humanity" (a phrase he originated) in the Belgian Congo. Some ten million people died in the brutal exploitation perpetrated by the Belgian government in the 1880s and 1890s. Williams' call for an international tribunal to expose and prosecute these wrongs awakened the moral conscience of people all around the world, in one of the most important early human rights campaigns.[21]

Another smaller incident also suggests that Newton's black students could play an important role on campus. At the anniversary exercises for 1881, an African American student, N. H. Ensley, "easily bore away the palm for oratory." Ensley's address entitled "The Colored Man's Claims to an Education" was a passionate defense of African American patriotism and of "the wrongs they have received from the government," beginning with the death of Boston Massacre victim Crispus Attucks to the indignities suffered by the Massachusetts Fifty-fourth regiment during the Civil War. Delivered with a "simple dignity and energy," and reprinted in the *Watchman* the following week, the oration inspired the learned Baptist audience to prolonged and "heavy cheering."[22]

Newton's first women students arrived in 1894. That year, at the request of the Women's Foreign Missionary Society, the faculty admitted four young female students as "guests" in the English class. "There is no reason to think that their presence has interfered in the slightest degree with the work of others," the faculty reassured the board of trustees. "Their bearing has been ladylike and their diligence commend-

---

21. The full story is told in Adam Hoschild, *King Leopold's Ghost* (New York: Mariner Books, 1999).

22. "Newton Anniversaries," *Watchman,* 16 June 1881, p. 188; "The Colored Man's Claims to an Education," *Watchman,* 23 June 1881, p. 194.

able." Within three years the number of women students had increased to ten, a distinct but visible minority within a student body of ninety-five. In 1900, with the establishment of Hasseltine House, a small dormitory, women established a physical presence on Newton's campus, the beginning of a long and eventful role in the school's later history.[23]

The Hills Library, dedicated on September 26, 1895, was Alvah Hovey's last and most fitting accomplishment as president of Newton. He left his post, though not all of his teaching responsibilities, in 1898. Funded through two large bequests — $20,000 in memory of alumnus and successful businessman Joseph Charles Hartshorn and $25,000 from Elizabeth M. Hills, an "esteemed neighbor and friend" — the library was the signal achievement of Newton's second half century. Hovey described the Hartshorne Memorial Hall, the name given to the library's graceful reading room, in glowing terms, as "a model of convenience and good taste." Amply furnished and well lit by gas appliances, the library was "a thing of beauty" that Hovey was certain Newton's students would "visit almost daily in their quest for truth."[24]

The English Course

Nathan Eusebius Wood, the pastor of Boston's First Baptist Church, followed Hovey as president of Newton in 1898. A traditional figure of the "Prince Albert" Victorian style, he was, according to Everett Herrick, "one of the most impressive and handsome men I ever saw in the ranks of the Baptist ministry." Wood brought a generous evangelical spirit and pastoral sensibility to his post at Newton, though, as Herrick recalled, he was a far more distinguished figure in the pulpit than in the classroom.[25]

Wood's discomfort behind the podium was emblematic of Newton's long struggle for institutional identity. Though the school had been established primarily for college graduates, two years after its founding, in 1827, the board of trustees voted to allow "students not

23. "Report of the Faculty," 1894, ANTS archives; "Report of the President and the Faculty to the Trustees, 25 April 1900," 1, ANTS archives.

24. Hovey, "Newton from 1875 to 1900," *Newtonian* 1 (June 1903): 1.

25. Herrick, *Turns Again Home: Andover Newton Theological School and Reminiscences from an Unkept Journal* (Boston: Pilgrim Press, 1949), pp. 32-34.

possessing the literary qualifications necessary for admission." Students in this so-called English course were to be instructed at the discretion of the seminary faculty, in courses "adapted to their age and circumstances." For the next several decades the school organized preparatory classes for students without college degrees.[26]

But continuing frustration among Newton's small and overworked faculty led to the abolition of the English course in 1899. The disparity between college-educated seminarians and their common school peers eventually required two separate tracks of instruction, which nearly doubled classroom time required of their professors. "In the end, therefore," the faculty warned the board of trustees, "your professors must do less studying and more teaching, which could certainly lower the standard of their scholarship."[27] "One must feel sympathy for men who feel that the struggle to take the college course is too hard and desire to enter the ministry earlier," faculty members admitted, "but at the same time one is compelled to feel sympathy for the churches also who need pastors of virility enough at least to gain a college training for themselves."[28]

Still, Newton's supporters fought a persisting sense among their fellow Baptists that a seminary education should be rightfully available to anyone who wanted it. As a layman reminded the Boston Baptist Ministers' Conference in 1905, "God has not limited His call to the ministry to men who have been . . . college trained." In fact, he insisted, "there is something needed in our pulpits more than mere intellectual training." Citing numerous examples, he argued that a young man with an obvious gift of preaching could be far more effective than even the most "cultured" prince of the pulpit.[29]

Newton students felt these same competing pressures. In 1903, a few enterprising souls organized the *Newtonian*, a student journal designed to build "school spirit" and provide a forum for theological discussion. An early issue featured a speech at the school's annual Thanksgiving banquet, in which the author began by citing the numer-

26. "Newton Theological Institution," *Christian Watchman*, 13 August 1830, p. 130.

27. "Report of the Faculty, 1889-1890," Records of the NTI Board of Trustees, ANTS archives.

28. "Report of the President and the Faculty to the Trustees," 25 April 1900, 1, ANTS archives.

29. William H. Breed, "Training for Religious Work," *Watchman*, 4 May 1905, pp. 9-10.

ous advantages of a Newton education, including the school's proximity to Boston and the achievements of its illustrious alumni. Academic rigor, he declared, was available to any student who desired it. Though some charged that "the lack of the Newton spirit is due to the low intellectual standing of some who at least pass as Newton men," those few egregious exceptions should not mar the reputation of the rest. "That there is room for improvement is very evident," he admitted, but "the Trustees have already moved in the right direction. The Faculty are quite willing to move quite as fast as we desire. And if every student will feel his responsibility and do his part even the present high standing of Newton will soon be surpassed."[30]

The Gordon School

Newton found a temporary remedy through an institutional partnership with the Gordon Missionary and Bible Training School in 1907. In some ways, the choice was counterintuitive, if not downright surprising. The Gordon school had been established in 1889 by A. J. Gordon, and for much of its early life was housed in his Clarendon Baptist Church in Boston's South End. The Gordon school offered basic biblical instruction to all comers, who usually arrived without a college degree. In fact, in its early days Gordon had no degree requirements of any kind or even a list of students. Institutional niceties were a luxury that the school's founders could not afford: they were ardent premillennialists, convinced that they were living in the world's last days and awaiting Christ's sudden, cataclysmic return.

The doctrine had a small following in Boston, primarily among Baptists, thanks to A. J. Gordon's role as author and editor of the fervent periodical, the *Watchword*. But premillennialism was widely known elsewhere, popularized in summer conferences and a myriad of local Bible institutes. The doctrine played an important role in the emerging fundamentalist movement in the United States, a movement with considerable support among northern Baptists. The distinct possibility that Christ might be returning suddenly and soon lent new urgency to the task of evangelism and foreign missions — according to premillennial-

30. "The Newton Spirit," *Newtonian* 1 (winter 1903): 15.

ist interpretation of biblical prophecy, Christ would not appear until all of the world's peoples had had an opportunity to hear the gospel.[31]

Given that timetable, it is not surprising that Gordon, and other American Bible institutes as well, endured regular criticism for being a "short cut school."[32] The curriculum centered on intensive survey of the English Bible, and branched out just slightly to include courses in the theory and practice of street evangelism, techniques in song leading, and modes of public speaking. To the dismay of seminary officials, some cash-strapped congregations found this education more than enough to qualify a young man as a preacher. Indeed, from its location in the middle of the diverse South End, the Gordon school attracted a regular stream of applicants from "the carpenter's bench, the painter's pot, [and] from the tailor's shop." As A. J. Gordon himself declared of his students, with no small measure of pride, "They are all poor." All of the talk about the dangers of an uneducated ministry was, in his view, "not a mark of genuine culture, but of intellectual snobbishness."[33]

Gordon was also, of course, a Newton trustee, a graduate of Brown, and no stranger to higher education. Moreover, as the school's supporters found, even the most ardent premillennial pragmatism could not be sustained indefinitely. A scant decade and a half after its founding, the Gordon school began to settle in for the long haul, regularizing courses of instruction and recruiting nationally known teachers. When A. J. Gordon died in 1899, the Bible school's faculty began searching for a permanent home, better financial backing, and a broader sense of purpose. Over the next several years, they explored affiliation with a variety of small evangelistically oriented schools including a small lay college in the Boston near suburb of Revere, and Dwight L. Moody's Northfield Academy.

On October 8, 1907, the Gordon Bible and Missionary Training School affiliated with Newton. The agreement specified that the now renamed "Gordon School of the Newton Theological Institution" would be administered by a committee of eleven, to be nominated by Gordon

31. George Marsden, *Fundamentalism and American Culture, 1875-1930* (New York: Oxford University Press, 1980); Virginia Lieson Brereton, *Training God's Army: The American Bible School, 1880-1940* (Bloomington: Indiana University Press, 1990).

32. "Missionary Training Schools: Do Baptists Need Them?" *Baptist Quarterly* 12 (January 1890): 69-100.

33. Gordon, "Short-Cut Methods," *Watchman*, 7 November 1889, p. 1.

people and then elected by the Newton board of trustees. The advantages to both institutions were clear: Gordon would have the administrative backing of an established school of theology, and Newton could, in effect, offer an English course to prospective students.

In the beginning, warm personal ties facilitated the union of the two schools. Newton president Nathan E. Wood was a close friend of A. J. Gordon's, both of them having served in Boston's Baptist churches. After he retired from his post at Newton in 1908, Wood continued on as a teacher on the Gordon faculty. His son and namesake, Nathan R. Wood, became dean of Gordon in 1911. Even after the partnership between the two schools ended, a few Newton faculty, including Galusha Anderson and church historian Henry Rowe, taught in both institutions.

But the affiliation lasted only until 1914, by which time the mismatch was obvious. At heart, the two schools were pursuing fundamentally different goals and serving two very different constituencies. Nor were they immune to institutional competition. According to one Gordon observer, some of the Newton faculty viewed the Bible school as "a rival theological school growing up in the same denomination and the same territory."[34] It did not help matters that Gordon flourished under the partnership, growing from twelve students in 1908 to seventy-two in 1914. Close to half of them announced plans to enter the ministry after graduation, even though few had even a high school degree.

Nor, most likely, did the school's predominantly female constituency give comfort to some up on Newton's hallowed hill. One of the little-known ironies of early fundamentalist institutions like Gordon was that the clear majority of their students were women. In the movement's early days, when evangelistic zeal trumped all other concerns, gender rarely proved a barrier; as the primary constituents of American religion in general, women quickly filled the ranks of Bible schools and missionary training institutes. This visible confirmation of religious "feminization," as it was often called, was not good news to schools dedicated to recruiting and training men for church ministry.[34]

Perhaps most important of all, Gordon was not really a Baptist school. By 1912, when a fire at Clarendon Baptist forced a move to a

34. Nathan R. Wood, *A School of Christ* (Boston, 1953), p. 68.
35. See Margaret Bendroth, *Fundamentalism and Gender, 1875 to the Present* (New Haven: Yale University Press, 1993), Chapter One.

nearby Presbyterian church, the school was already visibly interdenominational. The board of trustees included some of Boston's leading Baptists, including Edgar Lane from Tremont Temple and O. P. Gifford from the Brookline Baptist church, but also Park Street Congregational Church's A. Z. Conrad and William T. Rich, New England's leading Methodist layman.

The final straw, at least on the Gordon side, came in 1913, when its harried academic dean Nathan R. Wood received sudden word that he had only three days to produce a full academic catalog for the upcoming school year. As he later related the story, he managed to complete a task that normally took weeks in a matter of hours, sacrificing two nights of sleep in the process. The exhausted (and no doubt deeply irritated) Wood was "too dizzy to lift head or hand" by the time the catalog was finished.[36] The administrative glitch was, of course, only a symptom of a much deeper friction, and the beginning of the end of a short-lived institutional partnership.

In 1914 the Newton board of trustees entertained a recommendation to bring Gordon under more direct control of the Northern Baptist Convention. The new plan would have placed representatives from all of the denomination's mission boards on Gordon's administrative committee, and required all tuition grants from the Northern Baptist Education Society to go through Newton's business office before reaching individual students. A registration committee would have funneled ministerial candidates away from Gordon and into either college preparation or seminary.[37]

Infuriated, Gordon's leaders requested an immediate separation. The resulting motion passed by Newton's board of trustees on July 7, 1914, suggested that the parting of the ways was not entirely amicable. The seminary board charged Gordon to "pledge itself . . . to carry on in good faith the work for which it was founded *and for which it has until now been maintained.*" In other words, Gordon was to remain a Bible school, and nothing more.[38]

The end of the relationship also completed Newton's remaining ob-

36. Wood, *A School of Christ,* p. 69.

37. Donald Ashmall, "Newton Theological Institution during the Horr Presidency, 1908-1925," (B.D. Thesis: NTI, 1968), p. 60.

38. Ashmall, "Newton Theological Institution during the Horr Presidency," p. 61. In fact, however, Gordon separated into a liberal arts college and divinity school in 1931.

ligation to entry-level students. In the following years, the seminary began to offer more specialized courses that reflected current trends in pastoral work. Higher standards for students, larger course loads for faculty, and a board of trustees composed of ever greater numbers of professional educators, bankers, and lawyers reflected an emerging sense of new purpose up on Newton Hill — and few regrets over the failed partnership with Gordon.

George Horr

The driving force behind the shift was Newton's new president George Edwin Horr, who followed Nathan Wood in 1908. Horr represented a new breed of seminary president, emerging around the turn of the century. No longer just the leader of the faculty bearing a double burden of coursework and reporting to the board of trustees, the new seminary president was a public figure, representing the face of the school to the surrounding academic and denominational world. Horr arrived with a national reputation for his literary skill and scholarly accomplishments. A graduate of Brown University in 1876, he had studied under Phillip Schaff and Charles G. T. Shedd at Union Seminary in New York before finishing at Newton in 1879. He returned to Brown for a doctoral degree in 1896. Horr became pastor of the First Baptist Church in Charlestown, Massachusetts, in 1884 and in 1891 he became editor of the denominational journal the *Watchman*. He was well known among New England Baptists and across the country as an editorialist of uncommon skill, covering the full range of social debates about race, labor, and international politics. In 1904 he took a teaching post at Newton in a new field, the History of Modern Christianity. He seemed the obvious choice for the seminary's next president. As his old friends at the *Watchman* declared, "his election as president at Newton is but the first step in a series of developments and enlargements which will place the institution in the foremost rank of the divinity schools of America."[39]

The prediction proved mostly true. Under Horr's leadership, Newton's entrance requirements became more rigorous: in 1911 the faculty

---

39. "The Election of Dr. Horr," *Watchman,* 16 July 1908, p. 5.

ruled that all incoming students had to bring not only a good character but at least an 85% average in their college courses and a working knowledge of Greek and the English Bible. The school also shored up its academic offerings, adding a Master of Sacred Theology in 1909 for particularly able B.D. students who stayed on for an extra year of intensive study. In 1915, Harvard University began allowing academically able Newton students to register for two courses a year at the Divinity School and to compete for the prestigious Williams fellowships.

A series of curriculum reforms, carried out several times during Horr's presidency, also added academic luster. Its basic design emphasized three fundamental assumptions about "the needs of a competent ministry." The first, of course, was "a knowledge of the Holy Scriptures," including competency with the original languages; the second "a knowledge of the actual situation, critical, philosophical, religious, economic, social, and political" that the student would confront in parish life; and the third "practical skill" in relating the biblical message to "the needs of the present situation." Following this threefold emphasis, the academic year was divided into a fall, winter, and spring semester.[40]

Throughout their Newton program, all students received a vigorous course of instruction in the English Bible. Additional training in Greek was required for those arriving without previous college course work, with Hebrew available for the more ambitious. Though the curriculum required only one theology course every year, Newton students, like those at Andover, had access to a full range of elective classes. Juniors, for example, began their seminary course with the Psychology of Religion and a survey of The Church and Social Institutions, which spanned a range of current issues from family life to public education to the separation of church and state. The curriculum also emphasized the importance of preaching, with regular work in homiletics and "voice culture."

In 1919-1920, Newton introduced a program in religious education, reflecting the great enthusiasm in liberal Protestant circles for psychological study of child development and learning theory. Courses had begun as early as 1909, and the new curriculum required six hours of instruction for all B.D. students. But the new program established a

---

40. "The Newton Theological Institution: Revised Curriculum Courses for 1918-1919," *Institution Bulletin* 10 (1918): 5.

regular professorship in the field, filled for many years by James Percival Berkeley, a graduate of the nation's leading programs at Union Seminary and Columbia University's Department of Religious Education. As part of a movement led by John Dewey and George Coe, Newton's program was emphatically not intended for the old-fashioned Sunday school teacher. Modern religious educators required standard courses in Bible, theology, and church history, as well as psychology and sociology. In addition, students received specialized training in "pageantry" and pedagogical techniques.

The religious education program was also the first professional opportunity that Newton allowed to women. Though a few had attended classes as "visitors" training for missionary work, they were not regular degree candidates. The two-year Master of Religious Education program admitted women as full-time students, and for the first time, opened the door to full-time positions in local churches.[41]

But the professionalizing trends at Newton put a damper on whatever liberalizing impulses women's presence may have signaled. The guiding ideal behind women's education at Newton and elsewhere was practicality; old prejudices that viewed college-level schooling as a luxury would keep their numbers low, especially in more theoretically oriented subjects. During a time when barely 3 percent of American women attended college, Newton was not likely to produce many female theologians or biblical scholars. More often ambitious young women attended missionary training schools, or programs that promised an immediate vocational reward — teaching, library science, or secretarial work.

In fact, the underside of rising academic standards was an anti-liberal concern about admitting too many non-traditional students. Even the Gordon school, which was so heavily female that its founders briefly considered turning it into a women's academy, placed a quota on women students in the 1930s.[42] Newton was no different. In his autobiography, the famous African American theologian Howard Thurman recounted applying to Newton after seeing an advertisement in the *Watchman-Examiner*. "I wrote a letter to Newton Seminary inquiring

41. James P. Berkeley, "In Retrospect," *Andover Newton Bulletin* 46 (April 1954): 3-5.
42. "News," *Gordon News-Letter*, no. 25 (March 1931): 12; "News," *Gordon News-Letter*, no. 26 (November 1931): 1.

about admission," he wrote. "In reply, I received a very cordial letter from the president expressing his regret that the school did not admit Negroes, and referring me to Virginia Union, a Baptist missionary college in Richmond, Virginia." Though, as Thurman recalled, "the letter wished me well," the author (presumably George Horr) assured him that at Virginia Union, a black school, "I would be able to secure the kind of training I would need to provide religious leadership for my people." Thurman instead went to Colgate-Rochester, where he graduated at the top of his class.[43]

Some of the pressure on seminaries for professional "respectability" came from below. By the turn of the century, any congregation worth its salt aspired after the model of the "institutional church" popularized by the Social Gospel movement. Instead of a simple rectangle housing a sanctuary and a few Sunday school rooms under a vertical spire, the new church was a sprawling horizontal maze of clubrooms and parlors, with bowling alleys and basketball courts, kitchens and dining halls. "Late-Victorian Protestants were always busy doing God's work," historian Brooks Holifield writes, "pushing valves and pulling levers." The old ecclesiastical model, where the minister's primary job was to deliver a sermon and his basic training centered on Bible study and theology, would emphatically no longer suit. The modern pastor was, in Holifield's words, a combination "social director" and "physician of the soul." No longer a holy man or a saint, he needed to exhibit a "natural manly informality" that would make his parishioners comfortable, if not spiritually challenged.[44]

But most religious educators knew full well that they were not simply working to meet the expectations of an often fickle denominational constituency; they were also working alongside the nineteenth century's two other gentlemen's professions, medicine and law. After the Civil War, those two fields moved ahead rapidly, creating a standard regimen of post-college training and nationally recognized benchmarks for professional qualification. Organizations like the American Medical Associa-

43. Howard Thurman, *With Head and Heart* (New York: Harcourt Brace Jovanovich, 1979), p. 45. In 1953, the *Atlantic Monthly* erroneously reported that Thurman had been turned down by Andover. Newton's trustees did, however, vote to issue an apology. See Jean Burden, "Howard Thurman," *Atlantic Monthly* 195 (1953): 40.

44. Holifield, *History of Pastoral Care in America: From Salvation to Self-Realization* (Nashville: Abingdon Press, 1983), pp. 175, 178.

tion and the American Bar Association operated as powerful doorkeepers, winnowing out both the educationally and the socially unqualified — including for many decades, women and minorities.

Seminaries labored to follow suit, juggling competing obligations to churches, denominational leaders, and the larger academic world, and to the financial bottom line. Unlike many law and medical schools during this time, seminaries could not enjoy an economy of scale by affiliating with a secular university and sharing costs of library and dormitory space. Freestanding denominational seminaries like Newton faced a series of institutional challenges that they were only beginning to understand as the twentieth century opened.

Baptist Fundamentalism

Under Horr's presidency, Newton defined itself as a liberal school — a tricky task given the rising strength of the fundamentalist movement in Baptist circles during the 1920s. Already in 1918, Horr had had to defend Newton against scattered charges of lax doctrine, including one public attack by Boston pastor Cortland Myers.[45] In response, the school issued a short, single-paragraph "creed," probably written by Horr himself, that offered little direct comfort to conservatives. The statement made no mention of the virgin birth, the Trinity, or the authority of Scripture. Instead, it affirmed in strongly ethical, experiential terms the importance of Jesus as "the center of our religion." "Jesus' method is goodwill; his means is loving service of every sort," the statement declared; "his purpose is to bring every individual, who will yield to him, into personal communion with God, and to make human society in all its elements and relations what it ought to be, a loving brotherhood."[46]

Baptist liberals walked a fine line. In the early 1920s, the Fundamentalist Federation, a coalition of leading Baptist pastors and laymen, publicly challenged the standards of orthodoxy in the denomination's seminaries. New York City pastor John Roach Straton, Minneapolis pul-

45. Myers, "A Startling Peril in Our Schools," *Watchman-Examiner,* 31 October 1918, p. 1357.

46. George Horr et al., "The Newton Reply," *Watchman-Examiner,* 19 December 1918, p. 1562.

piteer William Bell Riley, and Boston's own J. C. Massee mounted a campaign at the Northern Baptist Convention meeting in Indianapolis, charging that modernism was being freely taught to hundreds of future clergy. Massee, the pastor of Boston's largest Baptist congregation, the Tremont Temple Baptist Church, had already conducted his own survey of seminary alumni, and circulated the alarming report that only 40 percent found faculty faithful to the Bible. In an article in the *Watchman-Examiner* in 1921, he had directly accused the denomination's Board of Education, which included two Newton faculty members, of breaking faith with historic Baptist belief. As proof, he cited a series of quotations from well-known seminary faculty — Walter Rauschenbusch, Shailer Mathews, W. H. P. Faunce — that indicated support for higher critical methods.[47]

Newton's board of directors lodged a protest, taking out a half-page advertisement in the *Watchman-Examiner* to denounce the "immorality and injustice" of the "covert propaganda" employed by Massee and the Fundamentalist Fellowship. Rather than answer any of the accusations against Baptist educators, the board appealed to the Baptist "heritage of freedom" and "heroic stand for religious liberty."[48] A week later, Newton Center's First Baptist Church issued its own full-page protest in the *Watchman-Examiner*. Names of Newton faculty and trustees, including W. N. Donovan and R. M. Vaughan, appeared prominently.[49]

Horr participated only reluctantly in the public controversy. Challenged by the *Watchman-Examiner* to provide specific proof of Newton's orthodoxy — editor Curtis Lee Laws was openly sympathetic with the fundamentalist movement's agenda — he refused to become caught in the growing "atmosphere of suspicion."[50] The strategy proved wise: by 1925 many Baptists, including even Massee himself, had lost enthusiasm for a theological witch hunt. By the late 1920s, the fundamentalist

47. J. C. Massee, "An Answer to the Board of Education," *Watchman-Examiner*, 16 June 1921, pp. 752-753. Mathews and Faunce were both NTI alumni. On Massee and fundamentalism, see Margaret Bendroth, *Fundamentalists in the City*, pp. 117-124.

48. "Newton Theological Institution: A Protest and an Appeal," *Watchman-Examiner*, 11 May 1921, p. 601.

49. Untitled advertisement, *Watchman-Examiner*, 18 May 1922, p. 635.

50. "Newton's Protest and Appeal," *Watchman-Examiner*, 1 June 1922, p. 678; "A Letter from Dr. Horr," *Watchman-Examiner*, 8 June 1922, p. 714; Ashmall, "Newton Theological Institution during the Horr Presidency," pp. 66f.

challenge to the Northern Baptist Convention resulted not in a take-over but in the departure of the conservatives.

The American Association of Theological Schools

As a former editor, George Horr was rarely afraid to express an opinion. Even while president at Newton he issued pronouncements on a variety of topics, from international politics to fishing treaties with Great Britain. In 1916, he wrote to President Woodrow Wilson to express his support for his foreign policy, and remained an avid public supporter of American involvement in World War I.[51]

Horr also intended Newton to take a larger public role. In 1918 he organized a conference of Baptist seminaries, aimed at a discussion of the wartime emergency, but in the long run groundbreaking for the future of American theological education. The meeting showcased Horr's Boston-area connections: Calvin Coolidge, the Massachusetts governor, gave a welcome and Abbott Lowell, the president of Harvard, hosted a dinner and gave a keynote address on "The Social and Religious Problems Which the War Has Presented to the Minister."

The rest of the conference, and the ensuing conversation, marked the first time that seminary officials had gathered on their own to discuss the future of their field. The timing was auspicious: after years of dealing with their problems separately, the leaders of theological education in the United States recognized that they could work together on setting standards for clergy preparation.

Over the next several years, Horr's conference of Baptist seminary leaders broadened into an ecumenical effort that would result in formation of the American Association of Theological Schools (AATS) in 1936. This remarkable achievement was a key step in the professionalization of clergy education, and one in which Newton and later Andover Newton played a founding role. In 1938, the AATS issued a set of guidelines for judging the quality of individual schools: rates of admission, the scope of the curriculum, the makeup of the faculty, as well as the state of finances and the number of books in the library. In other words,

51. "The Conference of the Baptist Leaders of New England," *Institution Bulletin* 13 (1921): 5-110.

prospective students and denominational officials now had an objective measure of what separated a "good" seminary from a substandard one. After rigorous inspection, 46 schools received full accreditation from AATS in 1938, out of 61 who had applied. Today the number of member schools has grown to 250, and the renamed Association of Theological Schools in the United States and Canada reflects the scope of its influence.[52]

Horr's meeting of Baptist seminary officials in 1918 had other portents as well. His developing friendship with Harvard president Lowell brought introductions to Richard Cabot and Nels Ferré, both of whom would later teach at Andover Newton; Cabot would introduce the concept of clinical pastoral education, a program which would ultimately transform the minister's traditional role as a healer of souls. The Harvard connection was also an early link between the two schools, though at the time more theoretical than real. In 1918, Andover was ten years into its abortive Cambridge sojourn, still certain of a long and productive future in partnership with the Harvard Divinity School.

All told, the late nineteenth and early twentieth centuries were a time of remarkable progress up on Institution Hill. Newton had emerged from the Civil War decades as a struggling, predominantly local Baptist seminary. Its loyal faculty were often stretched to the breaking point, as they attempted to bridge the demands of the international scholarly world with the needs of their students, many of whom lacked a college education. For a while, it seemed that Newton might tilt the second direction; indeed, had the affiliation with Gordon remained permanent, Newton would have likely been subsumed in the Bible institute's successful outreach to non-traditional students. But under George Horr, the Baptist school moved quickly in the opposite direction. Horr redefined Newton as a firmly liberal institution, playing a key role in an emerging national network of theological schools. He aimed high, and as Newton entered the twentieth century, his ambitious goals seemed, to many, well in reach.

---

52. Miller, *Piety and Profession*, pp. 451f.

Andover campus, circa 1820

Newton Theological Institution, 1866

Leonard Woods,
Andover's first Abbot
Professor of Christian
Theology

Moses Stuart, Andover's
Bartlet Professor of
Sacred Literature

Irah Chase, Newton's first faculty member

Alvah Hovey, the indispensable "utility player" of Newton's early years

Adoniram Judson, Andover alumnus and leading figure of Protestant foreign missions

Ann Hasseltine Judson, revered for her dedication and courage. Her untimely death inspired Newton students to begin a foreign missionary society in 1827.

Henry Opukaha'ia,
Hawaiian convert
and Andover student

Niijima Jo, Andover student from
Japan, founded the Doshisha
University in Kyoto in 1875

Edwards A. Park,
Andover's influential
and long-tenured
Abbot Professor

The Andover faculty, circa 1883

Puck Magazine comments on the Andover controversy: "A Glimpse into the Twentieth Century: What Andover's Methods Will Ultimately Bring Her To in an Age of Progress and Evolution"

Andover House, 6 Rollins Street, Boston.

Andover House, Social Gospel training ground in Boston's South End

William Jewett Tucker, Andover's leading Social Gospel figure

George Washington Williams, Newton Class of 1874, famed for his exposure of human rights abuses in the Belgian Congo

George E. Horr, Newton's forward-looking president who helped organize the American Association of Theological Schools

Andover Hall, a temporary home on Harvard's campus

Everett C. Herrick presided over the Andover-Newton merger in 1931

Student group at the Worcester State Hospital, 1929, with Geneva Dye (young woman on right), the first Andover Newton student to take supervised clinical training in a hospital setting

"Just As I Am: Young, Strong, and Free":
women students at Newton during the 1920s

Roy M. Pearson led
Andover Newton during
years of growth and
struggle

George W. Peck, son of an Australian coal miner, influential
church statesman, and visionary president

Orlando E. Costas, academic dean and Judson Professor of Missiology

Student organizer Carl McCall and Andover Newton President
Herbert J. Gezork at the Blue Hill Protestant Center, incorporated
as the Blue Hill Christian Center in 1964

Gordon M.
Torgersen, who as
president led a
critical financial
turnaround

Jane Cary Peck, social ethicist and one of
Andover Newton's first women faculty

Wilson Chapel

Nick Carter, named Andover Newton's president in 2004

CHAPTER SIX

Andover's Harvard Years: From Cambridge to Newton Center

———✣———

Andover marked its centennial year by returning to Cambridge. In a move that shocked some observers and delighted others, those two old mortal enemies, Congregationalist Andover and Unitarian Harvard, became neighbors once again — and on liberal soil no less. For a moment, it seemed, a hundred years of bitter separation simply melted into air; by 1922 the arrangement proved so successful that the two schools drew up a plan for full consolidation.

But it was not to be. While pens hovered scant inches over signature lines, the future union came to a sudden, humiliating end. Objections raised by Andover's old nemesis, the Board of Visitors, stopped the negotiations just weeks from their conclusion. In the months that followed, the Visitors issued a phalanx of legal questions so intractable that in 1925 Andover's stunned faculty and trustees prepared to shut down their venerable old institution for good.

Few observers, past or present, have managed to avoid marriage metaphors in telling the tale of Andover's Cambridge years, or of its subsequent union with Newton Theological Institution in 1931. Even harder to avoid have been the stock conventions of a morality tale, for the decision of 1908 had all these and more. As one disgruntled observer put it, Andover's move back to Cambridge was "the grimmest piece of irony ever known."[1] And indeed, as the episode unfolded there

---

1. John A. Faulkner, "The Tragic Fate of a Famous Seminary," *Bibliotheca Sacra* 80 (October 1923): 449.

was no denying the presence of a fatal flaw in Andover's past: the faculty creed, once forged as a permanent hedge against failure, very nearly became the source of its final demise. The rules and regulations so earnestly put in place by Andover's founding generation very nearly rendered the school incapable of survival. In Glenn Miller's apt summary, "Seldom has an institution suffered so long and so hard at the hands of its supposed friends and supporters."[2]

In the long run, however, all the upheavals of the 1920s were well worth the trouble. Andover came out of its legal morass with a broader sense of purpose, disencumbered at last of its nineteenth-century creed. Moreover, the transition from Cambridge to Newton finally dispelled the shadows of sectarianism that had haunted the school since its inception. As "act two" of the original Andover controversy, the Harvard merger provided a lesson that was at least as important as the courtroom battles of the 1880s: a decision largely engineered by a small group of men was not allowed to stand. Andover was not the property of a select few, or the instrument of a particular theological agenda. It was to be, along with Newton, a school of the wider church.

Why Harvard?

Even after a hundred years apart, Harvard was still an unlikely partner for Andover. Open hostilities over the Unitarian "schism," as it was often called, still lingered among rank-and-file Congregationalists. In many New England towns the paint was barely dry on new meetinghouses erected after the original buildings became the legal property of Unitarian dissidents. Not a few Andover alumni, schooled under controversialists like Moses Stuart and Leonard Woods, viewed the prospective move to Cambridge with open hostility. News of the plan provoked a flurry of letters in the Congregational press, and genuine alarm in local alumni associations. "Harvard University has always been looked upon as the center and source of Unitarianism in this country," one critic complained, "and it is peculiarly a perversion of the trust for the Seminary to establish such an alliance."[3]

2. Glenn Miller, *Piety and Profession* (Grand Rapids: Eerdmans, 2007), p. 134.
3. "The Andover-Harvard Merger Illegal. Remarks by Rev. William E. Wolcott before the Board of Visitors of Andover Theological Seminary, November 5, 1908," p. 10.

Harvard had its own issues, of course. As one former dean remembered, university authorities had tried to let the Divinity School "wither by neglect." The school had only one full-time faculty member, and two others filled a dual role as full-time pastors; the student body numbered only nineteen.[4] In 1869 Harvard's new president Charles Eliot, however, determined to "lift the Divinity School to honorable standing at Harvard."[5] In the 1870s and 1880s, a wave of distinguished faculty and endowment funds testified to his resolve to enforce university-level standards on theological instruction in Cambridge. The new direction required careful insistence that the Divinity School, though certainly seeking Unitarian donations, was not a Unitarian seminary. It was to be wholly nonsectarian, with no direct denominational obligation. Between 1880 and 1930, the rank of full professors included two Baptists, six Trinitarian Congregationalists, one Anglican, one Roman Catholic, one Jew, and five Unitarians. The student body grew equally diverse.[6]

Andover had considered other options. When the school looked to be failing for lack of enrollment, some alumni suggested that the best course would be to dissolve the educational apparatus entirely, and let Andover simply operate as a trust fund, supporting worthy Congregational causes. Others, recognizing the great influx of European immigrants into New England, including the factory towns of Lawrence and Lowell just a stone's throw from Andover, thought that the seminary might scale down its academic ambitions and become a training ground for an ethnically diverse array of new pastors. Or, some suggested, in keeping with its storied past and the rising popularity of practical Bible-school institutes, Andover could transform itself into *"the* foreign missionary seminary, the institution at which the candidate for the foreign field might get his entire education."[7]

---

4. William Wallace Fenn, "The Theological School, 1869-1928," in *The Development of Harvard University Since the Inauguration of President Eliot, 1869-1929,* ed. Samuel Eliot Morison (Cambridge, MA: Harvard University Press, 1930), p. 463.

5. Fenn, "The Theological School," p. 464.

6. Fenn, "The Theological School," p. 465.

7. Augustus Walker, "Another Suggestion for Andover," *Congregationalist and Christian World,* 12 January 1907, p. 61; "A New Departure for Andover," *Congregationalist and Christian World,* 8 June 1907, p. 782; "Is There Another Century for Andover?" *Congregationalist and Christian World,* 22 June 1907, pp. 823-824.

But momentum was moving the other way. The "Plan for Removal," approved by the board of trustees in December 1907, would merge both the faculties and degree programs of Harvard and Andover into a harmonious whole. Under the new arrangement, both schools would continue to issue their own Bachelor of Divinity degrees and publish their own course catalogs; Andover would maintain its own physically separate land and buildings near the Divinity School campus. But both Harvard and Andover students could register for any courses offered by either school, and Andover students could take full advantage of Harvard's libraries and museums. They were eligible for admission into Harvard's graduate degree programs as well.[8]

At Andover's commencement ceremony in June 1908, the last to be held on its historic hill, Harvard's Divinity School dean William Wallace Fenn voiced the hopes and anxieties of both schools. The risks to Andover were obvious, of course, but Harvard also needed confirmation that "our principle of non-sectarian theological education (in which we profoundly believe)" would not be jeopardized by overzealous Congregationalists. Andover would be encouraged to uphold its "great, uplifting, honorable traditions," but within a larger secular university structure. "We shall honor and love each other," he quipped, "but the word 'obey' is not in the contract. Neither is there, I trust, on either side the fond and foolish notion of marriage for the purpose of reformation."[9]

Why Cambridge?

In many ways, Andover's reverse pilgrimage made sense. By the turn of the century, simmering discontent with the Andover constitution had begun to loosen the hold of some of its more controversial traditions. In 1900, with the inauguration of Edward Hincks as Abbot Professor of Christian Theology, the Board of Visitors finally agreed that it was no longer necessary for Andover faculty to recite the old creed in public. It was enough, they said, for a professor to "approve himself a man of sound and orthodox principles of Divinity." The old anathemas against

8. Board of Trustee Minutes, December 1907, ANTS archives.
9. "Andover at the Parting of the Ways," *Congregationalist,* 20 June 1908, p. 808.

Socinians, Arians, and Mahommetans were gone; after years of strife, Andover was beginning to leave its truculent past behind.[10]

Andover's board of trustees was also convinced that the school's geographic setting, some twenty-five miles north of Boston, was no longer sacrosanct. The original endowment to the Andover Academy in 1780 had stipulated that the seminary would "never be removed from the South Parish in the town of Andover" unless "the good of mankind shall manifestly require it." The board of trustees reasoned that that time had come.[11]

Their official rationale for removal began with an enumeration of difficulties posed by the Andover location. Citing the "practical desertion" of the seminary by ministerial students, the trustees worried about the waste of funds solemnly consecrated by donors "to the great ends of religion." Trapped up in Andover, the school's gifted faculty faced a "narrow field of usefulness," and encountered great difficulty in recruiting new members to their ranks. All told, Andover's rural location made it impossible for the seminary to fulfill its original aim of "increasing the number of *learned* and *able* defenders of the Gospel of Christ, as well as of *Orthodox, pious, and zealous* ministers of the New Testament." To be true to the founders' ambitions, Andover had to pack up its tents and move southward.[12]

Clearly, something needed to change. Not only was Andover losing students, but the denomination's entire educational enterprise was running into difficulty by the 1890s. In 1897, the eminent Congregational historian Williston Walker estimated that barely half of the clergy ordained to churches in 1894 were seminary graduates. Even more startling, Walker estimated that in 1760, decades before Andover was even a Calvinist daydream, only 11 of the 258 Congregational ministers in Massachusetts lacked a college education. The schools themselves were hardly at fault; Walker blamed the lax standards of churches and installation councils for undermining the efforts of good denominational schools like Andover, Oberlin, and Hartford. "It is, indeed," he warned his audience at the Boston Congregational Club, "an ominous

10. The final clarification of this decision is in the Minutes of the Board of Trustees for January 1909.

11. Cited in Pierce, "The Legal Aspects of the Andover Creed," *Church History* 15 (March 1946): 43.

12. Cited in Pierce, "The Legal Aspects of the Andover Creed," p. 43.

token of a danger, in an age wherein training is increasingly demanded as a prerequisite to entrance on all secular professors, and in a denomination historically preeminent for a learned ministry, that an ever increasing proportion of the pastors of our churches are without thorough preparation for their work."[13]

The trustees were convinced that Cambridge, with its old Congregational ties, its proximity to Boston, and its critical mass of prospective students, was "best calculated" for carrying out the founders' original vision. Both students and faculty would benefit from larger course offerings, hearty intellectual camaraderie, and the stimulus of a university setting. "The effect of this," the Andover trustees promised, "would be to render the calling of the Ministry more honorable and attractive in the eyes of educated young men and draw a larger proportion of them into the profession." The Congregational churches, whatever their misgivings about Harvard, would clearly benefit from the partnership over time.[14]

Andover's urge to move and to merge was not unique. As theological seminaries entered the Progressive era of the early twentieth century, they readily absorbed its fascination with city life and its passion for efficiency. A meeting of the Evangelical Alliance at the Chicago World's Fair of 1893 found seminary officials in deep discussion about the best location of a theological school. While some worried about urban "distractions," most were convinced that city life offered the widest possible educational experience. The enthusiasm reflected the zenith of the Social Gospel movement among Protestant churches, a movement dedicated to the spiritual redemption of the nation's increasingly crowded industrial cities. Congregationalists in particular warmed to the idealism of Washington Gladden and William Jewett Tucker. In Boston, the Berkeley Temple, a vibrant "institutional church" in the South End, was the largest Congregational church in the city.[15]

---

13. Williston Walker, *Are Our Seminaries Maintaining the Quality of Our Ministry?* (Hartford, CT: Hartford Seminary Press, 1897), pp. 4-5, 6, 11. During this time, the National Association of Congregational Churches devoted significant attention to the problem of "acting" pastors in churches, i.e., men who had been selected by local churches without being approved by a local ordaining council. See *New-Fangled Congregationalism* (n.p., 1876).

14. Board of Trustee minutes, 12 March 1908, ANTS archives.

15. *Christianity Practically Applied: The Discussions of the International Christian Con-*

At the World's Fair meeting, seminary officials also talked at length about the advantages of connection with a university. This would prove, of course, to be the great trend of seminary education as the twentieth century unfolded, with schools like Chicago, Yale, Union, and Princeton leading the way. "The university throbs with life," Chicago Divinity School Dean E. B. Hulbert enthused, "and our young men are there and in vital union with it; and I believe it means a vast deal for them."[16]

This was also the great era of religious cooperation, of ecumenical partnerships for foreign missions and urban evangelization. The organization of the Federal Council of Churches in 1908 and the often relentless consolidation of denominational agencies and programs reflected a larger cultural assumption that cooperation meant efficiency and effectiveness. In the early twentieth century, Congregationalists regularly sought mergers with other denominations, including Free Baptists, Methodists, and the Disciples of Christ, always promising to overlook theological differences when a larger unity beckoned.[17]

Within this setting, Andover's trustees were following the lead of countless Protestant church men and women seeking a progressive liberal voice in a time of growing religious polarization. As one determined optimist argued, all of the worry about Andover being taken over by Cambridge Unitarians missed the possibility that "Andover's orthodoxy might reclaim Harvard's heterodoxy." Indeed, he declared, "people who believe in a truth ought to have faith in the power of that truth to overcome the error against which it is pitted, and the more faith as it gets into closer quarters with the error."[18]

The only whisper of trouble, a small cloud the size of a man's hand, came in a politely worded letter from the Board of Visitors. "It would seem," they noted elliptically, "that so important a step in the management of the Foundation and the carrying out of the purposes of the Founders should require in advance the consideration of the Board of

---

ference, Held in Chicago, October 8-14, 1893 (New York: Baker and Taylor, 1893), pp. 421-427; Jonathan Dorn, "'Our Best Gospel Appliances: Institutional Churches and the Emergence of Social Christianity in the South End of Boston, 1880-1920" (Ph.D. diss., Harvard University, 1994), p. 51.

16. *Christianity Practically Applied*, pp. 473-478.

17. John Von Rohr, *The Shaping of American Congregationalism* (Cleveland: Pilgrim Press, 1992), pp. 343-346.

18. "Apropos of Andover," *Congregationalist*, 30 May 1908, p. 716.

Visitors." They requested a copy of the action with a list of reasons, clearly intending to take the entire matter under review.[19]

But this time around the trustees were thoroughly prepared for the implied threat of obstruction. Well before the decision to move to Andover, they had taken out a separate act of incorporation, legally distinguishing the seminary board of trustees from those of the Phillips Academy. The move appeared to strengthen the Andover trustees' decision-making role, especially in regard to the seminary's financial assets and its overall religious purpose. In response to the Visitors' letter, the trustees insisted that the three gentlemen were confused about their role, which was never to be concerned with the day-to-day affairs of the seminary, only to oversee, in the most limited way, the proper administration of the Founders' original trust fund. "To invite the co-operation of others would be to increase the difficulties, confuse the processes and endanger the results of their efforts," the trustees warned. In 1908 the Board of Visitors meekly approved the decision to move to Cambridge.[20]

Merger Years

The Harvard Andover merger began happily. A portrait of the combined faculty and students of the class of 1910-1911 shows a relaxed and genial group, apparently untroubled by the historic enmities their schools represented [21] The Andover men included the elderly Edward Hincks and William Henry Ryder, "excellent scholars and Christian gentlemen." Albert Parker Fitch, a Harvard graduate and former pastor, was the president of the faculty and professor of Sacred Rhetoric; William Rosenzweig Arnold, a man of "stormy" moods and a "heart of gold," held the post in Hebrew Language and Literature. John Winthrop Platner, Andover's professor of ecclesiastical history and later its faculty president, had taught at Harvard until 1901. The Harvard faculty included nationally renowned scholars such as George F. Moore in Old Testament and History of Religions, Francis Peabody the great social re-

19. Board of Visitors Minutes, 9 September 1906, ANTS archives.
20. Board of Trustees Minutes, 1908, ANTS archives.
21. Levering Reynolds, Jr., "The Later Years," in *The Harvard Divinity School: Its Place in Harvard University and in American Culture,* ed. George Williams (Boston: Beacon Press, 1954), plate IX.

former, and theologian William Wallace Fenn.[22] "The affiliation was obviously a gentlemen's agreement which would require a certain amount of personal give-and-take if it were to work satisfactorily," one Harvard historian later recalled. "But there was no hesitation felt on that score, for both faculties had entered into the affiliation with all good will and with the expectation that they would be able to work together harmoniously and for the good of all concerned. The passing years proved these expectations well founded."[23]

Daniel Evans, who replaced Edward Hincks as Abbot Professor in 1909, remembered the Cambridge years with great fondness. After a year of study abroad, he arrived on the new campus eager to undertake an ambitious program of study and teaching. "In Andover-Harvard it was out of the question to use a textbook," Evans remembered. Every lecture had to be original and thought-provoking, no longer simply commenting on an assigned reading, but culled out of scholarly discovery. Evans' colleagues regularly inspired him to work his hardest. "For a young professor to be associated with such men was to be put on his mettle," he said, "to be tested day by day, to see what scholarship really is, to be able to observe how the scholarly mind works, and to realize that this is the ideal he must follow." As a teacher, Evans drew on his previous years of experience in the pulpit, incorporating sometimes difficult intellectual material, and encouraging his students to develop "empathy" for ideas they might find repugnant. Above all, Evans insisted that no intellectual pursuit was beyond the scope of a good pastor. "Practical interests might absorb the churches, the positivist temper might influence the psychological climate, the ministers might be engaged with the secondary and peripheral matters in religion," he wrote, "but sooner or later the churches and the ministers would discover that there is no substitute for profound thinking on the ultimate and primary matters of religion." Without a thorough grounding in theology, Evans argued, American churches would grow "vague and misty in respect to its great truths," and "the church and ministers are exposed to any wind that may blow."[24]

Construction on Andover Hall began in 1910. The imposing stone

---

22. Raymond Calkins, ed., *Daniel Evans: Teacher, Preacher, Theologian* (Boston: Pilgrim Press, 1944), pp. 100-101.

23. Levering Reynolds, Jr., "The Later Years," p. 193.

24. Calkins, *Daniel Evans*, pp. 101, 102, 103, 104.

structure, estimated to cost a quarter of a million dollars, included a dormitory wing and a library. It left no doubt about its historic legacy. The reference library was named the Moses Stuart Reading Room, and portraits of other Andover professors lined the walls. A gothic tablet engraved with the names of Andover's founders, and a tablet each for Leonard Woods and Edwards Park, served further notice about the seminary's peculiar theological lineage. The "terms of agreement" also involved both libraries. Andover's new building included space for a combined collection, with all of the books clearly identified by bookplates and catalog cards. The two schools evenly split the costs of maintenance and staff salaries, and administered the library through a Committee appointed from both faculties.

The inevitable drew closer, facilitated by the practical exigencies of the war years. In 1918, Andover allowed Harvard to use their new building "without financial consideration," in order to make room for the Cambridge Radio School, run by the United States Navy. In 1922, the two schools drew up a plan for "closer affiliation," designed to create a new entity, "The Theological School in Harvard." Under the plan, both schools would continue to exist but would unite to "form a non-denominational theological school, with single faculty, roll of students, administration, and catalogue."[25]

In many ways, the new plan simply formalized an arrangement that had become increasingly advantageous for both sides. Harvard and Andover would occupy Andover Hall together, splitting the costs evenly, though Harvard also threw in an additional $6,000 to offset Andover's contribution of its building and grounds. Faculty would be paid on the same scale, an immediate boon to Andover's perpetually struggling professors. With a proviso for a ten-year review and a two-year notice for termination, the plan was slated to go into effect on September 1, 1922.

The new arrangement promised much. An editorial in the *Congregationalist* declared it a new day in the history of American Protestantism. The affiliation marked an "undoing of the past" and all of the unnecessary rancor separating Christians. Indeed, "we regard this blending of evangelical and liberal traditions as prophetic of the day already begun, when men shall seek to study religion in the largest and most liberal atmosphere . . . of warmth, and wholesomeness, and reverence." Andover

25. *Dates and Data* (Cambridge, MA: Andover Seminary, 1926), pp. 24, 25.

was not being "swallowed up," as some critics charged, but would be "making a vital contribution in spirit and method to the life of a great university." "In the demonstration that evangelical religion can live and make its voice heard effectively in the presence of the freest, broadest and deepest quest of truth," he insisted, "Andover may enter upon a new day of opportunity and an accomplishment worthy of all that is best in her past."[26]

Halt

But the move to Cambridge had never solved Andover's financial problems. In 1912, Albert Parker Fitch, the president of the faculty, alerted the board of trustees that rising enrollments had created a critical need for more dormitory space and more teaching faculty. Though the trustees duly voted to undertake a capital campaign, they apparently did little; in 1916, Fitch returned to declare that "the work in Cambridge is rapidly going to pieces." Student enrollments were dropping, largely because the overworked Andover faculty could not provide a wide enough range of course offerings. "Two years ago," he wrote, "two juniors left Andover to go to Hartford [Seminary] because we had no courses in the department of Missions and Education. Last year a junior left to go to Union for the same reason. This year another junior and our most brilliant middler will follow him." Though Andover still provided standard seminary offerings in theology and biblical studies, "no adequate work is offered in the department of Social Ethics or Christian Sociology," or in the psychology of religion or religious education — all subjects considered indispensable to the education of a turn-of-the-century Protestant pastor.

By 1912 Andover was already running regular deficits, and with the additional burden of two key retirements (Hincks and Ryder), the Cambridge project looked dire. Fitch threatened to resign unless Andover's leadership recognized the "grave financial situation of the Seminary," and in June 1916, finally made good on his threat. Nehemiah Boynton, the president of the board of trustees, departed at the same time, a move that left the remaining trustees stunned and discouraged.[27]

26. "The Theological School in Harvard," *Congregationalist*, 22 June 1922, p. 774.
27. Albert Parker Fitch to ATS Board of Trustees, 15 April 1916, Trustee minutes, ANTS archives.

But the worst was yet to come. In December 1918, Andover's long quiescent Board of Visitors reappeared, this time with a carefully understated complaint about "certain changes in administrative practice . . . which apparently do not conform to the letter of the requirement as laid down by the Founders." The primary issue was not the creed or the Unitarian presence at Harvard, but three smaller infractions against the Associate Statutes. Specifically, Andover's faculty were no longer opening and closing lectures with prayer, as required by Article Five; the school was charging tuition (at the time $150 a year, following Harvard's practice) in violation of Article Six; and the trustees were allowing faculty positions to remain vacant, despite the requirement outlined by Article Eleven.

The trustees attempted to parry the complaint with an equally polite reply — certainly they had far more pressing problems to deal with than ceremonial prayers in lecture halls. Arrangements for the Theological School at Harvard were moving ahead swiftly, with the affiliation plan adopted by the Harvard Fellows on May 22, 1922, and Andover's trustees two days later.

The annual alumni dinner, held in mid-June, celebrated a promising future for both schools, set to go into effect September 1. As Andover trustee and Old South pastor George Gordon declared, the Theological School would open a new era of "freedom and faith." "So far as I can see in this new association," Gordon wrote, "there is nothing to fear, and everything to hope."[28]

The Board of Visitors thought differently. On July 18, 1922, they presented the trustees with a letter charging that the affiliation plan was "inconsistent with the Associate Foundation Statutes." Not only would Andover be "improperly managed" in its partnership with Harvard, but it would not "be conducted in accordance with the principles of its foundation."[29] The entire enterprise was, in effect, illegal. The trustees immediately began a "suit in equity" before the Supreme Judicial Court, attempting to restrain the Visitors from blocking the Harvard merger. In mid-August the Visitors returned fire, asking the court to find the affiliation plan null and void.[30]

While lawyers organized for battle, the Theological School opened

---

28. "Andover and Harvard Join Forces," *Congregationalist*, 22 June 1922, p. 784.
29. *Dates and Data*, p. 26.
30. Pierce, "Legal Aspects of the Andover Creed," p. 45.

for business. The 1922-23 school year began with hefty pay raises for Andover faculty and burgeoning classrooms. The combined enrollment numbered forty-seven Cambridge students, supplemented by a nearly equal number from other local seminaries (including two from Newton). The new total of ninety-three students marked an increase of twenty-five over the year previous.

But the enthusiasm proved short-lived. In January and May of 1923, the Visitors added two more legal complaints, alleging that the plan of affiliation would violate the ancient requirement of the Andover faculty creed. The new scheme did not, it almost goes without saying, require professors to "maintain and inculcate the Christian faith as expressed in the creed and in opposition not only to Atheists and Infidels, but to Jews, Papists, Mahometans, Arians, Pelagians, Antinomians, Arminians, Socinians, Sabellians, Unitarians and Universalists." The Visitors also charged that since 1908, when Andover came to Cambridge, its teaching had been inconsistent with the Westminster Assembly's Shorter Catechism and the Constitution and Statutes of the Associate Foundation. On January 26, 1925, the Andover case went before the full bench of the Supreme Judicial Court of Massachusetts. On September 19, 1925, the court ruled on behalf of the Visitors.

The Court's decision, laid out in a lengthy opinion written by the Chief Justice Arthur Prentice Rugg, was unequivocal. "The Andover Theological Seminary was founded by Calvinists," he declared, who made it "distinct and apart from every other theological school." What is more, the original "instruments of gift" from the Norris, Abbot, and Bartlet families included "definite theological denominational tenets," to "nourish, strengthen and extend orthodox, trinitarian, evangelical congregationalism." The original documents made clear that the founders of the school had no other purpose than to increase "'the number of learned and able Defenders of the Gospel of Christ, as well as of orthodox, pious and Zealous Ministers of the New Testament.'" Although social circumstances may have changed, and the theological gulf separating Unitarians and Congregationalists had closed considerably by the end of the nineteenth century, the legal issue could not have been any clearer: "the joining of the seminary with another institution to form a non-denominational theological school is contrary to the avowed end and aim of the founders." The Court declared the plan of agreement between Andover and Harvard void, and required the trustees to pay all of the court costs incurred by the Board of Visitors, some $50,000.00 [31] As Thomas Weston, attorney for the Visitors declared, the case came down to "the sacredness of trust funds": "when a man gives money to trustees for charitable purposes, these purposes as expressed in the instrument of gift must be carried out."[32]

The anguish of faculty, trustees, and students was palpable. The court decision was not just a legal defeat; it was also a tremendous embarrassment to Andover's friends and supporters. Harvard chose to shrug off the loss, allowing Andover to continue instruction for the 1925-26 school year. But Andover faculty now faced the reality that for the first time in twenty-five years, they would again be required to publicly recite the Andover Creed, with all of its ancient strictures against heretical Arians and Sabellians.

In the early spring of 1926, faculty members William Arnold, Willard Sperry, and Daniel Evans all submitted letters of resignation, declaring that the new situation was simply untenable. As Sperry wrote, "I do not conceive it possible under present religious conditions to increase the number of 'orthodox, pious and zealous Ministers of the New Testament' by being in any way concerned with the perpetuation of that Creed."[33] With "deep and poignant regret," Daniel Evans tendered his resignation, recalling that when he was hired, the Board of Visitors had received his prepared statement of belief, expressing support for the "great evangelical succession," their full approval. He had understood from the trustees that the creed "was not to control my thought." But now, Evans said, "Intellectual honesty and moral integrity makes subscription to this creed, in any strict sense of its historical meaning, impossible." The creed had "ceased to be the expression of the vital faith of our churches" many years ago. "Even if it were possible to believe and teach it today," he declared, "it would be of no use whatever to the men who are to serve our churches, nor to the churches themselves. I have conceived my task to be, to teach a vital theology to a living church which has cherished the conviction that there was more light to break forth from the Scriptures."[34]

Sympathy for Andover was widespread. The editorial board of the

31. *Dates and Data*, pp. 28-33.

32. "The Andover-Harvard Supreme Court Decision," *Congregationalist*, 1 October 1925, pp. 422, 423.

33. Board of Trustee minutes, February 1926, ANTS archives.

34. Calkins, *Daniel Evans*, p. 107.

Congregationalist rushed to defend the beleaguered faculty, declaring that "the so-called Andover Creed" had never reflected the beliefs of the denomination's rank and file. The Suffolk North Association of Congregational churches issued a statement arguing that if the creed were to be literally enforced, "the usefulness of Andover Theological Seminary to the orthodox Congregational churches of Massachusetts would be at an end."[35]

But in the fall of 1926, Andover closed its doors, apparently for good. Harvard gradually occupied the whole of Andover Hall for a small rental fee, and assumed responsibility for care of the building and grounds. When the Theological School in Harvard University, as it was then called, opened for classes, a few Andover faculty remained: William Arnold continued to teach Hebrew and Willard Sperry continued on as professor of homiletics and then as dean of the faculty. The Andover Library, with its books still earmarked and separately catalogued, also stayed in Cambridge, but was no longer used by Andover students or faculty. The final fate of Andover's endowment, which had reached some $800,000, remained an open question.

"The rest is history," as Andover Newton dean Vaughan Dabney remembered in 1957. "The professors resigned, the students folded their tents, and the Seminary fell asleep to await the coming of some Prince Charming, who five years later turned out to be Everett Carlton Herrick of the Newton Theological Institution."[36]

Newton

"One day," Herrick wrote, "I was talking over the telephone with Dr. Ashley D. Leavitt," the pastor of the Harvard Congregational Church in Brookline, Massachusetts, and one of the Andover Visitors. "In the course of the conversation he said, 'Have you ever thought about the possibility of some kind of tie-up with Andover? You know we have got

35. "The Andover-Harvard Decision," *Congregationalist,* 1 October 1926, pp. 420-421; "The Andover Seminary Creed: Massachusetts Conference Asked to Consider it," *Congregationalist,* 13 May 1926, pp. 591, 595; "Overture of the Suffolk North Association to the Massachusetts Conference," in *The Massachusetts Congregational Conference, 1926. Minutes of the One Hundred Twenty-Fourth Annual Meeting* (Boston, Jordan and More, 1926), p. 81.

36. Dabney, "Twenty-Five Years After," *Andover Newton Bulletin* 49 (April 1957): 10.

to do something and go somewhere.'" Herrick was intrigued. "To use an overworked word," he said, "I started out to explore the idea."[37]

In 1925, Newton celebrated its centennial year by weathering yet another financial crisis. Northern Baptists had placed high hopes on a massive fundraising campaign, grandly titled the New World Movement, and had promised Newton a million dollars if the effort was successful. But the decade of the 1920s found Baptists deeply mired in doctrinal controversy, an ugly public spectacle that pitted fundamentalists like John Roach Straton and William Bell Riley against anyone who stopped short of their standard of orthodoxy. The battle ultimately led to financial debacle, as local Baptist congregations, unsure about the denomination's future, began to withhold their annual donations. When fundamentalists squared off against Baptist financier John D. Rockefeller, tagged as a liberal, the New World campaign failed spectacularly, dragging many other Baptist institutions down with it. When Herrick became Newton's president in 1927, he encountered a financial situation he later described as "desperate." A hastily assembled effort, including a $100,000 gift from Rockefeller, netted $600,000, and temporarily halted the slide. But Newton's problems were far from over. As Herrick recalled, "People who lived very close to Newton were less familiar with the school than Baptists . . . who lived in Burma." To all but a relative few, the school was virtually invisible, even in the town of Newton itself.[38]

Nevertheless, representatives from the two schools began to meet, at first a bit awkwardly over dinner, and then with lawyers in tow. When Newton issued a formal proposal for affiliation in May 1929, the two institutions had invoked the legal doctrine of *cy pres* which, defined precisely, means that whenever the original purposes of a trust can no longer be fulfilled in strict compliance with its original terms, its trustees may ask the courts for a modification or even an annulment of those restrictions. "It is not enough," as one scholar writes, ". . . to prove that the terms are ridiculous or trivial or non-essential — it must be proven that they render the administration of the trust impossible," or subvert its primary purpose.[39]

---

37. Everett Carlton Herrick, *Turns Again Home: Andover Newton Theological School and Reminiscences from an Unkept Journal* (Boston: Pilgrim Press, 1949), p. 16.

38. Herrick, *Turns Again Home*, pp. 13, 14.

39. Pierce, "The Legal Aspects of the Andover Creed," p. 46.

The Newton-Andover partnership looked like the perfect solution. The two schools shared a common congregational polity and doctrinal background; Newton was, in many practical ways, the child of Andover. As the Andover trustees noted, the two seminaries had followed parallel tracts since their inception, with the same "high standards of theological education," "zeal for foreign missions," "general outlook toward the ministry," and "Calvinistic theological background." The only major area of difference was the Baptist principle of adult immersion, but in recent years Newton had ceased to teach that it was essential for conversion or church membership. Not least of all the advantages of partnership was the fact that the president of Newton's board of trustees was Justice Fred Field, who had sat on the Massachusetts Supreme Judicial Court and had heard every word of the Andover case.

One hurdle remained. A few critics pointed out that Newton was not Andover's only possible partner: Princeton, Westminster, and Gordon seminaries — all reliably Calvinist institutions — sent affidavits to the Massachusetts Attorney General, offering to provide a good home for Andover and its sizeable endowment. Since Andover's original charter allowed it to offer degrees only in the state of Massachusetts, Gordon emerged as the only realistic contender. As the Newton and Andover trustees began to hammer out the last details of their affiliation, leaders of the Gordon College of Theology and Missions began to discuss their own claim to partnership, apparently prompted by some of the more conservative members of the Andover Board of Visitors.[40]

A. Z. Conrad, the pugnacious conservative at the helm of Boston's Park Street Church, declared that he would have no problem finding new faculty members happy to fulfill every word of the Andover creed. But Daniel Evans, the sole remaining faculty member, refused to countenance any more delay. Combing through Conrad's published works line by line, he declared the Congregational pastor far too Arminian in his theology to be any judge of Calvinist orthodoxy.[41]

In fact, Gordon's trustees were understandably cautious. In the words of Gordon president Nathan Wood, the endowment belonged "doctrinally" to Gordon College of Theology and Missions as "the only

---

40. See Nathan Wood, *A School of Christ* (Boston: Halliday Lithograph Corp., 1953), pp. 156-159; Herrick, *Turns Again Home,* pp. 44-49.

41. Herrick, *Turns Again Home,* p. 45.

Seminary in Massachusetts qualified both by doctrinal position and by other educational standards to use these funds." But past history assured that any rival claim to the Andover endowment would quickly become "bitter and violent." After much deliberation, Wood determined that the money was not worth the risk. Besides a protracted and expensive legal battle, Gordon would also take on a partnership with the Andover trustees, whom he believed would ultimately prove themselves "an entanglement and hindrance to the free expression of the Evangelical Gospel for which Gordon stands. . . . Andover's thousands of dollars of endowments did not weigh in the scales as against Gordon's evangelical teachings."[42]

The Andover Newton partnership, drawn up in January 1930, laid out a plan for "a school of religious education for the training of evangelical Christian ministers." Instructors from both schools would form a single faculty, under the leadership of Newton's president; the president of the Andover faculty would become dean of the combined schools. Though Newton had recently rescinded its requirement that all of its trustees had to be Baptists, an administrative committee, composed of five representatives from each board, met to harmonize the separate workings of the two institutions. All resources would be shared in common, and students would receive either an Andover or a Newton degree, according to the requirements set forth by each board of trustees. Initially, the agreement provided for continued use of Andover Hall for specialized graduate instruction, with the understanding that Andover would not be abrogating any of its existing agreements with Harvard. The Newton collection would be the "working library" for both schools, though all students would have full access to the Andover books still down in Cambridge. And in keeping with the principle of *cy pres,* the old Andover Creed would never again apply to anyone; faculty had simply to meet the requirements of the Constitution and Statutes in regard to academic attainments and denominational affiliation, and to "adhere to the general doctrinal position of the evangelical churches."[43]

In Vaughan Dabney's words, Andover "came to live on Newton Hill, bringing her bags of gold, some painful memories, and a trembling

---

42. Wood, *A School of Christ,* p. 159.

43. Minutes, Andover Board of Trustees, 10 January 1930, ANTS archives; "Andover Newton Theological School," *Institution Bulletin* 24 (1932): 18-20.

hope." And in fact, familial metaphors proved difficult to pass up in describing the new partnership. "Some said that Newton married for money and Andover to get a good home," Dabney related, "and others saw the affiliation as a triumph of courage and tact." "In fact," Everett Herrick wrote, "Newton might be called the elder daughter, destined finally to receive her mother into her ample and hospitable home."[44]

Andover Newton

The early 1930s were not a good time for ambitious dreams. The Andover Newton merger began in the depths of the Great Depression, as the economy collapsed in on itself following the stock market crash of 1929. Over the next several years, as the gross national product spiraled ever downward, taking with it thousands of livelihoods and personal fortunes, the entire American project seemed in question. Organized looting and mass uprisings by hungry, desperate protesters pointed ominously toward all-out class warfare. In the spring of 1932, when American troops used tanks and bayonets to drive 20,000 unemployed World War I veterans out of Washington, D.C. — the famous "Bonus Army" — capitalism itself seemed teetering on the brink of chaos.

Speaking to Newton's last independent graduating class in June 1931, at the first public announcement of the affiliation, Everett Herrick chose the theme of "otherworldliness." "No less than a generation ago here in America," he said, "we believed, for the most part, in the finality of our Democracy." Yet, with the clear and growing instability of American civil institutions, "all about us in our land we see democracy breaking down. We are no longer sure of its finality, any more than we are sure of the finality of what we call Capitalism." Clearly, as Herrick said, "the world today is full of strange, portentous things."[45]

Continuity was the central principle of the merger, at least in its early stages. Daniel Evans came from Cambridge to teach theology in

---

44. Dabney, "Twenty-Five Years After," p. 11. Herrick, *Turns Again Home,* p. 30. Dabney also repeated the quip that the school should have been named "Handover Newton."

45. "Andover and Newton in Commencement," *Congregationalist,* 18 June, 1931, p. 833.

Andover once more, having met Herrick a few years before at the meeting of the American Theological Society. Vaughan Dabney, a Congregational pastor from Dorchester, stepped in as president of the Andover faculty, dean of the united schools, and Bartlet Professor of Sacred Rhetoric. All of the Newton faculty continued on as before.

Weary of creeds and restrictions, Andover Newton's supporters charted a broad and welcoming middle path. They emphasized the spirit of cooperation and compromise behind the merger, and the broad theological landscape still occupied by New England's Congregational and Baptist churches. With the earlier demands of creedal orthodoxy falling rapidly into the mists of historical memory, and the polarizing rhetoric of the "culture wars" many decades in the future, an interdenominational future seemed both prudent and appropriately idealistic. As the *Congregationalist* editorialized happily in the spring of 1931, "Andover Newton, we predict, will perform a valuable service for Congregational as well as for Baptist churches in New England and the rest of the country." And with terminology that, in the 1930s, still evoked an activist and theologically centrist purpose, the editors offered their full support for a "broad-minded evangelical theological education."[46] The years ahead, punctuated by world war and a string of social transformations, would both test and confirm that optimistic forecast.

Through all of their emotional ups and downs, the merger years yielded some important lessons. The partnership with Harvard was not ill-conceived or rash; in many ways it made good sense. Indeed, for all their differences, the two institutions had come from the same roots, going back centuries before Andover's founding. By moving back to Harvard's university campus, Andover was pursuing a strategy followed by many other independent seminaries at the turn of the century. By sharing costs and pooling resources, Harvard and Andover might well have created an important model of institutional cooperation. But the wishes of the founders were not so easily thwarted. Though long dead, they still wielded control over their wayward seminary's destiny, almost to the point of closing it down for good. In the end, the small group of men on Andover's board of trustees, intent on moving Andover back to Cambridge, could not undo the will of the founders. History would have its day in court, and, as always, came out the final winner.

46. "Andover Theological School to Reopen," *Congregationalist*, 23 April 1931, p. 539.

CHAPTER SEVEN

Andover Newton and Pastoral Education in the World War II Era

———&&&———

In 1932, Andover Seminary marked the 125th year since its incorporation, happily eyeing its future in partnership with Newton. "When the mother seminary of the land, the oldest Congregational theological school, unites forces with the original Baptist seminary of New England," Vaughan Dabney declared at the inaugural exercises that January, "we indeed have something new under the sun, a unique undertaking which should exert a tremendous influence on American Christianity."[1]

Technically, Dabney was right, but in 1932 his assertion was more of a prophecy than a statement of fact. Over the next three decades, Andover Newton grew steadily into an innovative institution with a clear liberal identity. It fostered important scholarship and led the nation in the introduction of clinical pastoral education, a program of psychological training for clergy. But those changes spanned some of the most dangerous and dramatic years of the twentieth century; Andover Newton came of age against a backdrop of economic catastrophe, world war, nuclear confrontation, and an emerging civil rights movement.

---

1. Dabney, "Andover Newton: Appreciation and Interpretation," *Institution Bulletin* 24 (February 1932): 13.

Traditions

Andover Newton began its corporate existence looking very much like a traditional New England theological seminary. The leading lights of the faculty were the professors of biblical interpretation, both with solid Victorian names — the crusty Frederick Lincoln Anderson and meticulous Winfred Donovan, New and Old Testaments, respectively. James Percival Berkeley, described by Herrick as the faculty's "grand old man," taught religious education. Daniel Evans, the sole survivor of Andover's Cambridge years, was the Abbot Professor of Christian Theology; he taught alongside Newton's Richard Miner Vaughan. Vaughan Dabney represented the Andover faculty as the academic dean, and held the historic post of Bartlet Professor of Sacred Rhetoric. Woodman Bradbury, "one of the gentlest and most saintly souls that ever opened a class or led a chapel," was the professor of homiletics. The catalog also included a "professor of country church life," one Charles McConnell, supported in part by the Interseminary Commission for Training for the Rural Ministry. The only woman on the faculty was Doris Bigglestone, an instructor in religious education and later dean of women.[2]

The course of study also reflected longstanding assumptions about the education of ministers. There was, of course, no tuition; students paid only boarding fees and supported themselves by occasional preaching and scholarships. All of them took the same "fundamental" courses in Bible, theology, and preaching. Classes were conducted Tuesdays through Saturdays, on the assumption that Monday was a day of rest after a busy Sunday schedule. Although the Greek and Hebrew requirement had long since fallen away, New Testament courses were still "conducted on the basis of the Greek text." Every member of the senior class wrote a 2,500-5,000 word thesis, the topic chosen independently or from a list compiled by the faculty: "The Spread of Secularism," "Paul's Doctrine of Justification by Faith," "Congregational Principles in England before 1600." Although the vast majority of stu-

---

2. This and most of the following material is drawn from the *Annual Catalog for the Academic Year 1931-1932* (Boston: Fort Hill Press, 1931). For Herrick's descriptions, see Herrick, *Turns Again Home: Andover Newton Theological School and Reminiscences from an Unkept Journal* (Boston: Pilgrim Press, 1949), pp. 77-80.

dents worked toward the B.D. degree, Andover Newton also offered a Master of Sacred Theology, awarded to exceptionally promising students who took an additional year beyond the B.D., and a Master of Religious Education, a two-year degree requiring a thesis.

Student groups on campus also followed along some well-trodden paths. The Students' Association was a present incarnation of the old Society for Missionary Inquiry, which in the late nineteenth century had fallen under the rubric of the Young Men's Christian Association. The Student Volunteer organization was also a survival of the turn-of-the-century movement led by Charles Mott and dedicated to "the evangelization of the world in this generation." They met every other week to discuss the problems and needs of missionaries.

During those early years, the student body also represented some deeply engrained traditions. Their numbers remained relatively small as the Great Depression tightened its grip on the economy, and the Second World War funneled hundreds and thousands of men out of classrooms and onto battlefields. From a high of 172 students in the 1932-33 school year, enrollment dipped to 110 in 1942.

They were, of course, nearly all single men. Out of a total of 133 students taking the B.D. degree in 1932, only 2 were women, a number that would barely budge throughout the decade. Thirty-two women, however, received master's degrees in Religious Education, a course of study designed to train "assistants and directors" in local churches, and specifically designated in the catalog as a track for women. Those numbers would remain relatively stable, even during the war years. The registrar did not yet track the number of married students, largely because the numbers were so few.

The students were also predominantly white, though also somewhat international, hailing from ten different countries.[3] The class of 1931 included three black students, Henry B. Harris, William R. Strassner, and Illmadelco Cooper Ravenell. The proportion of African American students would remain small throughout the decade, though several graduates would go on to make a permanent impact on the school as influential members of the board of trustees. The class of 1937 included both men for whom the Kelsey-Owens minority scholarship program is named: George D. Kelsey, later a professor of social eth-

---

3. "Complexion of the Student Body," *Institution Bulletin* 25 (October 1933): 5.

ics at Drew University, and Richard M. Owens, the pastor of the People's Baptist Church in Boston.[4]

In those early years most Andover Newton students were Baptist, reflecting Andover's relative weakness at the time of the merger. Many of those students held their undergraduate degrees from the Gordon School of Theology and Missions, which had a heavily Baptist constituency of its own. In the 1935-36 school year, Gordon graduates compromised the largest single group in the entering class, about 11 percent of the total. By the 1938-39 school year, the proportion had increased to 17 percent and it would not decline until the early 1950s.

Even the physical layout of the campus had changed relatively little since the nineteenth century. At the time of the merger, Andover Newton was composed of six buildings. The center of campus was the Hills Library, a solid square structure crammed to the ceiling with books, as well as the offices of the president and the dean. On its two flanks, two equally square and solid Victorian brick structures, Farwell and Sturtevant Halls, still functioned as dormitories for single men, as much disliked by twentieth century students as they were by their predecessors. Behind the library, Colby Hall, a dark stone edifice, housed both the school's lecture rooms and the chapel, which had been reappointed in 1930 with a new organ, pulpit, and stained-glass window. The colonial brick president's house sat, as it does now, on the library's other side. The newest building on campus was the gymnasium, built in 1876 and refurbished in 1930, complete with basketball court and showers. At the bottom of Newton Hill was Chase House, a residence for Andover Newton's rugged women students, who toiled up the school's long driveway for all of their classes and the meals they took in the seminary dining hall.

In 1931 the heart of Andover Newton's mission was to local Baptist and Congregational churches. "Though under no ecclesiastical control," the catalog affirmed, "the school has always recognized its responsibility" to the welfare of local congregations. The founding purpose of both schools was to "remain loyal to the spirit of their founders and true to the great common evangelical tradition which they have received," an aim that had not changed with the merger. Andover Newton's purpose was to "study and interpret, to defend and perpetuate,

4. Information on African American students is drawn from a memo in the President's Office Files, dated May 27, 1965.

the Christian religion; to make the spirit of Christ prevail in human life, and to realize the purpose of God in the affairs of the world." Indeed, in language that nearly echoed the old dictums of the Andover creed, the new school promised to "send forth well educated, deeply devout and thoroughly consecrated ministers and religious educators [so] that our churches at home and abroad may have able ministers of the Word and worthy pastors of the people and well-equipped workers in religious education and leadership."[5]

Andover Newton was, in other words, a quintessential New England institution. Even in the 1930s, the strength of Congregational and Baptist churches was still in their rural and small town roots; Boston, with its predominantly Italian and Irish-Catholic population, was at best a mission station. In the early twentieth century, eleven Baptist churches had folded their tents and left the city for suburban safety. "The city government is in the hands of those who are not descendents of Puritan or Pilgrim forefathers," a Baptist wrote in 1925. "Positions of public trust are held largely by those whose names have a foreign sound."[6]

Andover Newton also had practical reasons for treasuring its ties with Baptist and Congregational churches. Both denominations reported a surplus of clergy during the Depression years, as local congregations often resorted to the least expensive alternatives for filling local pulpits. On the national stage, church officials labored to enforce minimum standards for ordination, often in the face of studied indifference in the parishes.[7]

Innovations

The 1930s was an interesting time in the history of American seminaries. Andover Newton came of age in an era of transition in theological

5. *Annual Catalog for the Academic Year 1931-1932,* p. 15.

6. Arthur Leonard Wadsworth, "Boston as a Field for City Mission Work," *Watchman-Examiner,* 8 January 1925, p. 53.

7. See for example, *The Massachusetts Baptist Year Book, 1932: Minutes of the Proceedings of the Massachusetts Baptist State Societies* (Boston: Fidelity Press, 1932), pp. 55-57; *Digest of Minutes of the General Council of the Congregational Christian Churches of the United States, 1931-1965* (New York: Executive Committee of the General Council, 1965), pp. 99-101.

education, of growing enthusiasm for credentialing and standardization. "There is a wide-spread feeling," Abdel Wentz of Lutheran Theological Seminary wrote in 1937, "that we must find a better way to educate our ministers." The call was for a "comprehensive strategy" to bring the schools up to date and to educate clergy equal to the demands of their parishioners and of a surrounding world in turmoil. The terminology itself calls to mind the enthusiasm of Franklin Roosevelt's New Deal government for centralized bureaucratic solutions to local problems. Filled with Depression-era optimism, seminary officials also knew that tinkering and adjusting with old forms would no longer do.[8]

An exhaustive report of 161 American theological schools, published by Robert Kelly in 1924, found a broad and, to the author, distressing range of quality in faculty, facilities, and students. The typical seminary student was in his late 20s, "likely to have been brought up on a farm," and unlikely to have completed college. Less than half (44 percent) came to seminary with an undergraduate degree, and about a quarter of divinity students were themselves the sons of pastors; a majority still described their vocation as a "holy calling."[9] In most schools, denominational loyalties remained strong, with students fully intending to play out their careers in the denomination in which they had grown up. The conspicuous exception was Congregationalists, whose sons of the church were not likely to attend a denominational seminary and even more unlikely to have attended a denominational college.[10]

Seminary education itself was strongly vocational, with a typically overworked faculty devoting little time to research, or to writing not directly tied to a denominational publishing house. The curriculum was similarly uneven among the schools surveyed. Kelly was harshly critical of the antiquated teaching methods he found employed in many seminary classrooms, usually a combination of lecture and textbook study. "Some lectures," he complained, were nothing more than "rambling, hortatory sermons," and the "prevailing atmosphere is that of the church rather than of the school." Kelly, a strong advocate of academi-

8. Abdel Ross Wentz, "A New Strategy for Theological Education," *Christian Education* 20 (April 1937): 291, 292.

9. Robert L. Kelly, *Theological Education in America: A Study of 161 Theological Schools in the United States and Canada* (New York: George H. Doran, Co., 1924), pp. 152-153.

10. Kelly, *Theological Education in America*, p. 162.

cally oriented university-based theological education, reported entire class periods devoted to "reading from old manuscript lectures, line by line, as the students copy verbatim. On the margin of some of these manuscripts have been seen dates reaching back a quarter of a century, indicating the point the professor had reached in his annual journey over this well-traveled course."[11]

A subsequent study, published in 1934, confirmed many of Kelly's criticisms, but advocated a different solution. A team of researchers led by Mark May found that less than a third of American clergy, no matter what the denominational background, had both a college and a seminary degree; barely half of enrolled seminarians came with a college diploma. Libraries were poorly staffed, under-funded, and under-used, and most field education programs in similar disrepair.[12]

Arriving in the wake of the Kelly report, the May study provided more good reasons for standardizing seminary education. Its end result was the organization of the American Association of Theological Schools in 1938. The AATS laid out basic requirements for a Bachelor of Divinity degree — a minimum three years of work in the four basic fields of biblical, historical, theological, and practical study, and at least four faculty members teaching no more than twelve hours a week.[13]

By AATS standards Andover Newton was exemplary. In 1938 over 92 percent of its enrolled students had a college degree; the faculty numbered some twenty professors, lecturers, and instructors. In a number of ways, the aura of New England traditionalism was deceptive. On the faculty, for example, Henry Rowe taught the usual church history course as well as a "social science" regimen, reflecting the flowering of social gospel concern among Baptists. His primary interests were in international relations and labor issues. In 1931, the faculty grew to include the eminent British scholar Basil Mathews, installed as the Helen Barrett Montgomery Professor of Christianity and World Relations — a post honoring the first female president of the Northern Baptist Convention and long-standing leader of missionary work among the denomination's women. In 1933, Amos Wilder replaced Frederick Anderson in the New Testa-

11. Kelly, *Theological Education in America*, p. 55.

12. Mark May, William Adams Brown, and Frank Shuttlesworth, *The Education of American Ministers,* 4 vols. (New York: Institute of Social and Religious Research, 1934).

13. Glenn T. Miller, *Piety and Profession: American Protestant Theological Education, 1870-1970* (Grand Rapids: Eerdmans, 2007), 451-469.

ment department; the brother of the famous author and playwright Thornton Wilder, he was an accomplished poet and athlete. In the summer before his arrival at Andover Newton, he received his doctorate from Yale, his divinity degree from Hamilton College, and won the singles and doubles tennis championships in the state of Maine.

At its spot overlooking the Boston metropolitan area, Andover Newton was hardly a theological backwater. In 1933 the school hosted Andover alumni William Ernest Hocking for its inaugural Hyde Lecture on Missions. Hocking's widely read and deeply controversial report, "Rethinking Missions," would redefine the missionary task as an "exchange of spiritual ideas" rather than a one-way campaign of religious persuasion. Basil Mathews heralded Hocking's lecture as a means of developing a "unity of view among forward-looking people." That same year, Andover Newton hosted an Interseminary Conference, drawing students across New England, in which Yale luminary H. Richard Niebuhr spoke on "The Strategy of Christianity" and Union's Harry F. Ward on "Religion and the Decline of Capitalism." Andover Newton's own Basil Mathews gave an address on "Christ and the Present World-Conflict of Values."[14]

In the following years, the campus itself began to take on a more modern look. The increasing enrollments following the merger created a critical demand for housing, with only 90 spaces for 140 prospective students in 1932. A new dormitory, eventually dedicated as Herrick House and later set aside for married students, went up within the year. In 1935, the Andover trustees voted to sell their Cambridge building to Harvard for $300,000, though the Library would remain for the time being in their custody. The sale produced a spate of construction projects up on Newton Hill, and in the spring of 1937 two new buildings were on the brink of completion. The administration building, later christened Dabney Hall after the retiring Dean Vaughan Dabney, provided a new location for staff and faculty offices — to the vast relief of the beleaguered librarian William Cloues — as well as basement space for a museum displaying missionary artifacts collected by past generations of Societies of Inquiry groups on both campuses.[15] The Assembly Hall was

14. Basil Mathews, "Rethinking Missions" *Institution Bulletin* 25 (1933): 2-6; "The Interseminary Conference," idem, pp. 6-7.
15. Richard D. Pierce, "The Missionary Museum," *Andover Newton Theological School Bulletin* 33 (June 1941): 13-20.

renamed Noyes Hall in 1943 in honor of an Andover alumnus, trustee, and benefactor Charles Lothrop Noyes, the first Newton building with an Andover name. Its large open space seated 450 people and provided a venue for events too large for Colby Chapel or "of a character not appropriate" to its more ostensibly religious purpose. At either ends of the seating area were a stage and a projection booth. The Assembly Hall also included a post office, bookstore, kitchen, a club room with a fireplace, and a "voice laboratory" in the basement.[16]

In the 1936-37 school year, Andover Newton also began experimenting with one-day course offerings for local pastors, in response to a "widespread and insistent demand," as described in the school catalog for that school year. In the morning, after chapel, Henry Rowe offered a lecture on international relations and Vaughan spoke on "modern movements and cults." After lunch, the visiting pastors, some of whom came from as far away as New Hampshire, heard lectures about "modern preaching methods," "church school evangelism," and "care of the sick." The average attendance in each lecture was thirty pastors, with some courses twice that size.

Andover Newton's first visit, in 1938, from the Commission on Accrediting of the American Association of Theological Schools was a ringing success. Quoting from the committee's final report, Lewis Sherrill relayed to President Herrick their "outstanding impression" of "newness of life." "Andover Newton is a thoroughly live institution," they declared, with a "stirring of courage and hope" among the faculty and "energy and statesmanship" from Herrick. "The new buildings are visible evidence of this and the ideals of the institution are clearly moving in the right direction."[17]

Clinical Pastoral Education

During the 1930s, Andover Newton became a center of innovation. In 1931 the school invited Austin Philip Guiles to begin a program of clinical pastoral education, a cutting-edge idea in the emerging science of pastoral psychology. Andover Newton thus became not only the first seminary to incorporate clinical training into its curriculum, but it

16. "The New Building," *Institution Bulletin* 29 (April 1937): 1-2.
17. Lewis Sherrill to Everett Herrick, 1 February 1938, President's Office Files.

functioned as a coordinating center for programs in other schools, in effect adding an entirely new dimension to seminary education and to the professional role of the pastor.

By the 1930s the old model of ministry centering on the pastor's role in the Sunday morning pulpit had changed significantly. Depression-era conversations about standardizing seminary education mirrored a growing desire for professionalization among Protestant clergy. Traditionally, the care of souls had staked a great deal on exhortation and counsel; when a nineteenth-century sinner entered the pastor's study, he or she expected a good dose of direct moral guidance, often in the form of an extended quotation from scripture. But with the late-nineteenth-century "discovery of the subconscious," parishioners and pastors alike knew that even the sharpest biblical exhortations might not have much effect. The depths of the human mind held secrets that defied even the most theologically astute and biblically trained seminary graduate.

Furthermore, the psychology of religion was becoming a recognized field of academic study. Since the late nineteenth century, and especially in the wake of William James' *Varieties of Religious Experience,* first published in 1902, a growing body of scientific researchers and philosophers became intrigued by the role of religious belief in the internal workings of the human mind. In ensuing decades, James Leuba and Edwin Starbuck probed the meaning and mechanisms of religious conversion; G. Stanley Hall and John Dewey pointed the way for generations of religious education professionals by charting the religious development of children and young adults.

Especially in the Boston area, the possibility of religiously based healing had a fairly long intellectual pedigree. During the 1880s, Mary Baker Eddy's Christian Science movement had gathered a loyal following of female practitioners. In more conventional Protestant quarters, A. J. Gordon, the pastor of the Clarendon Street Baptist Church and former Newton trustee, taught that divine healing was a gift of the Holy Spirit. The Emmanuel Movement, centered in the Emmanuel Episcopal Church in Boston's Back Bay, advocated the cure of souls through more directly psychological methods.[18]

---

18. On Emmanuel, see Holifield, *The History of Pastoral Care in America,* pp. 207f.; Katherine McCarthy, "Psychotherapy and Religion: The Emmanuel Movement," *Journal of Religion and Health* 23 (summer 1985): 92-105.

Even more significant for the pastoral profession, during the 1920s, American society became enamored of popular psychology. Testing among army recruits in World War I had introduced the general public to an entirely new vocabulary of dark urges and painful fixations, the psychotic effects of repression and sublimation. The popularized Freudianism of the 1920s warned a willing public against the dangers of inhibiting personal desires, admonitions that found rapid acquiescence during a decade of unprecedented middle-class prosperity. During the 1920s, an emerging "white-collar" professional class began to expect clergy to provide not just a Sunday homily, but sensitive, well-informed personal counsel.

In 1924 Everett Herrick invited Richard Cabot to come to Newton Theological Institution to deliver a "Plea for a Clinical Year in the Course of Theological Study." Cabot was a formidable presence: a professor of social ethics at Harvard, a teaching physician at Harvard Medical School, and "a scion of the bluest of the blue-blooded families." As others later remembered the story, he had given this lecture in many similar settings, but at his Newton lecture in 1925, "more than at any other theological school, . . . the seeds fell on good ground."[19] Herrick and Vaughan Dabney recognized the significance of Cabot's proposal to provide ministers in training with hospital experience in psychological models and techniques. By the time that Cabot briefly joined the Andover Newton faculty a few years later, the school's leadership was thoroughly behind incorporating psychological training into seminary education.

Cabot was hardly a lone prophet. In 1925, Anton Boisen, a Congregational minister and chaplain at the Worcester State Hospital, had also begun training a small group of seminary students in clinical techniques. The survivor of a severe mental breakdown himself, Boisen was determined to place "sheltered students in contact with life including its sufferings." In Boisen's theoretical understanding, the proper study of theology required face-to-face encounter with people in trouble,

---

19. Austin Philip Guiles, "Clinical Education and Training," *Andover Newton Bulletin* 44 (February 1952): 40. Cabot's lecture, "A Plea for a Clinical Year in the Course of Theological Study," was subsequently republished in *Adventures on the Borderland of Ethics* (New York: Harper and Brothers, 1926). In 1918, he was invited by Newton Theological Institute to attend the Conference of Baptist Theological Seminaries, which was held in Boston and in Newton Centre. Miller, *Piety and Profession*, p. 595 n. 11.

what he referred to as "living human documents."[20] Boisen's three seminarians worked in the hospital as orderlies or with the department of psychiatric social work; the experience proved so successful that by 1927 he had seven prospective ministers under his wing. Boisen received strong support from the Massachusetts Congregational Conference and, interestingly enough, from Oliver Sewall, one of the Andover trustees. In 1929 he also received a promise of major funding from the Earhart Foundation; with Cabot's assistance, he created the Council for the Clinical Training of Theological Students, housed at 101 Brattle Street in Cambridge.

Under Cabot, Boisen, and Russell Dicks, the chaplain at the Massachusetts General Hospital, the so-called "Boston tradition" of pastoral care came to exercise enormous influence. In contrast to the Freudian professionals who dominated the movement in New York City, the Boston school was much more theologically and ethically oriented. Like other psychological professionals of their era, Cabot and Dicks emphasized the importance of "growth" as the core of life's meaning, but they never conceived of growth as an isolated personal quest. Their approach had a strong ethical edge, emphasizing balance between the needs of the self and the demands of the surrounding world. In their view, the purpose of counseling, carried out through "directed listening," was to bring the patient to meet his or her "growing edge," learning to "face and assimilate and obey the 'plan' of God for their lives."[21]

Cabot and his disciples had no doubt that they were prophets of a new era. As historian Brooks Holifield writes, they "deplored the cultural image of clerical prissiness" and worried openly that ministers were unequipped to meet the spiritual demands of the "real world." "They did not set out to train pastoral counselors," Holifield notes; "they intended to jolt the church."[22] The professional training they envisioned would not make ministers softer and more empathetic, but toughen and invigorate them. Cabot and his disciples often cultivated a stoic, often intimidating personal presence; Cabot himself enjoyed regular ocean swims and is said to have delivered a public lecture on the day of his wife's death.

20. "The Heritage of Anton T. Boisen," *Pastoral Psychology* 16 (November 1965).
21. Holifield, *History of Pastoral Care in America*, p. 237.
22. Holifield, *History of Pastoral Care in America*, pp. 231-232.

Austin Philip Guiles, a "debonair educational entrepreneur," carried on the work of Cabot and Dicks. He came to Andover Newton in 1931 with degrees from Princeton, Columbia, Union, and the University of Edinburgh, as well as clinical experience at the Massachusetts General Hospital.[23] Having married the sister of the famous Amelia Earhart, Guiles also brought a ready source of funding through the Earhart Foundation. He began his program by taking his students on field trips to local hospitals, mental facilities, and prisons. The master's degree program he established at Andover Newton emphasized all the latest techniques of group counseling, verbatims, and the case study method.[24]

Guiles insisted that a program in Clinical Psychological Education (CPE) was an essential to the making of good pastors and "well-rounded Christians." His Southworth Lecture, given in 1952, provided a litany of scientific discoveries in astronomy, biology, and physics, laced with admonitions to maintain an abiding curiosity in the world beyond the pastor's study. "If you are to get within sounding distance of many human souls these days, to whom you would sing the psalms, or 'tell the old, old story of Jesus and His Love,'" Guiles declared, "you may have to begin a study of the languages these people understand." Direct confrontation with human pain and suffering, "the dark and the cold," would deepen the student's personal faith. "We have reason to believe that the young pastor's capacity for endurance will inevitably be increased through clinical work," Guiles said, "if he is careful to walk hand in hand with the Master."[25]

During the 1930s and 1940s, Andover Newton played a leading role in developing the CPE curriculum. In 1933 with funding from the Earhart Foundation, Andover Newton developed and helped fund model programs at Bangor Theological Seminary, the University of Southern California, the Episcopal Theological School in Cambridge, Boston University, and the Chicago Theological Seminary.[26] Under John Billinsky, who succeeded Guiles as the director of the program, Andover Newton pioneered in the administration of psychological tests

---

23. Holified, *History of Pastoral Care*, p. 242.
24. Miller, *Piety and Profession*, pp. 596, 597.
25. Guiles, "Clinical Education and Training," pp. 47, 53.
26. "Andover Newton and Clinical Training," p. 20.

for all incoming students, described by one admirer as a "selective instrument for distinguishing the so called 'called' from *the* chosen."[27]

War Years

Andover Newton students were not a terribly serious group during the 1930s. No doubt their behavior reflected the lighthearted culture of college campuses that had developed during the 1920s heyday of flappers and fraternity men; for the first time in American history, advanced education was becoming a middle-class norm. In 1939 one student complained in the *Bulletin* of "horse-play" and "disrespect" in the school's classrooms. A campus visitor, perhaps expecting a buttoned-down group of pipe-smoking seminarians, wrote with similar dismay over the "disrespect and unpoliteness [*sic*] routinely exhibited by clergy in training." "You students talk to one another in class, you read books, you write letters, some of you go to sleep sprawled all over the desks, and in the midst of meditation and prayer some one gets up and closes a squeaky window." Echoing those same themes, a returning missionary noted with some bewilderment the "lack of respectful attention in class," and in particular the "nicotine aroma" clinging to some future men of the cloth.[28]

The onset of World War II brought a new seriousness to Andover Newton's campus. By 1944 at least 150 of the school's graduates were serving as military chaplains, and those who stayed behind could not avoid the war's implications for their own futures. The Selective Service Act, as it was originally instituted, provided exemptions for seminarians, and for college men in pre-seminary programs, just as it did for pre-medical students. The government recognized not just the value of military chaplains, but the need to "protect the supply of future ministers" by issuing deferments to college men. But once the draft age fell to eighteen, college curricula tended to fall fully in line behind government priorities. In April 1944 the Selective Service announced an end to pre-seminary deferments. In 1943 President Herrick voiced worries

27. "Andover Newton and Clinical Training," p. 19.

28. Raleigh A. King, "Thou Art the Man," *Bulletin* 1 (March 22, 1939): 3; Mrs. Harland Stuart, "Impressions," *Bulletin* 1 (April 1939): 3.

about a long-term drop in future enrollment, and of maintaining a high quality.[29]

Continuing graduate work while the world exploded into war was not an easy task. During the 1940s, student publications took on a more serious tone, with complaints about "the flabbiness of the ministry" up on Newton Hill. Especially in comparison to the strict physical discipline required in totalitarian societies, the average Andover Newton student looked to be a sorry specimen. "Exemption from military service is no excuse for softness," one student exhorted his peers, "but is rather an even greater challenge for physical fitness." Indeed, he continued, "We are professional men; does our general appearance reveal this? Clothes, shoes, shave, nails: are they acceptable? How about the taste we exhibit in our selection of clothes?" Even the easygoing atmosphere of classroom study needed toning up. "The great truths of life were being made banal by our flippancy," he noted ruefully, calling for a "greater regularity and discipline in our devotional life."[30]

During the war years many Andover Newton students took up team sports with new intensity, sensitive to the inference "poor draft dodger, the ministry is the only way out for him." Greeting the incoming junior class in 1943, an upperclassman challenged them to a "militaristic workout" in the gym — if they were up to it. "Until you show us differently," he challenged, "we will consider you either cream puffs or pansies depending on whether you choose to be delicate confectionaries or dainty flowers." A subsequent article in the *Bulletin,* simply entitled "Play Ball," offered an even more explicit challenge. "We are all well acquainted," the article began, "with the traditional stock picture of a minister as a rather fragile or otherwise otherworldly creature who is concerned with things totally apart from the world and who would not soil his hands or enter into the same activities with other men." But "many of us in this school feel that ministers must be real 'he-men' if they are to win places of influence with the people of the world today. It may be fine to be highly respected," he declared, "but we want to be one of the group as well."[31]

29. *Annual Report of the President, June 1943,* n.p.; *Annual Report of the President, July 1942,* n.p.

30. L.W., "The Hardening Process," *Bulletin,* 27 February 1941, p. 4.

31. "The Bulletin," *Bulletin,* 1943, p. 1; "Play Ball," no pagination.

The addition of social ethicist Herbert Gezork to the faculty in 1939 toughened Andover Newton's social profile. In 1936 Gezork, a leader of the German Baptist Youth Movement, fled the country, a "traumatic experience" that shaped his future scholarship. During the war years Gezork was also the faculty sponsor of a vigorous Social Action Group on campus. In 1940, a group of Andover Newton students were driving through the nearby village of Watertown and encountered a group of laundry workers on strike against the Lewandos Cleaning and Drying Plant. Their curiosity smitten, the students fell into conversation with the strikers, and soon became aware of appalling working conditions: 100-degree temperatures, low pay, and few breaks for rest. Over the next two months, they returned to the picket line some fifty or sixty times. "Most of us to that time had been at least mildly anti-labor," one student, Bedros Baharian, wrote in 1942, "preservers of the status quo born with the idea that if a man didn't like his job he could quit and look for another." But "this was the first time that many of us brought up in semi-capitalistic homes, had been brought in actual contact with strike conditions. For the first time the genuine spirit of social consciousness developed."

The Andover Newton Social Action Committee and a local chapter of the Religion and Labor Foundation quickly became two of the strongest groups on the school's campus. The students participated in another strike at the Boston Maid Company in Waltham, running the loudspeakers, giving speeches, and transporting strikers back and forth from home to protect them from the Pinkerton detectives working for the company management. In 1942 the Social Action Committee conducted an investigation of Herrick House, responding to complaints that faculty and school employees were taking up space that should have been reserved for married students.[32]

The Social Action Group also introduced Andover Newton students to racial issues. During the early decades of the twentieth century, Boston's black population was still relatively small, and clustered in the city's South End. The Second World War brought a new migration of working class blacks from other northern cities; as they became an increasingly visible presence in a predominantly white

32. Bedros Baharian, "A History of the Social Action Group Activities," *Bulletin* 12 (March 17, 1942): 4.

city, tensions slowly mounted. When the Social Action Group brought civil rights activist and pastor Adam Clayton Powell to campus in 1944, as part of a weeklong program that included peace activist Sherwood Eddy, Kermit Eby, the educational secretary of the CIO, and Myron Fowell, a leader of the Worcester Social Action group, they were well ahead of their times. Powell began his after-dinner speech by admonishing the Andover Newton community for perpetuating "racial tension." One African American student, Charles McCreary, regretted Powell's accusation, having lived in the South where the situation was far more dangerous than Newton Center. "However," he told his fellow students, "this does not mean that there is complete 'freedom and faithfulness of fellowship' on the Hill between individuals or races."[33]

The conversation would continue, far more eventfully, in later years. But as World War II drew to a close, Andover Newton students and faculty turned to other matters. In 1946 Everett Herrick retired as president. He was briefly replaced by Harold Tribble, who left to take a post at Wake Forest College in 1950, and then by Herbert Gezork in 1950. Herrick was a "little quiet gray man with a twinkle and a twang, the very embodiment of what it means to be a salty old-fashioned Yankee," whose presidency had brought a pastor's sensibility to the affiliated schools. He was, in the words of one admirer, "an institution among New England Baptists," a hugely popular "Christian diplomat" thoroughly at home in churches across the region.[34]

Postwar Renewal

By the time of Herrick's departure, other changes were in the offing. In the 1946-1947 school year Andover Newton introduced a new, much more intensive curriculum. Already in 1940 students had complained of the high number of required courses and lack of electives. In fact, compared to other leading seminaries, Andover Newton's curriculum

33. "The Fellowship on the Hill," *Bulletin,* 20 September 1943; Charles McCreary, "Racial Tension on the Hill," *ANTS Student Bulletin,* 24 February 1944.

34. Russell Henry Stafford, "The Builder Also Grows," *Andover Newton Theological School Bulletin* 38 (June 1946): 5; C. Raymond Chappell, "Dr. Herrick among the New England Churches," *Andover Newton Theological School Bulletin* 38 (June 1946): 25.

was fairly restrictive, with a 36/36 ratio of required to elective courses — compared to a 42/25 ratio at Princeton, 48/35 at the Pacific School of Religion, and 36/8 at Union. Students were particularly restive about the field education requirement, which was, in their view, inadequately supervised and inordinately demanding of their time.[35]

Another major impetus for the new curriculum was a national study of Northern Baptist Seminaries, conducted by Hugh Hartshorne and Milton Froyd in 1944-1945. Alarmingly, despite the standardizing trends elsewhere, Baptist institutions had made little progress beyond the numbers posted by the Kelly report in 1924. The Northern Baptist report was particularly critical of most seminary programs, described as "a liberal arts curriculum with some trade school practices added." Schools did little to prepare young men for the real-life demands of the local parish, sending them out to cure souls with relatively little practical experience. In comparison to medical schools, which routinely required clinical training as well as a year of internship, seminaries were far behind, and dangerously so. "No medical student would be allowed to go off by himself and try out his knowledge on unsuspecting patients," Hartshorne and Froyd complained. "Is the damage done here by blunderers no less serious than the damage to bodies that would result from the practice of fledgling doctors?"[36]

The new Andover Newton curriculum, launched in the 1946-47 school year, aimed to combine "learning by doing" with "learning by observing and thinking." The B.D. degree required four full years of study, the last semester of which was devoted to a supervised internship in a local church setting. The classroom regimen covered four basic subject areas, with a balance each semester between academic and practical subjects. In the mornings students took courses devoted to Bible, philosophy of religion, theology, and church history. In the afternoons they turned to classes in worship, homiletics, and religious education, which often met as seminars and workshops. Andover Newton was also one of the few seminaries to require speech classes of all its students, and so instruction in sermon preparation was followed during the senior year by instruction in "correct breathing, posture, bodily

35. "Report from the Curriculum Committee," *Bulletin* 2 (April 19, 1940): 4-5.
36. Hugh Hartshorne and Milton C. Froyd, *Theological Education in the Northern Baptist Convention* (Philadelphia: Judson Press, 1945), pp. 214, 215.

activity, [and] voice production." Seniors devoted a day a week to clinical training.[37]

A broad survey of American and Canadian theological schools, published in 1957, singled out Andover Newton's field education requirement for special mention. Only a few Lutheran seminaries had anything like the fourth-year internship, which in design and execution was a significant departure from most field education experiences. Andover Newton's fourth-year seminarians were working pastors, in much the same way that a medical intern fills a position in a hospital. They returned to campus every two weeks to meet with faculty supervisors, and to engage in discussions about parish work across the curriculum. "The students meet with theologians, psychologists, educators, and other members of the staff during the various sessions," the study reported approvingly, noting that the program was the work of the entire Andover Newton faculty, not just the field work department.[38]

During the late 1940s and 1950s, Andover Newton's faculty blossomed along with its new program of study. Roger Hazelton, who taught philosophy of religion from 1945 to 1957 and again from 1965 to 1978, was an authority on Blaise Pascal, and also devoted scholarly attention to the field of aesthetics.[39] Norman Gottwald, the first Lowry Chair of Old Testament, authored one of the most widely used introductions to the subject, *A Light to the Nations*. Paul Minear became Norris Professor of New Testament in 1945, and was a leading authority on Pauline literature. Gerald Cragg arrived in 1958, a historian with an international reputation for his work in Puritanism; he also authored *The Church and the Age of Reason, 1648-1789*, the fourth in an important and widely circulated five-volume church history series. During a decade that devoted enormous attention to religious education, Wesner Fallaw was a recognized authority in Congregational circles.

The psychology department also grew apace. In 1958 Henry Brooks arrived, the first African American on the faculty. John Billinsky, who

---

37. *Catalogue of Andover Newton Theological School, 1946-1947* (Newton Centre, MA, 1946), pp. 5-12.

38. H. Richard Niebuhr, Daniel Day Williams, and James M. Gusafson, *The Advancement of Theological Education* (New York: Harper and Brothers, 1957), pp. 119-121.

39. *Blaise Pascal: The Genius of His Thought* (Philadelphia: Westminster, 1974); *A Theological Approach to Art* (Nashville: Abingdon, 1967); *The Root and Flower by Prayer* (New York: Macmillan, 1943); *The God We Worship* (New York: Macmillan, 1946).

had studied under Carl Jung, arrived soon after. Billinsky, a war veteran with a combative personal style, did not endear the psychology department to the rest of the faculty. Yet he added to its reputation elsewhere: in 1969 Billinsky published an interview he had conducted with Jung, and reported for the first time on the personal reasons for his rift with mentor Sigmund Freud. Billinsky's revelation was that the presumably monogamous Freud was having an affair with his sister-in-law Martha Bernays.

The leading theologian on Andover Newton's campus during the mid-twentieth century was Nels Ferré. A Swedish immigrant who graduated from Andover Newton in 1934, he received his doctorate at Harvard under Alfred North Whitehead, and joined the Andover Newton faculty in 1937, the youngest man appointed to the Abbot Chair of Christian Theology. During an era when neo-orthodox figures like Reinhold Niebuhr and Paul Tillich dominated the theological landscape, Ferré defied simple categorization. Like Andover Newton itself, his early upbringing was conservative and pietistic, but he shed those convictions during his college years at Boston University, where he was influenced by the personalist school associated with Borden Parker Bowne. His study under Whitehead added awareness of process thought, and his friendship with Tillich a conversation with neo-orthodoxy. But Ferré was in many ways a liberal with a strong evangelical bent; and he was an "intellectual loner" who wrote steadily but did not inspire many disciples. His years at Andover Newton were sufficiently difficult that he made a brief sojourn at the Vanderbilt Divinity School from 1950 to 1958; Nashville's conservative ethos proved even more unwelcoming, and Ferré returned to Andover Newton for the remainder of his career.[40]

One ambiguous measure of Andover Newton's stature was the upward trajectory of its constantly disappearing faculty. Amos Wilder left to teach at Harvard in 1945; his replacement Paul Minear went to Yale in 1956. Walter Harrelson, who taught Old Testament from 1951 to 1955 and served on the translation committee of the Revised Standard Version Bible, became the dean of the Divinity School at the University of Chicago, finishing his career at Vanderbilt.

40. Gary Dorrien, *The Making of American Liberal Theology: Crisis, Irony, and Postmodernity, 1950-2005* (Louisville: Westminster/John Knox, 2006), pp. 39-57.

Another measure of success was the steady addition of new buildings on Newton Hill. Two were student dormitories: Kendall Hall opened for married students in 1954, and Fuller Hall in 1958. A living room and kitchen, named after religious education professor James Berkeley, connected the two buildings together and provided social space for the growing number of young families on the seminary campus.

The demand for space also reflected a 74 percent increase in enrollment between 1956 and 1963, the largest increase of any seminary in the United States and Canada. During the Cold War, the Depression-era surplus of clergy quickly turned into a shortfall, as Americans flocked to houses of worship. Few students encountered difficulty in locating placements after graduation. According to one report presented to the Board of Trustees in 1956, Congregational seminaries were graduating about 200 students every year — and still some 500 pulpits remained empty, with new churches being built every year.[41]

By a variety of different indicators, the 1950s were peak years for Protestant seminaries. Not only were mainline churches growing at an astounding rate, but seminarians were appearing just as quickly. A magisterial survey of theological education, conducted by H. Richard Niebuhr, Daniel Day Williams, and James Gustafson, found that since the Kelly study of the 1920s, Protestant seminaries had become healthy and strong. Enrollment figures had climbed dramatically, with a 151 percent increase in the twenty years since the academic year of 1934-35; the survey found a 33 percent increase just between 1949-50 and 1954-55. Whereas both Kelly and May had found uncomfortably low proportions of college graduates in the seminaries they visited, the Niebuhr study found little cause for concern. In 45 of the 178 schools surveyed, 100 percent of the students had college degrees; in 119 of the 178 the proportion was 75 percent or more.[42]

The Niebuhr report also unearthed some fundamental problems. To begin with, seminary faculties were overworked and underpaid: the theoretically endless demands of the professional curriculum failed to keep pace with most schools' ability to hire new professors. In constant dollars, the average salary of a seminary professor in 1954 (somewhere between $4,800 and $6,700) was below the same figure in 1934, during

---

41. Board of Trustees minutes, 1 February 1956, ANTS archives.
42. H. Richard Niebuhr et al., *The Advancement of Theological Education*, pp. 7, 11.

the depths of the Great Depression. In the meantime, as endowment funds dipped, an ever greater share of institutional budgets went toward administrative costs, including development departments and support staff.

Even during these years of high enrollment and academic productivity, Andover Newton began to feel a slight, discernable pinch. The school's budget grew dramatically during the 1950s, from about $214,000 to $501,000 over the course of the decade. By 1960, with the student body topping 250, the faculty-student ratio stood at 17 to 1, far higher than the 11 to 1 approved by the ATS. As faculty representative Gerald Cragg told the board of trustees in 1962, "We need better equipment, better classrooms, better professors' studies, a better library, and a salary scale on a level with any other school of outstanding excellence. These things we need," he warned politely, "to attract and hold a first class staff."[43]

But as Andover Newton celebrated Andover's 150th anniversary in 1957, the future looked bright. The Southworth lecturer for that year, Claude Fuess, was a member of the board of trustees and the headmaster of the Phillips Andover Academy. The title of his lecture, a wry historical retrospective on the seminary's history, was "Escape from the Dead Hand." Sketching out the old story of the Andover creed, the heresy trials of the 1880s, and the near-death experience at Harvard, Fuess declared that "Andover Seminary is no longer the Citadel of Orthodoxy but the Home of Protestant Freedom." It had "replaced dogmatism by questioning, believing leads in the end to prayer and a redemptive Christian faith which is intellectually respectable." "The cherished orthodoxies of one age," Fuess concluded, "are rightly rejected by the next."[44]

In many ways, Fuess was right. During Andover and Newton's first few decades together, they had emphatically moved beyond the past into something genuinely new. Barely pausing for breath after affiliating in 1931, they had launched a new program in Clinical Pastoral Education, bringing the latest advances in counseling psychology to the

43. "Record of the Joint Meeting of the Boards of Andover Theological Seminary and Newton Theological Institution, 1 February 1962," ANTS archives.

44. Claude M. Fuess, "Escape from the Dead Hand," *Andover Newton Bulletin* 45 (December 1957): 35.

world of the local parish. From a small, quintessentially New England institution, Andover Newton had become a school with a national, even international, sense of itself. Despite the upheaval of economic depression and world war, the seminary continued to reach out to the surrounding world, through a strengthened program of field education and a vigorous social action agenda. That world only grew more complicated in years to come, as the halcyon 1950s gave way to the tumultuous 1960s, and seminaries faced as never before questions of Christian faithfulness in the face of moral ambiguity and outright evil. Andover Newton would quickly find itself in the center of that difficult but deeply important time of testing.

CHAPTER EIGHT

Earthquake Years:
A Mainline Seminary Weathers the Sixties

—◦◦◦—

Herbert Gezork retired in 1965 with a profound sense of satisfaction. The full union of Andover and Newton was finally coming to pass, with an enthusiasm that affirmed the wisdom of the original decision to affiliate in 1931. Gezork's farewell presidential address, his "Retrospect and Prospect" to Andover Newton's students and faculty, listed some of the major achievements of the thirty-four years since Andover had left Cambridge. The Clinical Pastoral Education program was the school's shining light, changing the shape of seminary education and serving as a model for other programs sprouting up across the country. Andover Newton had also kept its social conscience: the Blue Hill Christian Center was, in Gezork's words, a "veritable beehive of religious, educational, social, recreational and tutorial activities" every day of the week. Andover Newton was also busy from morning till late at night, with evening and extension programs for laypeople. With a stellar faculty and an innovative curriculum, the school was fully on course to meet "the theological and educational ferment of our time." It had engineered a "sound balance" between "high standards of theological scholarship" and the "practical demands of the ministry."

The times were not, of course, all that easy. Even in the midst of his optimism, Gezork cited growing skepticism about the local church's ability to meet larger social needs. Did it make sense to continue teaching young men to marry and bury, to prepare the weekly sermon and supervise the Sunday school, when war was escalating in Vietnam and urban ghettos exploding into violence? "To be sure," Gezork conceded, "a renewal in the life and work of the residential parish is urgently needed. But," he challenged, "must we believe that the forms which God has used since the beginning of the history of His Church have to be discarded because of abuse, petrifaction or corruption?" Indeed, "what is needed is not a defeatism or cynicism about the Church as we know it, but the ardent prayer: Veni Creator Spiritus."[1]

During the 1960s many educational administrators on seminary campuses and in colleges and universities confronted unanticipated challenges. Widespread rebellion against the bureaucratic regulations of institutional life, the demand for "free speech" and relevant courses, would forever shatter the peace of the old ivory tower. Every social issue of the 1960s — war, poverty, racism, and sexism — sooner or later found its way into the classroom, and, even more inevitably, onto the desks of harried administrators.

In many ways, Andover Newton followed the familiar plot line of student unrest, confrontation, and educational reform. In scenes played out in many other theological schools from Berkeley to Cambridge, its difficult decade began with public confrontations over the school's racial politics and ended with an influx of women students who would forever transform the shape of seminary education. Without a doubt, the turmoil marked the end of an old era — and the beginning of a new one.

Halcyon Days

In 1965 Andover Newton's campus was literally in the midst of upheaval. Several new buildings were under construction at the end of the quadrangle, moving the old center of gravity away from the original Newton site anchored by the Hills Library. A large academic complex, with faculty offices and a lounge and seminar rooms (dedicated as Worcester Hall in 1966), honored the school's benefactors in the central Massachusetts area. Stoddard Hall, a lecture hall, was named for Newton trustee Harry Stoddard, whose family provided a major gift. A gift from the Arthur Vining Davis Foundation funded a classroom

---

1. Gezork, "Retrospect and Prospect," *Andover Newton Quarterly* n.s., 5 (March 1965): 5, 6.

building in memory of Perley Bacon Davis, who had graduated from Andover Seminary in 1861. Across the way, Appleton-Chase, a women's dormitory, was also under construction, and would be dedicated in 1967. Primary funding for the residence hall came from Mrs. Edward A. Appleton, whose great uncle Irah Chase was Newton's first professor.

The physical transformation mirrored other changes in administrative and faculty offices. Roy Pearson ascended from academic dean to the school presidency in 1965, bringing with him a strong empathy for church parish work. An Andover Newton alumnus from the class of 1938, he had served as pastor of the Hancock Congregational Church in Lexington (later United Church of Christ) before moving into the deanship in 1954. Described as a "clean desk administrator," Pearson was in many ways a quintessential New England churchman, known for his long, elegantly crafted prayers, and his enormous collection of refurbished clocks. With his loyal board of trustees, several of whom hailed from the Hancock church, Pearson aimed to cultivate a base of support among New England churches.[2]

In 1966, George Peck became Andover Newton's academic dean, bringing with him an entirely different academic toolbox. Peck was a native Australian, the son of a Queensland coal miner, who had spent forty years as a Baptist lay preacher. Beginning with studies at the Queensland Baptist College, Peck accumulated a steady flow of academic honors, all the while pastoring Baptist churches and lecturing in Greek and philosophy. Between 1958 and 1963 he served a highly successful tenure as dean and then principal at the Eastern Theological College in Assam, India. Peck was a clear rising star with an academic gift and a knack for administrative work; in 1961 he became president of the Council of Baptist Churches in Northeast India, all the while churning out a regular stream of books and articles. In 1963 Peck received a fellowship for doctoral studies at Harvard, and assumed his post at Andover Newton in the course of his work there. A self-described "Indophile," Peck brought an international awareness to Andover Newton's campus, along with his considerable administrative and academic talents.[3]

2. I am indebted to a variety of faculty interviews for much of the following information, particularly William Holladay, Earl Thompson, Max Stackhouse, Jerry Handspicker, Mary Luti, and Gabriel Fackre.

3. "Introducing George Peck: Andover Newton's Dean-Elect," *Today's Ministry* 1 (February 1966): 3, 12.

The mid-1960s also saw physical changes among the Andover New-ton faculty. In 1967, noting that six of the eighteen full-time members were in their thirties, school administrators predicted that "in the next five years the faculty will be larger, younger, and more heavily weighted in those departments which relate the School to the Church and the world."[4] In 1961, Andover Newton hired Meredith (Jerry) Handspicker straight out of Yale to fill this latter aim. Earl Thompson arrived in 1964, an American historian with a strong social justice orientation, trained at Union Theological Seminary and Princeton University. That same year, Joe Williamson also arrived to teach practical theology; Max Stackhouse, a student of James Luther Adams and Paul Tillich, arrived a year later in 1965 to teach social ethics. He replaced the outgoing Harvey Cox, who was part of a research project sponsored by the Baptist churches in Massachusetts. Cox was leaving for Harvard on the cusp of fame, having just published *The Secular City,* one of the defining books of that era, while he was at Andover Newton. But Stackhouse quickly es-tablished a strong academic profile of his own as a Niebuhrian realist with international interests that matched those of Peck. With Thomp-son and Williamson, he "stirred the pot" on campus, introducing stu-dents to the radical social vision of Martin Luther King, then in the midst of its dramatic unfolding in Selma and Montgomery, Alabama.[5] Not surprisingly, perhaps, the accreditation visitors for the AATS made special mention of the energetic spirit of the campus during the spring of 1967. "If a faculty, together with its President and Dean, are the heart of a theological school," they enthused, "this school has a strong and lively heart."[6]

The following years saw more strengthening of Andover Newton's faculty ranks, with Old Testament scholar William Holladay and theo-logian Gabriel Fackre arriving in 1970. Like Peck, Holladay came to Newton Center with international experience — he taught at the Near East School of Theology in Beirut from 1963 to 1970 — and an ambi-tious academic agenda. Already a well-published scholar before joining the faculty, Holladay became an acclaimed authority on the book of Jer-

4. ANTS Institutional Self-Study for the American Association of Theological Schools, February 1967, p. 24.

5. For an account of some of these events, see Max L. Stackhouse, "Ethical Decision-Making in Selma," *Metropolitan Boston Association Mission Witness* 1 (May 1965): 1, 3.

6. "Accrediting Report on ANTS, April 1967," President's Office Files, ANTS archives.

emiah. Fackre, who came to teach theology that same year, was also a prolific author with a broad background in the wider church. He commenced his academic career in the context of gritty urban parishes in Chicago and Pittsburgh, and then at Lancaster Theological Seminary in Pennsylvania. Rooted in the Evangelical and Reformed Church that joined with the Congregational Christian Churches to form the United Church of Christ (UCC) in 1957, during his lengthy career at Andover Newton, Fackre played a leading role in the theological identity discussions within the new denomination.

Along with the faculty, administration, and physical campus, Andover Newton's curriculum also changed in the 1964-1965 school year. The revision required incoming students to take four introductory courses, in theology ("The Faith of the Church"), Bible ("The Scriptures of the Church"), history ("The Life of the Church"), and mission ("The Task of the Church in the World"). After that, students had choices of upper-level electives, and were expected to complete one advanced seminar in each of the four areas. The clinical requirement continued, as did the fourth year of internship. But the new program encouraged more academically oriented students to pursue deeper study, by opting for Program Two, which allowed more independent study than the lecture and seminar requirements of Program One. In addition, academically competent students intending to move from seminary into graduate school were able under "Plan B" to skip the internship requirement and write a thesis.[7]

Restless Students

The cover of the 1964-1965 catalog tells its own story, of course. There the Andover Newton ideal was pictured as a clean-shaven white man in his mid-twenties; in a simple black and white photograph, he is staring firmly into the camera and standing in front of a neat brick colonial church. He is handsome but not overly so — a likely "Program Two," but not necessarily a "Plan B." His gaze is level and confident, anchored by a strong jaw that is dimpled by a slight cleft. It is apparently mid-

7. Andover Newton Theological School Catalog, 1964-1965, Newton Centre, MA, pp. 36-40.

winter — the trees are bare and there is a sprinkling of snow on the ground — but our seminarian is wearing only a sports coat over his white button-down shirt and tie. Unmistakably, any local church under his care would lie in competent hands.

What the picture does not show was that, by the mid-1960s, Andover Newton students were among the most liberal in the nation. A survey of American theological students, completed in 1966, offers a rather startling picture of the wide diversity of social and moral views among future men and women of the cloth, and of the relative scale of opinion at Andover Newton.[8] The divinity schools in the survey included, on the one end, established mainline institutions like Princeton, Northwestern (Garrett), and the University of Chicago, and two smaller evangelical ones, Gordon-Conwell and Trinity Evangelical Divinity School. The composite picture of theological education is both fascinating and revealing.

First, in regard to theological point of view, students were asked to rate themselves on a scale of one to six, from "very conservative" to "very liberal." None of the fifty-eight Andover Newton students who responded to the survey placed themselves in the first category, and all but 12 percent defined themselves as "moderately" to "very" liberal. No other school registered as high a percentage — and in fact, while 55.2 percent of Andover Newton students classified themselves as "liberal," the average percentage for that category among the rest of the seminarians was only 19 percent.

On the race relations scale, Andover Newton students also leaned toward the left end of the spectrum. They posted the second highest rate of support for the view that a "maximum of personal contact including intermarriage is the best way to overcome racial problems" (82.8 percent). Only students at the historically liberal University of Chicago Divinity School posted a higher score (95 percent). The survey also uncovered the "new morality" alive and well among Andover Newton students. They posted the third most liberal score, behind Chicago and Denver Methodists' Iliff Seminary, with 31 percent endorsing the position that "much personal freedom is desirable but the sex relationship is a personal one and partners should be selected discreetly." Only 13.8 percent believed that sex was allowable only within marriage, and till death

8. John T. Roscoe and Paul A. Girling, "American Theological Students: A Survey of their Value Commitments," unpublished paper, 1966; President's Office Files, ANTS archives.

ended the relationship, a figure more remarkable alongside the 75 percent of the Gordon students who believed so (and the zero figure for the University of Chicago).

On a variety of theological questions, Andover Newton students tilted toward the far end of the scale as well. Slightly more than half (53.4 percent) affirmed a "personal God who has revealed himself in the Bible," a response that garnered near unanimous support at Gordon (98.1 percent) and Trinity (100 percent). About 28 percent of Andover Newton students held to a universalist position, agreeing that knowledge of God was not confined to Christianity. This placed them further down the spectrum than students at the University of Chicago (15.3 percent) and Princeton (17.2 percent). Not a single Andover Newton student agreed that the Bible was the inspired word of God with unquestioned authority, though 100 percent of the Trinity students and 88.5 percent of the Gordon students did so. Almost every Andover Newton student agreed that the Bible "contained God's message," though it was not reliable in every instance, or that it was an inspired religious book similar to other religious writings.

The survey is indicative of new winds of doctrine roiling churches and seminary campuses during the early 1960s. As John C. Bennett wrote in 1969, seminary faculties were living with changes "that would have astonished a theological school faculty ten years ago." With the discipline of theology itself in a "state of flux," Bennett wrote, "it is difficult to state what the various positions mean for faith." In the "instant theology" of the decade, schools of thought came and went with bewildering rapidity. "[W]hat is the real meaning of the so-called 'secular theology'? What has happened to the 'death of God' theology and what did its emergency in the midst of the church mean? Where is the source of authority for the church or for the theologian? Even Roman Catholics," Bennett noted, "now are troubled by that question."[9]

Many students no longer entered seminary with a vocation for parish work. Underlining the iconoclastic thrust of 1966 survey, Episcopal churchman Norman Pittenger observed that the most striking aspect of the contemporary student was "the degree to which he *hates* the church." By that Pittenger meant that, like many other Americans rest-

---

9. Bennett, "Priorities in Theological Education," *Christianity and Crisis,* 14 April 1969, p. 87.

less for change, seminarians were distrustful of the self-perpetuating nature of religious institutions. Most ministers in training, Pittenger said, "manage to work out some kind of position which will enable them to serve the church as an institution while remaining critical of its *modus operandi;* but they are 'rebels,' even if in some sense 'loyal' rebels."[10]

Andover Newton students were no different. "During the past few days (and perhaps years) at Andover Newton," student William Whit wrote in 1966, "I have discerned a mounting restlessness within the student body." The presenting issues were not surprising, most of them centering on a few proposed curricular changes — including a proposed three semesters of "practice preaching" — that underscored the school's mission to local churches. But the real source of impatience went deeper and had little to do with the curriculum itself. The "free speech" movement that began at the University of California's Berkeley campus in the fall of 1964 — the year the first of the "baby boom" generation turned eighteen — was having an effect on universities and colleges across the country, and making its way up Andover Newton's hill. At the Berkeley uprising, students had refused to accept university officials' ban on "outside groups," and opened up a national debate about the need for more democratic school governance. Students began to demand the right to play a direct role in the decision-making process normally reserved for trustees or faculty committees. In that vein, Whit called on Andover Newton's administration to respect "the integrity of every student as a young *adult.*" Adding a theological twist to the Berkeley-inspired rhetoric, the seminarian of the 1960s demanded to be "taken seriously as a man who may have already formed many opinions as to his role as a Christian minister in the world today; he should be encouraged to pursue his ideal responsibly."[11]

Andover Newton students were already becoming more assertive in the early 1960s. In 1962, they presented the board of trustees with a petition asking for the full merger of the two affiliated schools, to more accurately represent the "unity of this school in its corporate, educational, and spiritual life." The student association, which had been

10. Norman Pittenger, "Theological Students Today," *Christian Century,* 26 April 1967, pp. 527, 528.

11. William Whit, "Magister Ex Machina?" *The Inconvenient Word* 1, no. 9 (10 February 1966): 1, 2. Student publications, ANTS archives.

formed in 1957, asked the faculty to raise money in support of Virgil Wood, an African American alum who had been active in the civil rights movement. In 1963, they heard reports from two students who had just returned from a nonviolent demonstration in Williamston, North Carolina. The following year, the Social Action Committee took part in voter registration efforts in Boston's Roxbury neighborhood. Even some wry indications of feminist discontent surfaced in Student Association minutes; in 1964 Lois Bond announced a "Name the Dames" contest, to finally put to rest the old "Divinity Dames" club for faculty wives and female students. When the student association was reorganized under a new constitution in 1965, it began to take aim at faculty and trustee decision-making, demanding a more direct role for the students in setting the future direction of the school.[12]

Student initiative also gave Andover Newton a foothold in Boston's inner city. In 1964, Carl McCall, an African American M.Div. student with a degree from Dartmouth College, recruited Jerry Handspicker for a project in the city's Roxbury neighborhood. Shepherded by Michael Haynes of the Twelfth Baptist Church, the Greater Boston Interdenominational Ministerial Alliance, and the City Mission Society, the Blue Hill Christian Center offered a range of classes, support groups, and practical help. Links with suburban churches brought in money and volunteers; Andover Newton paid McCall with funds from the field education department. For the first time since the days of Andover House in the turn-of-the-century South End, Andover Newton was back in the city of Boston.

Identity Crisis

Within a larger perspective, taking into account the changes on Andover Newton's campus and the deepening turmoil of the outside world, the accomplishments of 1965 would prove to be short-lived. In fact, Andover Newton's Institutional Self-Study, written for the American Association of Theological Schools in 1967, is a telling portrait of an identity crisis in the works. That did not make Andover Newton unique

---

12. "Minutes of Student Association Cabinet Meeting," 8 May 1961; "Andover Newton Student Association Minutes," 5 November 1962; "Student Association Minutes, 25 November 1963" in Student Organization files, ANTS archives.

among Protestant seminaries, of course; the language of crisis and up-heaval was common among theological educators in the late 1960s and 1970s. But in a school that was both very young and saddled with an unusually long institutional history, the uncertainties reverberated with considerable force.

The opening pages of the Self-Study documented a deep ambivalence toward the school's traditional emphasis on parish ministry. The narrative history began with an explanation of the creeds and founding documents that had shaped Andover's early years; it painted a picture of the school as a polemical institution with a strong sectarian bent, with Andover the lone warrior against a host of theological foes. Over the years, both Andover and Newton had struggled to locate a higher aim: academic excellence, denominational service, or professional preparation. Finally with the 1931 merger came a clearer, simpler purpose. Andover Newton existed primarily to educate men and women for the parish ministry. The school's statement of purpose adopted in 1960 is worth quoting in full:

> The objective of the school is the professional education of learned Christian ministers, persons called of God and equipped by faith and discipline to assume places of responsible leadership in the life and work of the churches. The School seeks to provide leaders capable of bringing others to the saving knowledge of God in Jesus Christ, guiding their growth in the Christian life, directing wisely and effectively the tasks of the church, and ministering with intelligence and devotion to the needs of the community and the world.
>
> Students, teachers, and administrative staff are members of a community of work and worship, study, and service. A fellowship of common interests and loyalties defines the spirit of classroom and dormitory, of personal contact and organized activity. The School welcomes those who share its purposes and give promise of real competence in attaining them.

Five years later, in 1965, a new statement took a different tack. It omitted the first paragraph describing the "professional education of learned Christian ministers" and the "life and work of the churches," and substituted a more nuanced statement:

The purpose of Andover Newton is education for Christian ministry. Our task is the equipment of men and women to be ministers
of a ministering community. We are servants of the churches, and
we believe in what we serve. But our deeper commitment is to the
world to which the church is sent, and whether that world be a factory or an office, a campus or a hospital, a lovely village or a city
slum, we dare not despise what God has so loved.

"At least in the understanding of staff, faculty and students," the Self-
Study report concluded, "the School which once sought to shape round
pegs for the round holes of the ecclesiastical organization strives even
more to create pegs of such immediately essential, though irregular
shape that the church will recreate its holes to fit them." Andover Newton was neither a "training school for parish plumbers" nor an ivory
tower for disengaged academics. "Its distinction," the report continued, "lies in its restlessness." But the real difference was more fundamental, as Andover Newton shifted from a basically passive relationship with local churches to an active one. The institution's real but
largely unstated goal was to transform those very churches it once existed only to serve.[13]

The restlessness resonated among students as well. The Self-Study
report cited a growing dissatisfaction with the so-called practical side
of the curriculum, centering on nuts-and-bolts preparation for local
church work. Observing a "notable tendency for students to avoid
courses in the area generally classified as 'church and ministry,'" the report identified a "growing suspicion that traditional styles of education
for the parish ministry are no longer adequate for that type of ministry."
As always, complaints circled back to the field education requirement,
where the majority of students worked in local parishes as youth directors, with varying degrees of supervision and often as much as twenty
hours a week.[14]

The accrediting report, issued by the ATS committee in April 1967,
affirmed the reality of these problems. If students were spending twenty
hours a week in field work, another fifteen or so in a part-time job, and
the requisite forty-eight to fifty hours a week meeting academic require-

13. "Self-Study Report," pp. 10, 11-12.
14. "Self-Study Report," p. 44.

ments, then, the accreditors concluded, "something is obviously wrong." Both faculty and students had expressed concern about the courses being offered in the "professional field," citing low academic expectations and "the stamp of a trade school." The ATS visiting team also reported "considerable evidence of a division in the Seminary community between those who are 'academic' and those who are professional and 'practical' in orientation. This quickly emerged as one of the most serious problems at Andover Newton." The school's flagship psychology department looked to be at the root of the problem, as it dealt with interpersonal issues while the rest of the faculty's academic interests centered on history, social ethics, and the role of the church in the wider world. Indeed, to the accreditation team, the psychology department appeared to be operating "almost adjunct to the Seminary itself."[15]

The solution to the field education problem was on its way, even before the accreditation process was complete. In 1967, in an effort to bridge the divide between "practical" and "academic," George Peck had created a department of Church and Ministry; its first task was to reform the old field work model. After Walter Telfer came on as the Director of Field Education in 1969, he and Jerry Handspicker began experimenting with different approaches to supervision. They enlisted area churches as "teaching parishes," training pastors to mentor seminarians and keeping tabs on these relationships through regular "sector group" meetings of clergy and Andover Newton faculty. Students had other opportunities for evaluating themselves and their parish experience in group meetings led by D.Min. candidates. By the spring of 1975, Andover Newton's revised field education program became the new model for the other Boston area theological schools as well.[16]

Race

But in 1967, other problems loomed which would prove much more difficult to fix. The following year was an epic one in American history, an

---

15. "Accrediting Report on Andover Newton Theological School," April 1967; President's Office Files, ANTS archives.

16. Walter Telfer and Meredith Handspicker, "Teaching Parishes — Partners in Theological Education," *Andover Newton Quarterly* 17 (November 1976): 109-117.

"earthquake year" according to *Time Magazine* essayist Lance Morrow. January began with news of the Tet Offensive, a sudden acceleration of the war in Vietnam, bringing North Vietnamese forces to the gates of the American embassy in Saigon. As popular support for Lyndon Johnson's war began to crumble, student protests escalated. Columbia University erupted in April, into an open air melee involving the radical Students for a Democratic Society, black power groups on campus and in the surrounding urban neighborhood, conservative counter-protesters, and students innocently passing by — one of the "most terrifying moments in the history of American higher education."[17] Later that spring, as more student protests spanned the world, from Tokyo to Prague to Mexico City, the assassinations of Martin Luther King and Robert Kennedy further stunned the American public. The chaos and violence of Chicago's streets during the Democratic National Convention that summer further paved the way for the election of a conservative Republican president, Richard Nixon.

Within the greater Boston area, Andover Newton's hilltop location provided little insulation. In January 1968, the Social Action Committee endorsed the antiwar statement put together by the Student Association of Harvard Divinity School, and vowed to provide financial assistance to any students who chose to resist the draft; they requested faculty support for a class moratorium in response to Lyndon Johnson's "carpet bombing" of North Vietnam.

Andover Newton's African American students also began pressing the administration to address racial issues. The presenting issue, simple but important, was a request for financial support for a proposed Consultation for the Study of Theology in the Negro Church. As organizers McKinley Young and Charles Brown described it, the consultation "arose primarily out of the distress of the Black Seminarians at ANTS" over the inadequate preparation they were receiving for ministry in African American churches.[18]

The accusation that Andover Newton was not serving its black students well took some administrators by surprise. Andover Newton had

17. Helen Lefkowitz Horowitz, *Campus Life: Undergraduate Cultures from the End of the Eighteenth Century to the Present* (Chicago: University of Chicago Press, 1987), p. 234.

18. McKinley Young and Charles S. Brown to Dr. Evans Crawford Dean, Rankin Chapel, Howard University, 16 February 1968; President's Office Files, ANTS archives.

one African American on the faculty, Henry Brooks, and took pride in the active role of students and professors in the civil rights movement. During spring vacation in 1965, according to one report, "more students and faculty members could be found in Selma or the emergency churchmen's meeting in Washington or on Boston common than on campus."[19]

Andover Newton also boasted stellar black alumni. Benjamin Anderson ('42) was the chaplain at Smith College, Thomas Freeman ('42) was professor of philosophy at Texas Southern University, George Kelsey ('37) a professor of Christian ethics at Drew, Richard McKinney ('34) a professor of philosophy at Morgan State College in Baltimore, and Joseph R. Washington ('57) was chaplain and assistant professor of religion at Dickinson College in Carlisle, Pennsylvania.

Andover Newton's black alumni also played major roles in the civil rights movement. Claude Black, who graduated in 1943, was known throughout the South for his work in Texas during the 1950s and 1960s. As pastor of San Antonio's Mt. Zion First Baptist Church and chair of the National Baptist Convention's Social Action Committee, he was a public ally of Martin Luther King, A. Philip Randolph, Thurgood Marshall, and Ella Baker. Virgil Wood ('56) and Carl McCall ('63), both associated with the Blue Hill Christian Center, had played highly visible roles in the aftermath of the Harlem riots in 1964 and during the voter rights campaign conducted by the Southern Conference for Christian Leadership. Wood had chartered two planeloads of clergymen to attend the memorial service for James Reeb, a Boston clergyman and co-worker at the Blue Hill Christian Center, who had been killed during the violence at Selma.[20]

Moreover, in April 1968, in the wake of Martin Luther King's assassination, the school offered a special course on racism, allowing students to take incompletes in other classes in order to participate. Arrangements had been made for a permanent course on race relations, to be taught through the Boston Theological Institute (BTI) by Boston University professor Preston Williams. Andover Newton also created a Social Justice Fund to assist local organizations in the black community during the summer months, and to promote racial understanding in

---

19. "The Months after Selma," *Andover Newton News Reporter* 11 (June 1965): 4-5.
20. "The Months after Selma," pp. 4-5.

Newton. School officials determined to select an African American as commencement speaker for the close of the 1968-1969 school year.

But as the summer wore on into fall the administration's slow response to the Consultation proposal rankled the small group of black students at Andover Newton — only 10 out of some 540 students. They did not feel welcome on Newton's white suburban streets, where police were known to harass black students walking up the hill from the subway. Nor could they change the fact that Andover Newton was a predominantly white school with a curriculum designed to train white pastors for ministry in white churches.

Seminaries and churches all over the country were slow to admit the problem. As Baptist pastor Henry Mitchell wrote in the *Christian Century* in April 1967, "It is ironic that, for all its belated but strong commitment to the civil rights struggle, the church has applied virtually none of [those] fresh insights . . . into public worship and theological education." Though black churches worshiped with a different style and theological understanding, and expected a distinct leadership style from their pastors, most seminary curricula were designed to serve the young white man on the cover of the Andover Newton catalog. "The Negro student," Mitchell wrote, "is either born into or brainwashed into white religious culture or he is, *ipso facto,* a poor theological student, often asked not to return after the first or second year."[21] Indeed, according to a survey commissioned by the American Association of Theological Schools, "no seminary offered courses in black religious studies before 1968."[22]

On October 9, 1968, Andover Newton's African American students made their dissatisfaction public. President Pearson had his first inkling of a confrontation around 10:15 that morning, when a local news station called to inquire about a campus demonstration scheduled for 11:00, to be followed by a news conference later that afternoon. The students — listed as McKinley Young, G. Wesley Raney III, Gerald R. Hoskins, Roscoe D. Cooper, Jr., Ronald W. English, William McKinley Freeman, and Michael Thornton — presented Pearson with a list of

21. Henry H. Mitchell, "Key Term in Theological Education for the Negro: 'Compensatory,'" *Christian Century,* 26 April 1967, p. 530.

22. "Black Theological Education: Successes and Failures," *Christian Century,* 27 January 1971, p. 130.

grievances and demands, citing "systematic exclusion from the main stream of life at ANTS." At the top of that list was the school's lack of support for the Consultation on the Black Church, but the other charges went far deeper. Not only did Andover Newton "provide inadequate education for its students," with little or no teaching about black history or religion, but "the overall atmosphere at A.N.T.S.," they said, "is a racist one." "Chapel, worship, lectures, course offerings, institutional priorities, and campus life are still those of the traditional white, Anglo-Saxon, Protestant institution with no genuine concern for the small Black constituency."

The heart of the students' concern was with the curriculum. They demanded a series of reforms aimed at educating both whites and blacks: a "remedial course in Black history" for all faculty and students, an endowed chair in Black Churchmanship, and a student-faculty exchange with a black theological institution. More pointedly, they called for an exemption for all black students from the clinical program, so that they might "engage their talents and energies in more fruitful and relevant programs in the Black Community." The deadline for meeting all demands was set for November 4, 1968, less than one month away.[23]

The administration, clearly taken off guard by the confrontation, and by a *Boston Herald Traveler* headline labeling the school as "racist," scrambled to put together a response. The development department was pressed into raising funds for the Consultation, which was held November 6-9 at Boston University, and within the year, a scholarship program was under way. Andover Newton also briefly explored an exchange with a black seminary, Virginia Union. The biggest changes, however, made their way into the curriculum. By March 1969, the school catalog listed five black visiting faculty, including two professors from nearby colleges and three local pastors.[24]

---

23. "The Demands of the Concerned Black Students," October 9, 1968; President's Office Files, ANTS archives. A summary of the administration's response is found in *Andover Newton News and Notes,* 10 October 1968. See also "Blacks Say Seminary Is Racist," *Boston Herald Traveler,* 10 October 1968, C3.

24. "News Release, 3/3/69," President's Office Files; ANTS archives. Charles Adams, the pastor of the Concord Baptist Church in Boston, taught a new course on "The Black Church," and Theodore Lockhart of Boston College co-taught another on "Black Religion in America" with Earl Thompson. Andover Newton enlisted Preston Williams, assistant professor of social ethics at Boston University School of Theology, to teach on "Christian-

Unfortunately, the matter was far from settled. In fact, during the winter and spring of 1969, student grievances of all types began to surface. Dorm residents complained about uncomfortable beds and rules against keeping pets; the student association demanded a larger role in decision making. Hoping to siphon off some of the rising discontent, Pearson called for a community forum. But the meeting, which began in the early afternoon and lasted until well after midnight, raised a new set of issues, centering around black representation on the board of trustees. The marathon discussion ended with a series of resolutions, including one that required the board to achieve a 20 percent black membership within the year, with a list of four names to be added immediately.[25]

Over the next several weeks, the board of trustees became the target of spreading discontent, as Andover Newton's predominantly white student body took up the black students' cause. Until that point, racial injustice was a prominent issue on campus but tied to the civil rights campaign in the South or the violence and poverty of inner-city Boston. Now it was coming home to Andover Newton. Though the board agreed to add African American members, they were not willing to accept the names given to them by the students. In return, John Kernodle, the president of the student association — now publicly aligned behind the black students — presented them with a new demand for a 25 percent representation and a list of eleven new nominees whom the students said more fully represented predominantly black denominations or inner-city churches. In the end, however, the board elected five new African American members. Three were the original board nominees: Rev. Dr. George Kelsey, professor of Christian ethics at Drew University; Julien Steele, commissioner of the Department of Community Affairs for the state of Massachusetts; and Mrs. Oscar Phillips, a prominent

---

ity and Race Relations." Earl Lawson, the pastor of the Emmanuel Baptist Church in Malden, lectured in Jerry Handspicker's course on Worship, and Eddie O'Neal, the pastor of the Myrtle Baptist Church in Newton, lectured in the preaching course taught by Joe Williamson and Ed Linn.

25. The four in question were Earl Lawson, Eddie O'Neal, Lucius Walker, and McKinley Young. "To All Friends of Andover Newton," 15 May 1969, President's Office Files, ANTS archives. The other resolutions called for the creation of a student-faculty decision-making body with seats on the board of trustees, more opportunities for participation in the BTI, and the immediate suspension of the CPE requirement. See "Town Meeting" and "Town Meeting #2," n.d., ANTS Student Association Files, ANTS archives.

American Baptist laywoman. Two were from the list of four names given by the students: Lucius Walker, the executive director of the Interreligious Foundation for Community Organization; and the Rev. Eddie O'Neal from Newton's oldest African American congregation, the Myrtle Baptist Church.[26]

The emerging coalition of white and black students called for a full meeting of the board of trustees on May 12, with a petition demanding the addition of five more black trustees and greater student representation on the board. On Friday, May 9, the "Concerned Christians of the Andover Newton Community" held a protest rally, charging that the board had "failed to deal responsibly with white racism," by "failing to consult either with the leadership of the black church, leadership of the black community, or the student body" before electing their new members. "These actions," they declared, "continue Andover Newton's long history of white racism and paternalism." Saturday morning newspaper accounts showed black and white students, complete with obligatory beards and clipboards, standing around several trash cans, burning the "Opportunity" brochures created by the development department to showcase the school's black students.[27]

The week of May 11 was pivotal. President Pearson had called for a special meeting of the board of trustees for Monday morning, but by late Sunday, students were convinced that the meeting would not take place. With exams scheduled to begin on Tuesday, they circulated a petition announcing their intention to "refrain from any official activities of Andover Newton" until the board of trustees answered the demands of the Concerned Christians. Although the executive committee met early that Monday to consider restructuring to allow greater student participation, there was no board quorum for the 10:00 meeting. The students refused to participate and fifty-five of them promptly "liberated" the administrative offices in Dabney Hall.

---

26. The students' objections to the board nominees were laid out in a flyer, "Why All the Noise on Our Quiet Hill?" Student Association Files, ANTS archives. For a "bipartisan" synopsis of events, see "History of Events from May 7-14," ANTS Student Association Files, ANTS archives.

27. "Statement of the Concerned Christians of the Andover Newton Community," Student Association Files, ANTS archives; "Students Charge Andover 'White Racism,'" *Boston Herald Traveler,* 10 May 1969; George M. Collins, "Newton Campus Erupts," *Boston Globe,* 10 May 1969.

According to press accounts (where the number of protesters was estimated variously from seventy-five to ninety), the Andover Newton sit-in was relatively brief and well mannered. The students marched into the building and sat down in the entryway, effectively blocking passage in or out. Within a short time, they met briefly with Pearson, who agreed to call another public trustee meeting for the following day; by the end of the afternoon, most of the demonstrators had left, with only a small group remaining behind sitting in the lobby of Dabney Hall for four-hour shifts through the rest of the night.

But the Andover Newton confrontation was mild compared to dramatic events elsewhere. For most of the previous month, Harvard University had been virtually shut down by student unrest. The public learned of the uprising on Newton Hill during a week in which protests roiled Dartmouth, the City College of New York, and Union Seminary. At Union, some seventy-five student demonstrators occupied their administration building in support of black power activist James Forman's demand for $500 million in reparation payments.[28]

Supporters and alumni of Andover Newton were not pleased. "What kind of a Theological School are you running up there?" a "Congregationalist and Citizen" demanded of Pearson. "You and your school have gone down in the estimation of many thinking people who are loosing [sic] faith in you and your school." "I wonder where dedicated Christian students find so much time to sit on their cans," another angry constituent agreed, "and in Dabney Hall no less."[29]

The Tuesday evening "town meeting" of May 13, 1969, began at 7:30 and did not end until dawn the following morning. The often heated discussion involved students, faculty, and trustees, as well as alumni and members of Boston's black community. The students demanded the addition of ten more black members to the board of trustees, specifically men who would represent the concerns of the city's poor, urban African American churches. After lengthy discussion, the executive committee of the board of trustees voted to increase their number from forty to forty-five, thus making space for half of the students' nominees;

28. "Lawyers Seek Bail for Jailed Students," *Record American,* 13 May 1969; "Seminarians in Campus Revolt," *Herald Traveler,* 13 May 1969; "Andover Newton Students Seize Building," *Herald Traveler,* 13 May 1969; "Andover Seminarians Sit In," *Globe,* 13 May 1969.
29. Unsigned correspondence, President's Office Files, ANTS archives.

they also offered to allow the faculty and students to select two persons each to sit in on the nominating committee's deliberations.

As the night wore on, however, the Concerned Students realized that they had not achieved their goal: even with the additional five board members, added to the two already elected the previous week, they were still three seats shy of the 25 percent representation they had called for. But by then, weary trustees had begun to depart. The original group of twenty-three dwindled down to nine who refused to take any further action on their own. In anger and frustration, all but two of the black students and community representatives left the meeting.

The group who remained behind signed a final agreement at 3:15 A.M. The board members present committed themselves "in good faith" to add five more black trustees from the list generated by the school's African American students, before the end of September 1969. Two days later, representatives of Andover Newton's black students publicly endorsed the decision. As the school year drew mercifully to its close, the crisis looked to be nearing its end.[30]

Aftermath

In the years that followed, the goals set at the May 1969 town meeting proved difficult to realize. That October the faculty voted unanimously to discontinue a search for a position in World Religions, and to concentrate on adding black faculty. In short order, the faculty voted to invite Eddie O'Neal, who had been lecturing in homiletics courses, to join the Church and Ministry department; in 1975 they named Boykin Sanders, then still at work completing his Ph.D. in New Testament, to a five-year initial appointment. The board of trustees also set out to enroll twenty black students by the fall of 1971, and to raise $60,000 in scholarship aid.

Nevertheless, by the end of the decade, black enrollment remained very low. In 1976 only four African Americans completed their M.Div. degrees; a report from the Educational Affairs Committee in 1979 admitted that Andover Newton had "gradually ceased to be regarded as a major contributor to the ministry of the Black community." Once listed

---

30. "History of Events from May 7-14"; "Statement by the Andover Newton Black Community," 15 May 1969; President's Office Files, ANTS archives.

among the top three or four Northern schools for black students, Andover Newton had fallen below most of its BTI partners, including Harvard Divinity School, Gordon-Conwell, and Boston University's School of Theology.[31]

Institutional Pressures and Solutions

But Andover Newton's troubles, like those of many other independent Protestant seminaries during that climactic decade, did not end with race. By a variety of different measurements, they were financially and institutionally at risk. A survey of fifty-three seminaries in the mid-1960s found most in an institutionally untenable position: in spite of the Selective Service draft, enrollments were "erratic" and mostly declining — yet the schools had continued to hire an average of 31 percent more faculty members. In some schools the faculty/student ratio was a comfortable twelve to one. The average cost of educating seminarians was uncomfortably high, however, averaging $2,760 per student when the cost of a university education hovered around $2,100. But faculty salaries were not the reason why nearly half the schools in the survey reported deficit budgets: the average take-home pay of a seminary professor was $2,000 less than his university counterpart. The researchers declared that a sizeable number of American Protestant seminaries were in "de facto bankruptcy," continuing to spend far beyond their means. The main thrust of the survey was a warning against undertaking any new construction or program improvements that would increase debt. During the 1960s, the American Association of Theological Schools reinforced that point by regularly counseling independent seminaries to join forces with each other in "clusters" or other cooperative arrangements. By 1980, 44 percent of ATS schools had followed their advice.[32]

Andover Newton was no exception. In January 1968, it joined with six other theological schools in the Boston area — Boston College, Boston University School of Theology, Episcopal Divinity School, Har-

31. "Enrollment Trends at Andover Newton: A Report from the Educational Affairs Committee to the Board of Trustees," Board of Trustees Minutes, Supporting documents, 1978-79, ANTS archives.

32. "The Future of Protestant Seminaries: A Conference for Seminary Trustees" (Alban Institute, 1982), pp. 26-30.

vard Divinity School, Saint John's Seminary, and Weston Jesuit College — to form an "interdenominational theological university." With 167 full-time and 88 part-time instructors offering 918 courses, and combined library resources of 750,000 volumes, the Boston Theological Institute offered the city's seminary students an unparalleled educational opportunity. The seven institutions agreed to coordinate class schedules to allow for maximum cross-registration and eliminate unnecessary duplication. Students registered in one school could take courses in all of the others.[33]

Also in the 1970s, Andover Newton entered into a joint doctoral degree program with Boston College. The program immediately boosted the offerings of both schools, particularly in medieval studies, where both were strong. But more importantly, the joint program was an ecumenical venture that followed logically from Andover Newton's role in the BTI.

Andover Newton continued to expand other academic programs as well. In 1971 the faculty approved two doctoral degrees, a D.Min. with a concentration in psychology and clinical studies and one in church and ministry. Students could also take additional work beyond the M.Div. (which replaced the traditional Bachelor of Divinity in 1971) for an S.T.M., a more academic degree to complement the practice-oriented D.Min. The additional fourth internship year was dropped.

In spite of all these changes, Andover Newton struggled with difficult financial realities. In 1952, with a total enrollment of 247 students and 24 full and part-time faculty, the school expenses ran upwards of $211,000. Twenty years later, in 1972, Andover Newton had almost doubled the number of students on campus, with 421 degree candidates; these were supplemented by an additional 297 cross-registered or summer school students. Though the number of faculty also doubled to 48 members, the faculty-student ratio grew from ten to one to fifteen to one. Total expenses, however, grew by a factor of ten, reaching $2.1 million. Though tuition had grown from $200 in 1951-52 to $1,300 in 1971-72, by 1971 the operating deficit was closing in on $60,000.[34]

33. "Seminary Cooperation in Greater Boston," *Christian Century* (June 1968): 76-78; Brian Boisen, B.D. Thesis, 1994; "Boston Theological Institute Formed," *Today's Ministry: A Report for Andover Newton* 3 (January 1968): 1-2.

34. Paul R. Dunn, "Financial Crunch Reaches Andover Newton," *Today's Ministry* (November 1971): 8-9.

Gender

From 1970 to 1975 Andover Newton encountered another series of profound changes. In the 1971-72 school year the entering class of 65 students included only one woman, barely 1 percent of the total. Two years later, the number had shot up to twenty five, and women comprised 41 percent of the entering class. By the fall of 1974 they accounted for one-quarter of the total enrollment.

The changes may have appeared sudden, but they were long in coming. Women had been taking classes at the Newton Theological Institution since the late nineteenth century, largely by virtue of their role as missionaries in training. Newton established the Master of Religious Education as a professional degree for women in 1919, opening the B.D. degree at the same time. The Dean of Women at the time, Priscilla Fowle, had a Ph.D. from Radcliffe College. Echoing the words of the popular hymn "Just as I am, young, strong, and free," the catalog of 1923 underlined the fact that the Newton woman student was "free to choose for her profession or her life work any one of a large number of fields. . . . Opportunities for work and service are open to her in every direction as they never were before."[35]

Throughout the 1930s and 1940s, women enrolled regularly in Newton's M.R.E. program, and occasionally received the B.D. In 1933-34, for example, out of a total of 170 students, 23 were women in the M.R.E. program, with 5 pursuing the B.D, and 8 "unclassified" — over 21 percent of the student body. The onset of the economic Depression cut quickly into these ranks; in churches under financial pressure, the female Director of Religious Education was very often the first employee to be let go. But in a few years, as World War II began affecting male enrollments, the Andover Newton catalog included a special statement that "Women are welcomed as candidates for all degrees." Responding to the growing popularity of "release time" classes for elementary school children, the catalog encouraged women to "pursue studies in the field of Christian education." For some women already trained as public school teachers, the program was a second career option, qualifying them to teach in "week-day schools of reli-

35. "The Newton Theological Institution School of Religious Education for Women," *Institution Bulletin* 15 (1923): 11.

gion."[36] By 1951, Andover Newton had 144 male and 33 female students; close to 20 percent of the total student body were women.

Ironically, as the major white denominations began to open ordination to women in the 1950s, women began to disappear from Andover Newton's campus, a trend repeated around the country. The decision to discontinue the M.R.E. degree signaled the end of an era, and a shift away from the traditional female track in local church work. With the influx of married students after World War II, women maintained a presence on campus, but farther from the classroom. During the 1950s, the "Divinity Dames" emerged as the primary women's organization on the Hill, a club for faculty and student wives and female students. Its purpose was social — the Dames sponsored everything from informal dinners to hat designing demonstrations — but also religious, featuring opportunities for prayer and spiritual retreat.

The rapid emergence of women students at Andover Newton was, of course, part of a national trend. By the 1980s, female enrollment in Protestant seminaries was approaching 30 percent of the total, and by the decades end, women clergy would comprise 10 percent of the profession. Some of the most dramatic changes occurred in northern mainline churches like the United Church of Christ, where women would become the majority of seminarians by the 1990s. Between the mid-1970s and mid-1980s, the number of ordained Presbyterian women increased by 310 percent.[37]

Andover Newton attracted a steady array of talented female faculty. The first woman appointed to a full-time tenure-track position at Andover Newton was the biblical scholar Phyllis Trible in 1971. Already a leading figure, she published her landmark book, *God and the Rhetoric of Sexuality,* shortly before leaving for a post at Union Seminary in 1979.

---

36. *Andover Newton Theological School, Maintained by Newton Theological Institute and Andover Theological School, Catalog for 1942-1943* (Newton Centre, MA, 1942), pp. 20-21.

37. Mark Chaves, *Ordaining Women: Culture and Conflict in Religious Organizations* (Cambridge: Harvard University Press, 1997), p. 1. See time line in *Religious Institutions and Women's Leadership: New Roles Inside the Mainstream,* ed. Catherine Wessinger (Columbia: University of South Carolina Press, 1996), pp. 347-97; Laura S. Olson, Sue E. S. Crawford, and James L. Guth, "Changing Issue Agendas of Women Clergy," *Journal for the Scientific Study of Religion* 39 (June 2000): 140-153. For a useful overview, see Gary Ward, "Introductory Essay: A Survey of the Women's Ordination Issue," in *The Churches Speak On: Women's Ordination,* ed. J. Gordon Melton (Detroit: Gale Research, 1991), pp. xiii-xxxv.

Emily Hewitt arrived from Union in 1972 to teach Christian education, replacing Wesner Fallaw. An ambitious scholar and a committed feminist, Hewitt was one of the "Philadelphia Eleven," the women who were irregularly ordained for the Episcopal priesthood in 1974, before that denomination formally approved female priests. She left for Harvard Law School and a legal career soon after, eventually ending up on the judge's bench. Maria Harris, a former Roman Catholic nun, came to fill Hewitt's spot, and enjoyed a long and productive time on the faculty before leaving for Fordham University in 1986, a well-known figure in her field. In 1975, another Episcopalian with a specialty in late medieval Catholicism, Eleanor McLaughlin, replaced the retiring Gerald Cragg. She was joined in 1982 by Elsie McKee, a prolific Calvin scholar. In 1976 Jane Cary Peck, a southerner with a scholarly focus on race relations, arrived to teach social ethics.

Andover Newton took special pains to adapt to these changes. In the fall of 1973 the United Church of Christ Task Force on Women chose Andover Newton's Department of Church and Ministry to test a model program for female seminarians. The year-long curriculum included two semesters of seminars dealing with the specific vocational and intellectual issues facing women students, followed up by a summer of supervised ministry experience. The program emphasized a team approach, with shared leadership and many opportunities for serious theological conversation. It addressed directly the specific concerns facing that first generation of female seminarians: isolation, invisibility, powerlessness, and vocational identity.[38]

Though the program was counted a success, it brought to light some important problems. Citing the "enormous diversity" among the participants, the report noted their "sense of struggle and lack of clarity" as they attempted to deal with theological questions. "It is one thing," the report said, "to debate different views of eschatology from within the perspective that one has been saved. It is quite another to explore the meaning of a theological doctrine when one is asking, 'Does this have anything to say to me?'" Many women were arriving at seminary deeply "ambivalent about the Christian tradition and their place in it." In many cases, the study of Christian theology and church history brought

---

38. Barbara A. Gerlach and Emily C. Hewitt, "Training Women for Ministry," *Andover Newton Quarterly* 17 (November 1976): 133-142.

women students face to face with centuries of misogynist thought and practice; instead of confirming a sense of call, seminary education made it problematic.[39]

Ambivalence about one's sense of call did not originate with women students. Already in 1962, Roy Pearson (then dean) and student association members talked at length about the lack of "spiritual life" on the Hill. "Dean Pearson noted that there has been a decided increase in recent years of men who come to seminary in search of the Christian faith, rather than as convinced and dedicated disciples," the association minutes noted. Citing "unrest and dissatisfaction" spreading among the student body, both Pearson and the student leaders wisely conceded that "there is no single answer to this problem."[40] A psychological assessment of Andover Newton's incoming class in 1974 and 1975 found widespread vocational confusion. Barely a third of the students demonstrated an "average degree of enthusiasm for traditional ministerial activities"; the majority did not seem to have strong vocational interests at all, beyond a desire to "work with people."[41]

The results were broadly typical of many college and graduate students pursuing careers in the wake of the 1960s and at the cusp of the lean economic times to follow. Nor were they surprising, given the studied vagueness of many mainline Protestant churches during those decades. Furthermore, they reflected some of the natural hesitations felt by women students undertaking seminary training for the first time in large numbers.

By the end of the 1970s, Andover Newton was a fundamentally different place than it had been in 1965. The protest instituted by black students in the winter of 1968 set in motion a series of changes that would challenge the seminary for years to come. Andover Newton students and faculty achieved a larger say in the running of the school; the faculty and student body became less male, and in a more limited way less white. But the questions raised by the black students in 1968 only became more pointed and difficult as Andover Newton became less

39. Gerlach and Hewitt, "Training Women for Ministry," p. 141.

40. Student Association Minutes, 5 November 1962, Student Organization Files, ANTS archives.

41. John Robert Harris [Visiting Lecturer in Tests and Measurements], "A Report on Psychological Assessment of the Junior Class at Andover Newton," President's Office Files, ANTS archives.

male and more female. The church, once assumed to be the largely unquestioning partner of the theological seminary, was now under the scrutiny of students who did not take its existence for granted. Moreover, during a time of deepening financial scarcity and startling personal loss, the last two decades of the twentieth century would prove to be some of the most challenging in Andover Newton's history.

At bottom, the turmoil of the 1960s and 1970s was not just unavoidable — it was necessary. The long, weary "town hall" meetings in the spring of 1969 and the years of institutional soul-searching that followed were acts of faithfulness, by people working to keep Andover Newton true to its Christian calling. It is not surprising that issues of race and gender provoked long and painful discussions up on Institution Hill: after all, those inequalities were centuries in the making, rooted deep in the past history of Christian churches and of the United States itself. An easy solution would have been a foolish one. What is remarkable about those years is the moral persistence of Andover Newton's students, faculty, and administrators, their willingness to open up those ancient evils for a new round of honest confrontation. They could have chosen another way — certainly plenty of other institutions found ways to circumvent public protests during the 1960s and 1970s. The fact that they did not is an important part of Andover Newton's history, and a central piece of its emerging identity in the 1980s and 1990s.

CHAPTER NINE

Andover Newton's Turn of the Century

⸺෴⸺

Thisis chapter is more a series of reflections than it is a true final episode, covering some key events of the 1980s and 1990s. A safe strategy for a historian, perhaps — but also a respectful distance. In a very
real way, the recent past is still the property of the people who are living
through it day by day.

Much of the narrative is familiar ground. The last two decades of the
twentieth century were historically difficult years for mainline
Protestant churches, and seminaries quickly felt the impact of shrink-
ing budgets and dwindling spiritual morale. Like most other theological schools unaffiliated with a university or college, Andover Newton
could not take its survival for granted.

Every school faced those years with different resources from the
past. In Andover Newton's case, a long history of institutional partnerships enabled the school to take a leading role in establishing new
ones, first with its neighboring Christian seminaries in the Boston
Theological Institute (BTI) and ultimately with Hebrew College and
Rabbinical School in 1995. New forms of outreach, including distance
learning and online instruction, continued the school's historic role as
an innovator in theological education. Andover Newton's public struggles with racial justice during the 1960s also became a central shaping
force for institutional decisions in the 1980s and 1990s, culminating
with the appointment of David Shannon, its first African American
president, in 1991.

But some challenges of those years were unprecedented. Andover

Newton's story of the past several decades is in many ways a typical mainline Protestant one, of setbacks in some areas and progress in others. But in this case, the narrative is punctuated by personal loss. The deeper story of the 1980s and 1990s is Andover Newton's response to the deaths of important, and in some cases beloved, colleagues and friends — in many ways still an unfinished story, but still an instructive one.

The Eighties

The 1980s dawned gloomily for mainline Protestant churches. While the political world celebrated a new "morning in America" with the landslide election of Ronald Reagan, the old line white denominations — United Methodists and American Baptists, Episcopalians, Lutherans, northern Presbyterians, and the United Church of Christ — faced a steady, demoralizing drain of church members. As two eminent sociologists concluded in 1988, "The liberal Protestant community is mired in a depression, one that is far more serious and deeper than it has suffered at any time in this century."[1]

If anything, the seminary world felt even more on the defensive, its malaise deepening under an avalanche of cold hard facts. During the 1970s, as denominational support dried up, tuition had increased by an average of 118 percent, outpacing even the consumer price index of that inflationary decade. The costs of seminary education had grown even more quickly, and nearly all schools found themselves facing debilitating financial scenarios. Indeed, in the ten years before 1981, fourteen seminaries had closed down for good; another fifteen had survived only by merging with other equally fragile partners. With budgets increasingly tuition driven, mainline seminaries turned away relatively few applicants, fueling complaints that churches were getting students who did not have the requisite grades for law or medical school.

Seminary faculty were also feeling pinched. After the heyday of the 1960s, when salaries declined across the academic world, professors in

---

1. Wade Clark Roof and William McKinney, *American Mainline Religion* (New Brunswick: Rutgers University Press, 1988), p. 150.

theological schools bore a particularly heavy burden. Though enrollments had increased by 71 percent during the 1970s, and new degree programs multiplied equally rapidly, the number of seminary faculty grew by only 6 percent. It is not surprising that optimism was in short supply. As one report concluded in 1981, seminaries were "facing the start of the new decade in much the same way they faced the beginning of the '70s — hard-pressed and anxious about survival."[2]

Andover Newton faced the same hard cold dawn; in many ways, its passage through the Reagan years and beyond was not particularly unusual. The school entered the 1980s under severe financial constraints, and though a regimen of hard work and discipline lifted these temporarily, difficult times were not over. Rising faculty workload and questions about academic standards flowed together into a constant undertow of worry. The end of one leadership crisis always seemed to bring another in its wake. For Andover Newton, as for many other mainline Protestant institutions, the late twentieth century was a jarring and painful time.

When Gordon Torgersen succeeded Roy Pearson as president in September 1979, he spent his first few months trying to grasp the scale of Andover Newton's financial difficulties. Warned that the deficit for that year might reach $50,000, he soon discovered it had actually surpassed $200,000, more than doubling the shortfall of the previous year. With the endowment declining and alumni support painfully small, around 15 percent of Andover Newton graduates, a combination of aging buildings and escalating energy costs left the budget mired in red ink. When Torgersen approached philanthropic foundations for help, he received a painful truth: no institution with a history of deficit budgets was eligible for grant money.[3]

Emergency measures quickly went into effect. Torgersen instituted a three-phase "crash program," a vigorous fundraising campaign aimed at raising four million dollars to counter the financial slide. While the development department and the board of trustees worked to right the ship on the income side, Torgersen imposed strict budget-

---

2. Christopher Walters-Bugbee, "Hard-pressed and Anxious: Seminaries Face the '80s," *Christian Century*, 4-11 February, 1981, p. 102.

3. Mid-Winter Trustees' Meeting, 9 February 1983, Board of Trustees, supporting documents, ANTS archives.

ary controls on students and faculty. Everything from the use of the Xerox machine and departmental stationery to lights in the classrooms and funds for faculty travel underwent close scrutiny. The *Andover Newton Quarterly* ceased publication; both the president and the faculty had to forego annual raises. Even so, difficult budget cuts loomed. Torgersen's emergency measures required eliminating two faculty positions in the middle of the school year, including that of Boykin Sanders, the recently hired black New Testament scholar.[4]

Amazingly, by the end of Torgersen's tenure in 1983, the financial ship was upright and looked to be moving ahead. Against the "somewhat grim and pessimistic" events of the years previous, he told the trustees in a departing memo, ". . . we have good reason to move into the future on a note of optimism and hope."[5]

In many ways, the positive outlook was justified. Even in the midst of distress on the ledger books, Andover Newton was finding ways to prosper. In 1982 the school formalized its relationship with the Laity Project, an effort that had been launched in the late 1970s, later renamed the Center for the Ministry of the Laity. The leader of this effort was Dick Broholm, a management consultant with ten years of experience studying the ways in which laypeople brought their faith into the secular workplace. He arrived at Andover Newton in 1977 and immediately inspired joint efforts by faculty and clergy from area churches, aimed at lowering the bar between pew and pulpit. In Broholm's initial five-year project, six Massachusetts churches participated in a Model Congregation Task Force, engaging faculty and students in conversation with laypeople hoping to integrate their Sunday faith with weekday issues on the job.[6]

New leadership also brought new life. In the fall of 1983, George Peck became Andover Newton's president, bringing fresh energy after the lean years under Torgersen. Peck's sense of Andover Newton's past and his hopes for its future were clearly evident in his optimistic, care-

---

4. The other position was that of speech professor Edmund Linn, who successfully sued Andover Newton in 1987 for age discrimination, with a jury award of over half a million dollars.

5. Mid-Winter Trustees Meeting, 9 February 1983.

6. John S. Hoffman, "The Laity Project: What's That?" *The Lantern: A Student Journal of News, Arts, and Opinion at Andover Newton* 2 (February 1982): 10, 12; Gabriel Fackre, "Personal Reflections on the Laity Project," idem, p. 11.

fully worded inaugural address. Peck declared his intention to make Andover Newton a "transpositional" institution, borrowing a theological term from Asian liberationist scholar C. S. Song. That meant that the school would learn to embody its old truth in a new setting; it would continue to maintain its old reality with integrity, but would view it from a different angle, under a new light. "It is not surprising," Peck said, "that in the 19th and 20th centuries we became, as both Andover and Newton, then as Andover Newton, an institution strongly involved with intersections and re-embodiments of all kinds." All through its storied history, "this school has done more than its share to help transpose a faith and a tradition into different keys under a great many different conditions both at home and abroad."

Peck proposed several key initiatives. The basic curriculum needed attention, as always, but the critical need focused on Andover Newton's ties with the surrounding world. He urged more integration of the Center for the Ministry of the Laity into the life of the school, a strong relationship with minority churches. In order to become a "seminary for all the people," Peck said, "we must break out from our predominantly white, suburban, middle-class orientation." He also urged a recovery of Andover Newton's missionary past, "as the seminary of Adoniram Judson, and of Samuel Newell, and the great missionary movement of the last 175 years." The school's historical legacy required it to seek "a contemporary version of a role which once dominated the spirit of both the institutions which make up our heritage." Finally, Peck proposed a new round of discussions about the relationship between theology and the arts. "Do I perpetuate a *non sequitur* by throwing in that issue unannounced at the end? Surely not," he declared. Transposition was not just a social or theological matter, but also opened the way for "an encounter with the world of the imagination." Without a sense of creative passion, asked Peck, "how can we expect that the Word will become truly our flesh and the flesh of the world?"[7]

Peck's new academic dean, Orlando Costas, embodied much of Andover Newton's emerging new identity. Costas, a native Puerto Rican with roots deep into both the liberationist and evangelical Latino communities, was also named as the Judson Professor of Missiology. With a doctorate from the Free University of Amsterdam, and a formidable

---

7. George Peck, "The Seminary as Transpositional: An Inaugural Address," Board of Trustees, Supporting documents, 1984.

publishing record — some thirteen books by the end of his career — Costas cut a strong profile on the old Newton Center campus.

Within just a few years, Andover Newton began to attract Hispanic students. An Urban Ministries program, established in 1986, funded scholarships for fifteen Latino students, provided new courses, and conducted programs and workshops for lay leaders in a network of seventy-five Hispanic churches. The Center also helped facilitate Clinical Pastoral Education placements for Spanish-speaking students and churches. In subsequent years, Andover Newton brought in Hispanic faculty — Robert Pazmino in religious education, Samuel Solivan in theology. The Orlando Costas Hispanic and Latin American Ministries Program, established in 1989, further institutionalized the school's work with the rapidly expanding Hispanic community in the United States.

Andover Newton broadened in other ways during the 1980s. By 1986, Andover Newton students included seven African Americans, thirteen Latinos, and eighteen international students — about 15 percent of the total student body. A Committee on Racism, formed in 1982, presented a thorough critique of the school's recruitment, curriculum, and student placement to the board of trustees in 1984, calling for a permanent Committee on Institutional Racism, and a commitment to affirmative action that would bring all minority enrollments into line with their proportion in the general population. The Kelsey-Owens Black Ministries program was established in 1989.[8]

Both Peck and Costas attempted to till the fruitful middle ground between mainline and evangelical Protestant communities. During a time in which the "culture wars" between social conservatives and liberals were nearing their height, this was no mean feat. A profile of Peck in *Christianity Today* depicted Andover Newton as broadly Reformed and characterized by a "warm evangelical spirit." Whether or not the characterization was true — privately Peck thought it overdrawn — the ecumenical impulse was clear. "The last thing we need is another round of party squabbles," Peck told the evangelical magazine's readership. "We don't want to belong to a party. We want to affirm the gospel and get on with God's work in the world."[9] Similarly, Costas pushed against

8. "Committee on Racism, Report to the Board of Trustees," Board of Trustees, Supporting Documents, 1984.

9. Steve Crowe, "A Stray Seminary Wants to Find Its Conservative Roots," *Christianity Today*, 16 September 1983, pp. 38, 39.

the simple dualisms that animated so much of the religious world in that decade. "He did not envision a Latin American seminary in the confines of a white institution," one observer noted. "He came with a much broader vision: a multiracial and multicultural seminary in which other languages besides Hebrew, Greek, and English would be spoken." Costas was by his own declaration neither liberal nor conservative; a friend later recalled, the "constant and dis-respectful way in which he crossed frontiers was a call to define ourselves without fear." This was the message of Costas' last published work, *Liberating News: A Theology of Contextual Evangelization,* what he called a "radical evangelical" perspective from the margins of power in American society.[10]

Rainy Season

Even as optimism began to gather, Andover Newton, like nearly every Protestant mainline seminary, still faced daunting institutional problems. During the 1980s, the biggest enrollment perplexity was not race or gender, but the growing number of part-time and commuting students, many of them older adults pursuing a second career in the ministry. By the end of the 1984-1985 school year, the ratio of full to part-time was 186 to 269. It would only grow in following years, creating a financial lag in tuition revenue without decreasing the administrative and faculty workload. By the end of the 1990s, 90 percent of Andover Newton's students were commuters and over half, about 240 out of 458 total, were part-time.

To an old institution like Andover Newton, with roots nearly as deep as the nation itself, few practical problems were truly brand-new. The money supply rises and falls, students appear and disappear, faculties come and go with steady regularity; adjustments are made and the institution moves on. But every once in a while, a set of circumstances becomes extraordinary. Looking back in 1998, Andover Newton's faculty wryly remembered the late 1980s and early 1990s as the seminary's "rainy season."[11]

10. "In Tribute: Friends, Colleagues Offer Tributes to Orlando Costas," ANTS archives.

11. "Report of a Comprehensive Visit to Andover Newton Theological School, Newton Centre, Massachusetts, for Association of Theological Schools in the United States and Canada and New England Association of Schools and Colleges," 1998, p. 2.

Beginning in the fall of 1987, Andover Newton endured a series of painful losses. Orlando Costas died of stomach cancer on November 5, 1987. George Peck memorialized him as a "shooting star," who had in his short tenure fundamentally shaped the school's future direction. And just months later in May 1988, Andover Newton lost the chair of its board of trustees, Frank Parrish, a man with simple tastes and a long history of generosity to the school. "More than once," Peck eulogized, "when I went to breakfast with him burdened by something we needed to do but lacked the means, I came away with the promise that we could go ahead because Frank Parrish would make sure the bill was paid, if not by someone else by him." "He loved to give," Peck said, "and he did it munificently."[12]

The next blow to hit the school was the death of George Peck. He died of a massive heart attack on January 17, 1990, just days after returning from a sabbatical in Czechoslovakia. After six months of observing first-hand the radical changes taking place in eastern Europe, Peck was ready to expand Andover Newton's global reach into new directions. His death was, as one Baptist educator said, "a dreadful, terrible loss to the seminary, to theological education and to his colleagues."[13]

Later that year, Andover Newton endured another bereavement: social ethicist Jane Cary Peck died of cancer on September 10, 1990, just months after her diagnosis. "Many of us are still shaking our heads in disbelief that Jane Cary has died," one of her students wrote. Peck's combination of scholarly gift and personal warmth made her a popular figure in the classroom, and for many students a distinct personal loss. "I came to [her] class knowing nothing," this young woman said, "now I have a million questions."[14]

The Nineties

Andover Newton's accreditation report from the Association of Theological Schools in 1998 included both good news and bad. Recognizing the "extraordinary amount of stress and pain" the school had

---

12. George Peck, "Reflections in Gratitude: Frank Parrish, May 4, 1988," ANTS archives.
13. American Baptist News, 17 January 1990, ANTS archives.
14. "Remembrance of Jane Cary Peck," ANTS archives.

endured over the past eleven years, the report found much to praise. The visiting committee found that at all levels, Andover Newton's employees "expressed great loyalty to and affection for the school." In its daily life the campus "breathe[d] a spirit of freedom of inquiry," and a reinvigorated board of trustees took to its task with new seriousness of purpose.[15]

Andover Newton's faculty were also a source of pride. In 1998, the Templeton Foundation recognized theologian Mark Heim's course in the relation of science and theology as one of twelve best in the field. His ecumenical interests, teaching experiences in India and China, and provocative theological work (including that old Andover question about the possibility of salvation outside Christianity), brought international attention to the school. A theology and the arts program, approved in 1996 and implemented by historians Robin Jensen and Mark Burrows, opened whole new spiritual and intellectual ground.

By 1998 the protracted struggle of the 1960s and 1970s over racial justice had also born fruit. "The school rightly points to diversity as one of its chief values," the ATS report confirmed, noting the successful efforts of the Kelsey-Owens and Costas scholarship programs and the institution of a required course, "Engaging Racism, Sexism, and Other Forms of Oppression." A growing number of international programs also brought in students from abroad, especially in the academically oriented theological degree program, or S.T.M. Andover Newton's teaching ranks also mirrored the changes in the student population: of the twenty-three full-time faculty members, three were African American, three Hispanic, and one Asian-American. Eight of the total were women.[16]

The ATS report also applauded the theological diversity on Andover Newton's campus, recognizing that the school was in many ways testing the limits of that commitment. "While the overall ethos of the seminary is that of liberal, mainline Protestantism," the student body included growing numbers of Unitarian Universalists as well as conservative evangelicals. Unstated in the report, but certainly significant in this respect, was the growing number of gay and lesbian students on campus, preparing to test not only Andover Newton's but the mainline church's limits of diversity. With nearly all of its students living off campus,

15. "Report of a Comprehensive Visit," pp. 5, 6, 16.
16. "Report of a Comprehensive Visit," pp. 3, 12.

drawing emotional or spiritual support from many different sources, Andover Newton was "more a community of communities than a community itself."[17]

In 1998 Andover Newton was struggling for common ground on a number of fronts. The most difficult and public was the resignation of the school's first African American president, David Shannon, in 1994. His arrival in 1991 loomed bright with promise, a capstone to years of work toward racial reconciliation begun in the 1960s. But whether the appointment was premature or ill-considered, it did not take; after only three years, Shannon departed, leaving behind an institution in turmoil.

Under interim president George Sinclair and his successor Ralph Eliot, Andover Newton's leaders worked diligently to right the ship. In 1995, under the incoming president Benjamin Griffin, the trustees declared a "state of financial exigency," recognizing that heavy budget deficits, increasing fourfold between 1989-90 and 1997-98, threatened the school's future stability. The ATS visitors underlined the seriousness of the situation, voicing a "deep concern about the long term health and viability of the institution" if significant changes did not occur. Even with major cuts in staff positions and institutional resources, especially in the library, stretched to the breaking point, the financial situation was dire.[18]

Perhaps not surprisingly, Andover Newton's leadership struggled to articulate workable goals for the future. A detailed strategic plan, written in 1992, fell under the weight of events during the next few years. After a period of "profound and pain-filled administrative change," the school had shifted toward what the ATS visitors described as a "reactive mode."[19]

Prospect

But this not where the story ends. For one thing, the broader picture of American religious life was changing by the late 1990s. The old truisms

17. "Report of a Comprehensive Visit," pp. 7-8.
18. "Report of a Comprehensive Visit," pp. 19-29.
19. "Report of a Comprehensive Visit," pp. 37, 38.

of mainline decline began to give way to more nuanced understandings of their historical role. Moderate and liberal Protestant churches began to rediscover Christian practices of prayer, hospitality, and witnessing; they found new ways to address once-polarizing issues about the family.[20] Their old position at the center of American culture was surely gone forever, but mainline churches were still finding ways to reinvent themselves.

Andover Newton experienced similar growth in new directions. In 1995 Ben Griffin forged a partnership with Hebrew College and Rabbinical School, allowing the two schools to share physical space at the top of the old Institution Hill. The arrangement not only helped balance Andover Newton's financial ledger; it also introduced both schools to the intellectual and spiritual challenges of interfaith dialogue. Journeys on the Hill began as an interfaith dialogue for students on practical issues of congregational leadership; the Interreligious Center for Public Life drew together leaders from the Christian, Jewish, and Muslim communities to reflect on pressing public issues. Andover Newton and Hebrew College also began to offer classes co-taught by faculty from both schools, an effort which eventually led to a joint certificate in Intercommunal Leadership.

The arrival of new president Nick Carter also brought renewed focus. The board of trustees announced their new strategic plan for the school with a clear and ambitious opening statement: "The model for graduate theological education in North America was conceived at Andover Newton and now we are about to break it." Defining Andover Newton as a "liberally oriented, tradition-grounded institution," the plan emphasized ministry to "progressive congregations" through "creative alliances" and the nurture of "outstanding men and women." "No border or ocean," the school's leadership stoutly declared, "will limit our search for partners to help achieve this vision."[21]

---

20. See, for example, Dorothy Bass, *Practicing Our Faith: A Way of Life for Searching People* (San Francisco: Jossey-Bass, 1997); Diana Butler Bass, *The Practicing Congregation: Imagining a New Old Church* (Herndon, VA: Alban Institute, 2004); Don Browning, Bonnie Miller-McLemore, Pamela Couture, K. Brynolf Lyon, and Robert Franklin, *From Culture Wars to Common Ground: Religion and the American Family Debate* (Louisville: Westminster/John Knox Press, 1997).

21. "Andover Newton Theological School Board of Trustees Strategic Plan, Adopted December 14, 2005," http://www.ants.edu., accessed 7/26/2007.

In many ways, the document made deft use of Andover Newton's past. Since the earliest days of Andover Seminary, when Old Calvinists and New Divinity men decided it was better to forge a working compromise than to press for theological purity, creative alliances have been essential to survival. Since the days of the Haystack prayer meeting and the missionary diaspora of Newton and Andover students all across the world, international outreach has been a way of life. Since the days when Moses Stuart and Alvah Hovey toiled in their respective classrooms, bringing the latest scholarly knowledge to young ministers in training, respect for intellectual questions and regard for tradition have shaped the history of both schools. Whether or not Andover Newton will in fact inaugurate a new era in seminary education is, of course, a story not yet written — but there is not doubt that, historically speaking at least, the school has an undisputed claim to that larger purpose.

Undeniably, as it approached its bicentennial year, Andover Newton moved into uncharted territory. The shifting contours of modern American religious life were also evident in Andover Newton's student body. By 2007, they numbered 390, with well over half of them (62 percent) women. No longer a simple coalition of Baptists and Congregationalists, Andover Newton was training students from thirty-five different denominations. The largest group (around 42 percent) hailed from the United Church of Christ (UCC), making it the single largest concentration of UCC students in the country. The number of Baptist students was somewhat smaller, around 12 percent, but even that figure made Andover Newton one of that denomination's larger source of trained pastors. The student body also included smaller numbers of Methodists (9 percent), Episcopalians (11 percent), and Roman Catholics (3 percent); most remarkably, however, some 16 percent of Andover Newton students were Unitarian Universalists (UU). Andover Newton in 2007 was home to the largest concentration of UU students in the country.

By some measurements, especially this last, Andover Newton has distinctly parted ways with its past. One can see the old theological imprecations of the Andover creed, against Unitarians and Arminians, Catholics and "Mahometans" visibly transgressed just by a casual walk across the campus. The largely unstated assumptions of nineteenth- and early-twentieth-century seminary life, that students were to be male and heterosexual, have also fallen by the wayside. In this sense, the past two hundred years of history have relatively little to do with the modern rhythms of Andover's campus in the opening decades of the twenty-first century. But historical legacies are tricky things, and rarely obvious. The various meanings drawn from Andover Newton's long past require a bit more space for reflection.

The Andover Newton Legacy

———◦◦◦———

At the far end of the reading room of the Congregational Library, set high on Boston's Beacon Hill, marble busts of Alphaeus Hardy and Edwards Park hold down two adjacent corners. The Library, where I work and where much of this book was written, is, much like Andover Seminary, a testimony to the intellectual aspirations of nineteenth-century Congregationalists. These folks did not worry much about their place in history; by the mid-nineteenth century it seemed all but guaranteed. The tall graceful windows in the reading room overlook Boston's famous Granary Burial Ground, the final resting place of many Congregational worthies, and the Park Street Church, organized the year after Andover, in 1809. It is not hard to imagine that both Park and Hardy would find their ancient surroundings, though recently transformed by the hum of computers and telephones, eminently fitting.

But they would not necessarily enjoy their immediate company. At the height of the Andover controversy in the 1880s, Park and Hardy were adversaries. Park led the charge against the accused professors, certain that they were destroying not only his legacy as Abbot Professor but Andover's orthodox underpinnings. Hardy is best known as the sea captain who befriended the young Niijima Jo, and opened the way for him to attend Amherst College and Andover Seminary. But he was also president of the Andover board of trustees during the 1880s, and, as the record suggests, a defender of the embattled professors. He was no great friend of Edwards Park or the Board of Visitors.

Now, either by some historical accident or purposeful irony, their marble memorials sit side by side. The passage of time sometimes makes for strange juxtapositions, and it is not hard to imagine a general air of disapproval emanating from that corner of the reading room. Yet in the course of my research, I was fascinated to discover that much of the material about Andover Seminary in the Library's collection has Park's distinctive signature on the inside cover. As one of the Library's founders, he likely took the opportunity to ensure that future historians, like myself, would not fail to encounter his side of the Andover controversy, and he no doubt hoped, to tell it properly.

Though, thankfully, Professor Park is no longer around to issue judgment, the past that he and Captain Hardy represent still resonates far beyond the walls of the Congregational Library. It is still, in its own way, very much alive — and rightfully so. History offers a line of interpretation, a sense of place, a well from which to draw fresh sources of identity.

Legacy

First of all, there are the historic achievements. Andover was the first American theological seminary, and the model for all others to follow. The ambitious vision of its founders changed the way that all Protestant clergy would be prepared for ministry forever after. No longer a private, largely ad hoc affair conducted in the study of a busy working pastor, theological education became a serious intellectual endeavor requiring years of concentrated time, and the full support of all Protestant churches. Andover faculty also made ministerial training into an intellectual adventure. Moses Stuart, Leonard Woods, William Jewett Tucker, and Daniel Evans — all leading scholars in their separate fields — dedicated their lives to training preachers. The Andover model, which was quickly replicated by the Newton Theological Institution, linked head and heart, library and pulpit, the life of the mind and the yearning for God

Andover also introduced American Protestants to the idea of mission, the conviction that the Christian gospel was a message for the entire world, not just the faithful in their pews. Andover did not originate that idea — the call to evangelization is as old as New Testament Christianity — but its busy students and faculty provided a new model of urgency and commitment. The hundreds of graduates who departed Andover for Hawaii, Syria, China, and the ends of the earth; the Andover Bands on the western frontier; the students at Andover House in Boston's South End and at the Blue Hill Christian Center in Roxbury — all drew from the same missionary impulse. Certainly the scope of mission has changed over the years: no longer just simple proclamation, it has evolved into more nuanced encounters with other cultures, recognizing the need to both give and take, speak and listen. But the germ of the idea came from Andover.

Newton helped usher in a new era of cooperation among Protestant seminaries. In 1908, its ambitious president George Horr presided over the gathering which eventually became the American Association of Theological Schools. That fact alone is noteworthy. From small beginnings as a school for New England Baptist preachers, Newton played a shaping role in the professionalizing world of modern theological education, where standardization and collaboration would become key virtues.

Andover Newton also played an important role in the professionalization of the pastor's role, with the introduction of Clinical Pastoral Education into the seminary curriculum and some creative new models of field education. The new role of the twentieth-century pastor, as both resident theologian and psychologically trained healer of souls, began with a course of study and practice first instituted on Andover Newton's campus in the 1930s. The fourth-year internship was also an idea pioneered by Andover Newton, as was the model of a "teaching parish" and the Center for the Laity in the 1980s. All of these work-intensive programs reflected the school's fundamental commitment to training pastors for leadership in local churches.

Lessons

This is not the whole story, of course. Behind all those historic achievements are many less public and less celebrated years of determined effort. Over the course of the past two centuries, both Andover and Newton have returned from more than a few near-death situations. Andover did in fact close its doors in the 1920s; Newton swung perilously close any number of times, and Andover Newton faced tremendous financial pressures in the 1980s and beyond. A series of untimely deaths also set the institution on its heels, and recovery proved difficult and slow.

Certainly, in some deep way, human organizations, much like individual people themselves, mourn their losses. Long after conscious memories fade, difficult events still linger in the larger ethos; it is not all that hard to imagine that institutions, just like people, undergo grief.

But repeatedly, both Andover and Newton discovered a path toward survival. They succeeded through a bit of luck and timing, perhaps, but also perseverance and a high level of tolerance for discomfort. Indeed, the past two hundred years amply demonstrates that they are resilient institutions — not infallible or perfect, but certainly flexible and determined.

Clearly, the past two hundred years of Andover and Newton's history demonstrates the depth of their achievement as independent seminaries. Both schools, but Andover in particular, regularly faced questions about ownership and control. Both were organized by discrete groups of people who had a particular purpose in mind. Twice, in the 1880s and in the 1920s, Andover nearly faced extinction because its trustees and Board of Visitors believed they had the power to recreate the school anew, on their own terms. In one case, the three men on the Board of Visitors attempted to impose its particular interpretation of the Andover creed; in the other, the board of trustees pursued a goal widely repudiated by the school's alumni and supporting churches. The re-creation of Andover Newton in 1931 embodied a wider, nonsectarian mission, both legally and institutionally, to be simply a "school of the church."

But that has not proved to be a simple task. To begin with, the sectarian impulses in American religious culture are strong; within the freewheeling spiritual marketplace of churches and denominations in the United States, groups that generated the strongest "brand name loyalty" have tended to rise to the top most quickly. In recent years, the theological schools growing most rapidly have been conservative, ensuring doctrinal standards with procedures that would have certainly been familiar to Andover's founding faculty. The other alternative for Protestant seminaries has been to seek affiliation with a university or college. Beyond the simple economic benefits of the partnership, divinity schools have benefited from the regular infusion of fresh scholarship from the secular university campus.

Between both of these two models — a theologically defined "niche" school or a spoke within the wheel of a secular university — Andover Newton sought to become a broadly conceived "school of the church." The goal is in many ways profoundly counter-cultural, running against the increasingly sectarian grain of American religious life and the secularizing trends of higher education. Those schools like Andover Newton, who have hewed to a larger religious purpose, have survived by learning to become institutionally nimble.

In 2007, Andover Newton dedicated the Wilson Chapel. Situated at the far end of the grassy rectangle long anchored by the Trask Library, it physically completed the campus, finally closing in the empty fourth side. The new chapel also marked the end point of a physical migration from an old campus once dominated by Newton's original buildings, Farwell Hall, Sturtevant Hall, and Colby Chapel. The new campus, with almost all of its buildings erected after 1931, now literally looks in a different direction than the old, standing above suburban developments that have been creeping ever closer since the late nineteenth century.

The chapel's architectural design is a metaphor of that historical progression. Its front exterior is white, with a regular pattern of square windows designed to imitate a seventeenth-century New England meetinghouse. The rear is a wall of glass, looking out toward the Blue Hills in Boston's far suburbs, and, by conscious design, toward the world's southern hemisphere, the new source of Christian vitality and growth in the twenty-first century.[1]

It's a neat trick for one building to hold together both the reality of the old and the promise of the new. The chapel's exterior design is an important statement about Andover Newton's sense of its past and its intentions for the future. But far more important than the outside walls is what will happen within them: how worship, music, the visual arts, and a purposeful sense of community will shape new generations of students and faculty, preachers and pastors, for many years to come. If anything, history teaches that nothing is ever really settled, and that few predictions made in the present day ever amount to much in the future. Those who are paying close attention will learn some humility. But above all, to its most avid students, history teaches that it is always a good idea to be prepared for new surprises.

---

1. The description is drawn from Mark Burrows, "The Wilson Chapel: A New Church for a School 'Set on a Hill,'" *Faith and Forum,* December 2007.

Index

⸺𝒶𝓋𝓋⸺

205